THE UNITED NATIO
NEW WORLD ORDER

Also by Dimitris Bourantonis

THE UNITED NATIONS AND THE QUEST FOR
NUCLEAR DISARMAMENT

Also by Jarrod Wiener

MAKING RULES FOR AGRICULTURE IN THE URUGUAY
ROUND OF THE GATT : A Study in International Leadership

The United Nations in the New World Order

The World Organization at Fifty

Edited by

Dimitris Bourantonis
Lecturer in International Relations
Athens University of Economics and Business

and

Jarrod Wiener
Lecturer in International Relations
University of Kent at Canterbury

First published 1995 by
MACMILLAN PRESS LTD
Houndmills, Basingstoke, Hampshire RG21 6XS
and London
Companies and representatives
throughout the world

ISBN 0–333–63122–6 hardcover
ISBN 0–333–63123–4 paperback

A catalogue record for this book is available
from the British Library.

10   9   8   7   6   5   4   3   2
04   03   02   01   00   99   98   97   96

Printed in Great Britain by
Ipswich Book Co. Ltd, Ipswich, Suffolk

Published in the United States of America 1996 by
ST. MARTIN'S PRESS, INC.,
Scholarly and Reference Division
175 Fifth Avenue, New York, N. Y. 10010

ISBN 0–312–16118–2

Contents

Acknowledgement

The editors would like to express their appreciation to the contributors to this volume, without whom it would not have been possible. Our thanks also to Professor A.J.R. Groom for his help with the project, and to Mr. T.M. Farmiloe at Macmillan for showing an interest in it at an early stage. Many of the articles in this book first appeared in a special issue of *Paradigms: The Kent Journal of International Relations* of the University of Kent at Canterbury. We therefore would like to thank the editorial staff of the journal for their assistance above and beyond the call of duty. Assisting with the technical aspects of production, Dominic Powell, the editorial wizard behind *Paradigms*, deserves much credit for the herculean tasks of typesetting the manuscript and indexing, and much thanks indeed for working his usual magic. Thanks also to John Kennair and Amanda Linter for their help in proof-reading. The assistance of Marilyn Spice, the Secretary of the Department of Politics and International Relations at the University of Kent, and Justine Clements in the Rutherford College Secretarial Office was invaluable.

Notes on the Contributors

Peter R. Baehr studied political science at the University of Amsterdam and Georgetown University, Washington, D.C. He is now Professor of Human Rights at Utrecht University and Leyden University, and Director of the Netherlands Institute of Human Rights of Utrecht University. He is co-author of *The United Nations in the 1990s*, and author of *The Role of Human Rights in Foreign Policy*.

Dimitris Bourantonis is Lecturer of International Relations at the Athens University of Economics and Business. He specializes in the politics and institutions of the European Community and the United Nations system. He is the author of *The United Nations and the Quest for Nuclear Disarmament*.

Vojin Dimitrijevic is Professor of International Law and International Relations, University of Belgrade Law School. He is currently Visiting Professor at the University of Lund and Vice-Chairman of the UN Human Rights Committee. His latest book is *The Insecurity of Human Rights After Communism*.

Marios Evriviades is Assistant Professor at the Athens University of Economics and Business. He holds a Ph.D from the Fletcher School of Law and Diplomacy, Tufts University and has been a research associate at the Center for Middle Eastern Studies, Harvard University.

Alan James is Research Professor of International Relations at Keele University, UK. A former chairman of the British International Studies Association, he was recently Chair of the International Law Section of the (US-based) International Studies Association and Guest Professor at Japan's National Institute for Defence Studies. His recent publications include *Peacekeeping in International Politics* and *States in a Changing World*, edited with Robert Jackson.

R.J. Barry Jones is Senior Lecturer and Head of the Department of Politics at Reading University. His interests are in international relations theory and international political economy. He is the author of *Conflict and Control in the World Economy: Contemporary Economic Realism and Neo-Mercantilism*.

Georgios Kostakos has a Ph.D in international relations from the University of Kent at Canterbury and is an associate of the Hellenic Foundation for European and Foreign Policy (ELIAMEP). He was a member of the United Nations Observer Mission in South Africa (UNOMSA) from February to May 1994.

Edward Newman graduated from Keele University in 1992 and is currently conducting research at the University of Kent at Canterbury on trends in the international civil service.

Jelena Pejic is Assistant Lecturer in International Law and International Relations, University of Belgrade Law School, and is a former journalist with TANJUG press agency.

Benjamin Rivlin is Director of the Ralph Bunche Institute on the United Nations and Professor Emeritus of Political Science at the Graduate School of the City University of New York. He is co-editor of and contributor to *The Challenging Role of the UN Secretary-General: Making "the Most Impossible Job in the World" Possible* and editor of and contributor to *Ralph Bunche: The Man and His Times.*

Lev Voronkov is Director of the International Institute for Peace in Vienna. From 1985 to 1988 he was General Secretary of the Scientific Council of Peace and Disarmament Research of the USSR. He has published widely, and is the author of *Public Opinion and Foreign Policy of the Nordic Countries* and *Non-Nuclear Status to Northern Europe.*

Jarrod Wiener is Lecturer in International Relations at the University of Kent at Canterbury and Managing Editor of *Paradigms: The Kent Journal of International Relations.* He is author of *Making Rules in the Uruguay Round of the GATT: A Study in International Leadership.*

Introduction

Jarrod Wiener

To present a book about the United Nations in the New World Order is difficult, given that the organization is in the process of redefining its role and that the international system is still dealing with the consequences of dramatic structural transformations. Yet, it is necessary to contextualize the "New UN" within the prevailing international system. The world organization always has reflected, and continues to reflect, the realities of the international political order. Notwithstanding the mandate of the UN Charter on paper, the Cold War established the parameters within which the organization could act in practice. The bipolar confrontation proscribed, or at least imposed limits upon, collective UN activities. The end of the Cold War signalled the first time that a new international order has inherited the organization of its predecessor. It is the first time that a structural change has occurred not as the result of a hegemonic war. Hence, this is the first time that a world organization has had to adapt to a new political order, which makes the analysis of the former all the more inextricable from the latter: to understand the shape of the "New UN" requires an analysis, however difficult, of what the "New World Order" wills of it, and will permit it.

Necessity has not made our task any easier. At the time of the organization's fiftieth anniversary, the New World Order remains undefined. This has not prevented some scholars from seizing the moment: some daring voices have prophesied "the end of history"; other, more idealistic, ones have heralded the dawning of a new system of morality unconstrained by political imperatives where the concern for cosmopolitan values, human rights, and justice can be pursued; some more prudent have asked whose morality will be advanced, and have questioned whether the substance of politics really has changed beneath the new agendas that have come to the surface; the more cautious have warned that the great powers may disengage from the system where they perceive their interests not to be immediately at stake, providing for a set of insular communities, whether they be military security complexes or trading zones; and, more pessimistic voices have argued that the future of the international system lies in its reversion to a more or less "classic" form of balance of power configuration. Depending on one's viewpoint, the New World Order may have elements of all or none of these elements, given that this thumbnail sketch is probably not exhaustive.

Introduction

The fact remains, however, that all that can be said with certainty is that at this point in time the international system remains fluid and evolving – an evolution that depends on the unfolding of conflicting trends.

The authors in this volume do not predict what the future shape of the UN will be, but they do aim to provide navigation points in examining some of the main challenges that confront it during the transition to the post-Cold War system. These are, namely: the opposing forces of globalization and regionalization, and the changing conception of security from a mainly military one, to one that encompasses global issues; the interplay between the rule of law and cosmopolitan ethics that inform the UN Charter and the interests of states; the stability that is promoted by the leadership of the strongest states, and their tendency not to lead unless vital national interests are perceived to be at stake; and the need to reform the UN to cope with its increasing role, particularly in peace-keeping, and the financial burden with which it is encumbered. These themes, discussed in the first three chapters, permeate the more detailed case-analyses of the remaining ones, which are concerned with such issues as the role of the Secretary-General, disarmament, peace-keeping, the use of sanctions by the Security Council, human rights, and humanitarian intervention.

Lev Voronkov sets the agenda with, "International Peace and Security: New Challenges to the United Nations". He argues that the UN's future role depends on how it copes with the conflicting forces of globalization on one hand, and those of regionalization on the other - the consequences of either of which can promote or frustrate efforts to maintain international peace. The trend towards regionalization can be seen in such economic groupings as the EU, ASEAN and NAFTA, or in international security structures, such as the CSCE, NATO and the WEU. But as Voronkov points out, neither economic nor security regionalization is *prima facie* detrimental to international cooperation. The members of regional trade zones belong to the World Trade Organization, for example, and regional security arrangements can be supportive of the UN agenda of maintaining international peace, as indeed the cooperation between NATO and the UN in the former Yugoslavia illustrates. Globalization can involve such things as the growth of economic interdependence, which, while heightening a state's vulnerability and sensitivity to external forces, provides for increased contacts and cooperation at the political level. Another positive aspect of globalization can be seen in the increased membership of international organizations as the remaining developing countries and newly emerging states of Eastern Europe accede to them. On the other hand - Voronkov's central point - globalization increasingly entails a growth in the number of problems of common concern to all states as the world community shrinks into a "global village", particularly as this relates to non-military threats to humanity, such as the proliferation of nuclear weapons, the protection of the environment, the use of natural resources, the spill-over of ethnic and nationalist unrest into international conflicts, population growth, mass migrations, and famines.

A central issue that arises from the transition of the international system with which the UN has to cope is whether the United States will assume the central leadership role for the system - meaning, at its most basic level as holding to a particular vision of order and persuading others to follow it - or whether the system will be more diffuse and multipolar. The consequences of a lack of hegemony are explored by R.J. Barry Jones. His chapter, "The United Nations and the International Political System" situates the UN within an international system that is composed of states, and as such, is constrained by their pursuit of their own agendas. In his words, this basic contradiction is how to construct a "viable international order based upon cosmopolitan ethics" within a society constituted by the "imperatives of a system of sovereign states". Jones argues that while the "foundational principles" of any political order may evolve over time, that order will reflect the "profound value preferences" of its most powerful members. He discusses the residual effects of US hegemony on the world order, and concludes that notwithstanding the development of a complexly interdependent international system that, in theory, can become self-sustaining after the structure of power that brought it into being erodes, "serious questions remain about the prospects for any new international order that is not promoted, and subsequently sustained, by one or more dominant states". Comparing the inability of the League of Nations to take effective action against Italy's invasion of Ethiopia, the UN' success in Kuwait, and the lack of coherent action over the conflict in Bosnia-Herzegovina, Jones concludes that the onus for the effective management of collective security continues to be placed on the "big powers". However, he argues that the system itself is imbued with structural constraints that prompt developments which challenge order, while at the same time restrict the ability of states to adopt effective solutions to them - a paradox that has often assumed a deadly mandate.

Introduction

Jarrod Wiener agrees that the international system can suffer from instability if it lacks the commitment and leadership of its largest states. However, he argues that a distinction must be made quite clearly between a lack of power to lead, a lack of an interest in leading, and most importantly, the issues that demand leadership. In "Leadership, the United Nations, and the New World Order", he observes that much of the discourse about the conflict in the former Yugoslavia, particularly as this has related to the inability of the United Nations to take effective action to mediate its successful conclusion, has centred, implicitly if not at times explicitly, on the assumption that the organization has lacked leadership, particularly from the United States. Wiener examines various theories of international leadership, particularly the Theory of Hegemonic Stability, which suggests that a state must be predominant in terms of resources in order to lead in the international system. He argues that the theory has some intrinsic difficulties on a theoretical level. However, practically, its application to this particular conflict may be misplaced, particularly if it is for the purpose of extrapolating a general political paralysis due to a lack of leadership in the New World Order. The conclusion is that in the post-Cold War system, the US will continue to react to those issues in which it perceives an interest, as it always has done. That there may be more conflicts arising to which the UN does not respond effectively, and that the consequences of these will at times present an affront to the cosmopolitan values of human consciousness may give the illusion of drift, but merely reflects the consequences of an international system of security driven by the imperatives of state interest.

In "UN Reform: The Post-Cold War Organization", Georgios Kostakos examines the impact of changes in the international system on the transformation of the organization itself. With the overall emphasis on the area of peace and security, the author considers four main aspects. The first is the political changes that have accompanied the increased number and diversity of the organization's membership, and in this context he discusses the proposed additions to the permanent membership of the Security Council. The second area is structural and administrative reform, which have brought about changes to staffing at the level of the international civil service. Related to this are economic considerations, the third force promoting change, which mainly has to do with proposed financing arrangements for the UN's expanded role while at the same time the largest states are in arrears in their commitments to it. He suggests that whereas the UN had suffered from more or less irrelevance, or at least impotence during the Cold War, its main danger is now financial overstretch. Finally, Kostakos relates these changes and the proposals for the UN's further reform to the overarching conceptual framework of the Secretary-General Boutros Boutros-Ghali's *Agenda for Peace*. Kostakos makes some interesting recommendations as to the manner in which the UN should develop to meet the challenges of the New World Order. Most notable is that the Office of the Secretary-General should remain authoritative, "side by side with states and their governments", and that more duties should be delegated to the Under-Secretaries-General and Directors to form a responsible "international cabinet". Kostakos advocates a "stand-by" international force for peace-making and enforcement which is trained in the art of conflict management. However, given financial constraints, the UN should adopt a "selective" approach that is quantitatively decreased, but qualitatively much stronger and authoritative.

Benjamin Rivlin then elaborates the role of the Secretary-General. In "The UN Secretary-Generalship at Fifty", he considers how the Secretary-Generalship has changed since the inception of the office, if at all. The author begins by contextualizing the Office within the fluctuations of the UN over the past fifty years, which itself responded to variations in the international political climate. Notwithstanding the inherent vagaries, he isolates and discusses seven constants that have rendered the execution of the Office particularly difficult, namely: role ambiguity; an overburdened office; ambivalent relations with the Security Council and the General Assembly; constraints as head of the Secretariat; minimal authority to coordinate the heads of the specialized agencies; limited means to lead, resulting from a lack of a political base and constituency, lack of human and financial resources, and a dependence upon outside sources of information; and finally, the changing international political climate. Rivlin pays particularly close attention to the pressures that have been placed upon Boutros-Ghali as he has been expected to anticipate developments, to provide intellectual leadership by formulating ways of meeting new challenges, and persuading the Security Council to accept them, the latter of which is perhaps the most difficult of all. However, Rivlin concludes that the Office has essentially not changed, and that "all of the negative limitations and positive attributes of the office that governed the first Secretary-General are still in force". Rivlin examines proposals to strengthen the Office, and concludes that this deserves particular attention given the intense debate taking place over the future of UN peacekeeping.

Indeed, an increase in the number of peacekeeping operations perhaps has been the most visible characteristic of the New World Order. Yet, in addition to signalling the effective pursuit of the UN's mandate, this can also entail some negative implications for the UN, such as financial overstretch. In "UN Peacekeeping: Recent Developments and Current Problems", Alan James elaborates both the conceptual and practical difficulties that the recent flurry of peacekeeping missions presents. Conceptually, James argues that the traditional distinction between "peacekeeping" and "enforcement", measured by the degree to which the parties to a conflict have "consented" to UN intervention, has become blurred. A conceptual problem has arisen out of larger, often more powerfully armed, and sometimes more assertive "peacekeeping" operations, such as those in Cambodia, Bosnia-Herzegovina, and Somalia. While he doubts that there is a sufficient basis to develop a third concept to cover this new activity, he does offer a sub-categorization of peacekeeping into "pacific peacekeeping", which refers to traditional sorts of operations, and "prickly peacekeeping", which refers to operations with which it is painful to tangle. James then discusses the practical problems of peacekeeping from the perspective of contributing states, host states, and the UN.

Another instrument at the disposal of the Security Council in its efforts to ensure international peace and security is economic sanctions. And, the post-Cold War period already has witnessed the implementation of the most comprehensive set of sanctions in UN history in the attempt to arrest the conflicts in the former Yugoslavia. In "UN Sanctions Against Yugoslavia: Two Years Later", Vojin Dimitrijevic and Jelena Pejic investigate the effectiveness of such multilaterally sanctioned instruments of economic coercion. They find that the precise targets of the sanctions remained unspecified. Formally, the Security Council had targeted the Federal Republic of Yugoslavia, whereas official Serbia was the most powerful player, and subsequent political signals seemed to indicate that there was an intent to pressure the federal government and the Montenegrin authorities to cooperate in finding an internationally acceptable solution. Moreover, the aims of the sanctions were unclear, ranging from the cessation of hostilities to the removal of political figures, namely Slobodan Milosovic, and these continually changed with developments on the ground. Consistent with the theoretical literature on sanctions in general, Dimitrijevic and Pejic find that sanctions did not achieve the main objective of stopping the war. They review the economic situation under sanctions, the political effects in terms of elections results, and popular opinions of the peoples affected. The finings from this case suggest a reconsideration of the reliance upon economic sanctions as an instrument of the Security Council.

In "New Directions in Disarmament", Dimitris Bourantonis and Marios Evriviades review the arms limitation treaties in the history of the UN and point out that the strictures imposed by the Cold War impeded constructive advances in this, as in most other areas. They point out that the UN has been more successful in overseeing disarmament since 1987 than in all of the organization's previous years combined. This, they argue, makes it all the more imperative for the UN to develop a "more forward-looking, efficient, and results-oriented" role. The authors review the functioning of the UN disarmament machinery, namely the First Committee, the Conference on Disarmament, the Disarmament Commission, and the Office of Disarmament Affairs, and suggest that the UN should adopt a new agenda for arms limitation that relies on a complementary division of labour between regional and multilateral fora. Given that the UN operates in the global context, it would be better for it to focus "purely on multilateral aspects.. such as the strengthening of the non-proliferation regime", rather than become involved in specific arms control treaties, where regional organisations such as the CSCE, OAS, OAU, and ASEAN can be effective in, for example, the creation of nuclear-free zones, and bilateral fora, such as SALT/START which have proven its successes between the superpowers. To assist in this, they advocate the strengthening of the authority of the UN, the Security Council, and particularly of the Office of the Secretary-General to sanction states that violate the norms of non-proliferation.

The final two chapters deal with the issue of human rights. In "Human Rights Organizations and the United Nations: A Tale of Two Worlds" Peter Baehr examines the interaction of non-governmental organizations with the UN. He argues that there is an in-built tension between such non-governmental organizations and the UN, mainly because there is a tension between such organizations and states. NGOs often pressure governments to take measures that exceed what governments are prepared to take, and suspect governments of insincerity, while governments view such NGOs as interfering in their domestic and foreign policies. Baehr illustrates this tension with an examination of the

Introduction

World Conference on Human Rights in Vienna in June 1993 and of the appointment of a high Commissioner for Human Rights.

In "Realpolitik and the CNN Factor of Humanitarian Intervention", Edward Newman draws out the various perspectives of humanitarian intervention and seeks to identify the indicators which would point to post-Cold War trends in this issue-area. Drawing on a seminar at the British Foreign and Commonwealth Office which represented government and non-governmental organizations, academics, and the UN Secretariat, this chapter presents the converging and competing agendas of those involved. It concludes that political will on the part of UN Member States and the dynamics of public opinion make it a volatile subject. It also results in a case-by-case approach to humanitarian intervention, so that this area appears inherently inconsistent in policy terms.

The reader of this Introduction may well have the impression by this point that the outlook of this book is essentially pessimistic. But perhaps "cautious optimism" is a better characterization. It is true that many of its contributors are concerned about the manner in which the imperatives of power and interest can constrain the construction of a greater project for international peace and security. However, all implicitly warn against dramatizing the negative aspects of the international system, as indeed many prophets of doom have done. Indeed, all point rather pragmatically to practical ways in which the UN can evolve towards a more comprehensive system that is more effective and responsive to the new imperatives which the New World Order will present to it. As well as new challenges, there are indeed new vistas and opportunities.

1 International Peace and Security: New Challenges to the UN

Lev Voronkov

The founding fathers of the United Nations established the organization with the purposes of maintaining international peace and security, of developing friendly relations among nations, and of taking other appropriate measures to strengthen universal peace. They also wished to achieve international cooperation in solving economic, social, cultural, and humanitarian problems, and to promote respect for human rights and for the fundamental freedoms for all.

The political, military, economic, ecological, social and cultural environment in which the UN operates has changed considerably and continues to evolve. The organization was established by the victorious states of the Second World War. To this day, several provisions of the UN Charter, (for example Article 53), are directed against the former "enemy states", Germany, Italy, Japan and their allies who are now full and equal members of the UN. Some of them even wish to become permanent members of the Security Council. Moreover, many members of the UN did not exist as sovereign independent states at the time that the organization was established. Now such members are in the majority.

The UN has become the most universal international organization in the world, embracing under its aegis the activities of governments from 184 states, as well as hundreds of national organizations, international governmental organizations (IGOs), and international non-governmental organizations (NGOs). The norms of international law derived from the UN Charter and from other international agreements, treaties, and conventions signed under its auspices play a vital role in regulating the internal life of states and the world society.

What is currently happening to the UN system now that the political objectives and priorities of many modern states are undergoing large-scale qualitative changes? The world is in transition from the Cold War

1

structure of international relations towards a new system. The 50th anniversary of the UN and the forthcoming entry of the world into the 21st century give us an additional impetus to analyze the role and significance of the UN in maintaining international peace and security, and to elaborate a vision of its future development. The focal point of this chapter is the interaction between the UN system and the changing nature of world society.

THE HERITAGE OF THE COLD WAR

The international community is not yet fully aware of the scale of the changes which are under way during the process of overcoming the heritage of the Cold War in contemporary international relations in general, and in the activity of the UN in the field of international peace and security in particular. To assess accurately the impact of these changes on the UN system, one must analyze at least the main features of this heritage.

The confrontation between East and West which dominated world politics for over forty years was ideologically motivated. The confrontation between opposing social systems was based on the perception that the other system was a threat to the basic values of human society. This polarized the world along political, military, economic, cultural and ideological lines. Each side tried to reinforce the strength of its ideology, and its domestic and foreign policies by military might, which was justified in the public mind as being necessary to guarantee peace and survival. This confrontation was expressed institutionally in the alliances of the North Atlantic Treaty Organization (NATO) and the Warsaw Treaty Organization (WTO), which not only performed military functions, but which also tried to consolidate political, economic, scientific, technological, cultural and ideological policies between allied countries.

The need to maintain the unity of the military alliances within a confrontational atmosphere provided the United States and the Soviet Union with the status of "superpowers". This bipolar structure of international relations left a substantial mark on the UN, as the stand-off pervaded all spheres of life, and was reflected in the functions, powers, structures and programs of the UN and its special agencies.

The founding fathers of the UN intended to unite their strengths in maintaining international peace and security, and to this end committed themselves "to take effective collective measures for the prevention and removal of threats to the peace, and for the suppression of acts of aggression or other breaches of the peace..." (Article 1 of the UN Charter). To ensure prompt and effective action, Article 24 stipulates that UN members "confer on the Security Council primary responsibility for the maintenance of international peace and security, and agree that in carrying out its duties under this responsibility the Security Council acts on their behalf". However, due to the confrontation between some of its permanent members the Security Council could not act in such a manner. States were forced by the existing military-political circumstances to seek an effective substitute for the functions of the Security Council, and to rely on military-political alliances for their security (or on the right for individual or collective self-defense in accordance with Article 51 of the UN Charter). Under these circumstances the mechanisms of the Security Council's enforcement measures could not be developed properly.

In the atmosphere of East-West global confrontation, the UN became, to a certain extent, a field for ideological competition and propaganda campaigns, supplemented by various other measures to convince world public opinion in general, and the Third World in particular, to support a particular type of socio-economic and political development. In this manner, the superpowers and their allies tried to enlarge their spheres of influence among developing countries, where two-thirds of the world's population lives, by turning them into their clients. After the General Assembly's proclamation in December 1960 of the Declaration on the Granting of Independence to Colonial Countries and Peoples (resolution 1514 (XV), East-West competition in the Third World sharpened significantly. Some of the peace-keeping operations in the Third World initiated by the Security Council during the Cold War were undertaken by the major players with the hope of achieving their own political objectives, but through the mechanisms of, and under the auspices of, the UN.

The East-West confrontation gave an impetus to the emergence of the Non-Aligned Movement, which gradually became an influential political factor not only within the UN, but in world politics generally. Its importance lay in the affiliation of a great number of the UN member states to the movement, as well as in its ability to play a conciliatory role in the settlement of East-West conflicts.

However, the real problems of development within Third World countries were neglected, and buried under the weight of the bi-polar confrontation. Ideological bias prevented superpower cooperation in addressing the real problems of development. As a result, a coherent worldwide strategy which should have been a matter of concern for the whole world community was not created. These vital problems, however, could not be ignored by the developing countries themselves. Beginning in 1960, the General Assembly proclaimed four successive United Nations Development Decades in order to focus international action on programmes to aid development.

Before the end of the first United Nations Development Decade (1961-1970), the need for a world strategy for development became evident. In 1974, the General Assembly adopted the Declaration and Programme of Action on the Establishment of a New International Economic Order (NIEO), which was based on "equity, sovereignty, interdependence, common interests and cooperation among states, *irrespective of their economic and social systems*".[1] In their quest for development, Third World countries created the Group of 77 and other economic mechanisms within the UN. These were founded to overcome ideologically biased approaches to development and to promote worldwide cooperation on the global problems of humanity, including environmental protection, energy supply, the rationalization of natural resource utilization, population growth, and health care. But, as the head of the World Commission on Environment and Development, Gro Harlem Brundtland concluded, "the United Nations system was on the whole too weak and fragmented to deal with human needs in an integrated way".[2] These and other problems of global magnitude, which can be characterized as non-military threats to the security of humanity, were constantly aggravated by the inability of the superpowers and their allies to address them in a spirit of international cooperation.

The whole range of problems relating to the protection of human rights was perceived, by both East and West, first and foremost as an ideological tool to be used in combat with the opposite side. These vital problems also were subordinated to the political strategies of both sides within the framework of the Cold War. Problems of human rights in Third World countries likewise were seen in this light.

In spite of such a deeply penetrating atmosphere of East-West confrontation in all aspects of its activities, the UN was at that time one of the very few fora where official representatives of different military-political alliances could meet and discuss the problems of world politics, as well as their own bilateral relations. The UN was a model of so-called "negative peace", providing the military-political alliances, and their members and clients, with the opportunity to coexist and to elaborate some kind of behavioral code to regulate their hostile relationship. The vital role of the UN in maintaining international peace and security during these times took the shape of preventing the Cold War from becoming a hot one, in military terms.

Peace-keeping operations and enforcement measures could be neither efficient nor a focal point of UN activity during this time of mutual distrust between the permanent members of the Security Council. Naturally, the UN bodies which had been established for peace-keeping and conflict resolution neither could, nor did, become operational (such as the Military Staff Committee, for example). The funding of these operations created many conflicts among the main contributing states, whose willingness to pay was very much dependent on the political and military outcome of the operations.

The dependence of regular payments to peace-keeping activities on the outcome of conflicts, which quite rarely could satisfy both sides, contributed to the emergence of financial problems within the UN. And, the practice of delayed payments to the regular budget of the UN for political reasons, which resulted in no serious consequences for those who delayed payment in breach of their obligations as UN member states, created the preconditions for the gradual aggravation of the financial crisis within the UN.

To sum up, the dominating conceptions of security during the Cold War promoted UN involvement in diplomatic efforts to address problems of military doctrines and strategies, arms control and disarmament, arms trade, confidence and security building measures in their military dimensions, and verification and control over existing military potentials and agreements in the field of arms control and disarmament. The prominent role of these problems to the detriment of non-military security issues at that time was reflected in the structure and programs of the UN.

In addition, regional aspects of the system of international peace and security, stipulated particularly in Chapter VIII of the UN Charter, could not work in the way that they had been designed by the UN's founding fathers. Under conditions of confrontation between some of the permanent members of the Security Council the provisions of Article 53 which states that, "no enforcement action shall be taken under regional arrangements or by regional agencies without the authorization of the Security Council..." could not be used in practice. This promoted the efforts of both NATO and the WTO to justify their existence and strategies by referring to the right for individual or collective self-defense in accordance with Article 51 of the UN Charter. According to this interpretation, regional security arrangements on a pan-European level, as well as regional enforcement measures in the spirit of Chapters VII and VIII of the UN Charter, could be substituted with different regional arrangements and agencies acting in accordance with Article 51.

Countries belonging to the same military-political alliances and economic institutions experienced intensive economic and social integration, far greater than that which developed between allied countries and those belonging to different military, political and economic structures. A slight interdependence between members of different military-political and economic institutions did occur, but broad economic integration and real interdependence between them did not. Countries belonging to opposing military-political alliances tried to avoid extensive economic interdependence with their adversaries due to their concern that such interdependence could be used against them in a hostile situation.

The following will focus on the new challenges that the UN has to meet within the framework of the transition from Cold War practices to the cooperative security and peace structures of the post-Cold War era.

UN REVITALIZATION IN SIGHT

Attempting to maintain international peace and security through a system of military blocs is now part of the past. The WTO has ceased to exist. The disintegration of the USSR, ongoing socio-economic and political changes in the countries of Central and Eastern Europe, economic reforms in the People's Republic of China, the gradual resolution of conflicts inherited from the Cold War, and the further development of integrative processes in the world economy and of growing interdependencies are all visible signs of the overwhelming changes under way in contemporary international relations. Such changes are of great importance for the whole UN system.

The Cold War atmosphere of confrontation is being supplanted by the development of a spirit of partnership among the permanent members of the Security Council. If these processes are strengthened and deepened a new chain-reaction of revitalization of the UN system of international peace and security will become a reality. There are many signs that this chain-reaction already has begun.

The emerging conditions conducive to the intensification of cooperation between states on bilateral, sub-regional, regional or broader levels should be supplemented by an increasing role of institutions in general, and of the UN system in particular, in promoting and facilitating this cooperation. The role of the UN in maintaining international peace and security has to be revitalized and supplemented in accordance with the UN Charter, and the *Agenda for Peace* formulated by the UN Secretary-General Boutros Boutros-Ghali, as well as in accordance with changing perceptions of security. In fact, one can speak in terms of the conversion of the UN system of maintaining international peace and security from the Cold War paradigm of military-political and ideological confrontation to a pattern of cooperation in the resolution of crucial problems of common concern.

To be in a position to meet effectively the new challenges, the UN has to be reformed in accordance with new political, economic, social, ecological, technological, cultural and humanitarian realities. Many proposals for this have been made by governments, diplomats, academics, research centres, IGOs, and NGOs. Many of these proposals originated from the former inefficiency of the UN during the Cold War years. Although a considerable number of the causes for this inefficiency are disappearing in the post-Cold War era, some of them still exist.

An ideal and quick reform of the whole UN system is hardly within sight, in view of the divergent interests of member states, the transitional nature of ongoing changes and the practical difficulty of amending the Charter. Reform is a sensitive and complicated issue which should be treated with caution and political realism. But the UN system of international peace and security is ripe for reform, and different approaches should be discussed among diplomats, politicians and the research community.

NEW CHALLENGES TO THE UN

As the heritage of the Cold War is being overcome, processes of internationalization and globalization of the economic and political life of contemporary states are taking deeper roots, and their interdependence is growing. These processes are exerting a mainly positive influence upon the development of the world economy and trade, the distribution of technological achievements and public wealth, democratization, and the protection of human rights.

At its special session in 1990, the UN General Assembly adopted the Declaration on International Economic Cooperation, in which the member states proclaimed their, "strong commitment to a global consensus to promote international economic cooperation".[3] The General Assembly in 1991 adopted a resolution on restructuring and revitalizing the UN in the economic, social and related fields, largely aimed at the role and functioning of the UN Economic and Social Council.[4] The completion of the Uruguay Round of the General Agreement on Tariffs and Trade (GATT) and its future transformation into a World Trade Organization within the UN system clearly demonstrates that economic globalization is being effected in the activities of the UN. To monitor agreements and to improve the conditions for revitalizing the UN in economic, social and related fields, various safeguards are emerging in the form of different international arrangements and structures.[5] The World Summit for Social Development, to be held in Copenhagen in 1995, the United Nations Conference on the Environment and Development (UNCED) in Rio de Janeiro, and the World Conference on Human Rights in Vienna, in addition to other meetings of this kind under the auspices of the UN, are a clear indication of the efforts undertaken by the UN in these fields.

The international community must recognize, however, that the processes of globalization are indivisible from such phenomena as migration, more transparent borders, ecological interdependence, and the spilling-over of internal problems to neighbouring countries, the region, or the global community. These processes could be associated by different ethnic groups and national minorities with threats to their national or ethnic identity, languages, cultures, and national and ethnic rights. Their inclination to defend these values by means of self-determination or sovereignty is often skilfully heated by nationalistic leaders to strengthen their own political position. Eugene Rostow rightly stated that:

> ...rather than yielding automatically to every call for self-determination, however unwise, policy should ... concentrate on seeking the acceptance by all states of rules and practices which could assure that those who live within their borders share the right to participate as equals in the processes of responsible democratic governance.[6]

The violation of human rights of ethnic and national minorities is causing violent conflicts on an international scale. The lack of acceptance of these rules and practices in the former Yugoslavia, Moldova, Georgia, and Nagorny Karabakh are cases in point. There are unfortunately many other places in the world which can erupt into conflict (among which are Latvia and Estonia) where these rules and practices are not accepted in full. Proper attention to these rights and their protection should become a vitally important element of any preventive diplomacy.

The animation of radical nationalistic movements in different countries, including those of the West, is the result of not only worsening economic and social conditions, but also one of the consequences of the rapidly developing process of internationalization and globalization. The

UN Secretary-General in his lecture at Columbia University on 7 February 1994 remarked that indirect forces of globalization are felt everywhere: "This has created an overwhelming sense of insecurity. As a result, tribalism, nationalism, protectionism and fundamentalism increasingly appeal to the alienated individual."[7] The international community in general, and the UN in particular, have to address both the positive and negative implications of these processes.

Along with these processes of internationalization and globalization is the fragmentation, or regionalization, of many aspects of world society. In the Cold War era, most instances of meaningful multilateral cooperation occurred outside the UN system, particularly in regional areas. There is an extensive network of intergovernmental and non-governmental organizations in different regions dealing with problems that concern the UN. To name but a few: in international peace and security, there is the Conference on Security and Cooperation in Europe (CSCE); in economic cooperation, the Association of Southeast Asian Nations (ASEAN); and in human rights, the Council of Europe. However, many of these organizations are either only formally connected with the UN, or not associated with it at all. The Palme Commission in 1982 proposed a strengthening of regional cooperation and the establishment of links between regions and the UN. According to Mrs. Brundtland, the Norwegian Prime Minister:

> Regional and global organizations must be mutually reinforcing, each organization doing what it can do best. Our goal must be to create an appropriate division of responsibility between regional organizations and the UN systems... The UN's Regional Commissions should also play a growing role in this respect.[8]

The promotion and further development of regional cooperation constitutes a stabilizing factor in the system of international peace and security. The experience of western Europe already has demonstrated that the deepening and widening of regional integration creates extensive spheres of common interests in different fields and lessens the threat of violent resolution of possible conflicts. In this way, regional integration could contribute to the strengthening of international peace and security.

In an address to the Inter-Parliamentary Conference held in Canberra in September 1993, the Australian Minister for Foreign Affairs, Senator Gareth Evans, identified the ASEAN Regional Forum as the most important development in regional security which is indicative of the growing sense of a regional community. He stated that, "[n]ations that increasingly see and do things the same way — economically, politically, socially — are nations that should find it easier to talk together, to build processes and institutions together and advance common interests or resolve common problems."[9] Until now however, there has been an unfortunate inclination to underestimate the significance of regionalism in favour of investigating mainly global concerns.

In this context one could mention the principle of "consensus minus one" adopted by the CSCE in its decision-making procedures in respect to its conformity with principles and procedures of the UN; in particular with the principle of the sovereign equality of all its members. Of course, absolute sovereignty is no longer possible. In many cases states have voluntarily accepted certain limitations to their sovereignty by signing international agreements and treaties in the fields of human rights, protection of the environment, maritime law, disarmament, and confidence-building, or by giving aspects of their sovereignty to supra-national and multilateral bodies. The state is being transformed in the interdependent world, but no alternative to the state as the cornerstone of international order is in sight. Taking into account the principle of sovereign equality, any international attempt to resolve conflicts in accordance with the principle of consensus minus one or to the principle of individual or collective self-defense without the authorization of the Security Council would be at least questionable, if not counterproductive.

To prevent violent ethnic or national conflicts the international community must combine the forces of internationalization and global-ization with purposeful measures to provide different ethnic groups and national minorities real opportunities to exert an influence on the economic, social, cultural and humanitarian aspects of their lives. Every nation or ethnic group should have the opportunity to determine voluntarily the scale of its involvement in internationalization processes, and also the conditions of its involvement. Successful preventive diplomacy has to promote such opportunities. To make the system of international peace and security more stable, the world society has to find a proper institutional expression for this vitally important interaction between globalization and regionalization.

In his *Agenda for Peace* of June 1992, the UN Secretary-General proposed that changes in UN mechanisms for maintaining international peace and security should be linked to the increasingly prominent role that regional organizations were playing in preventive diplomacy, peacemaking and peace-keeping.[10] A modern system of international peace and security should have a vertical structure, relying on an interaction of global arrangements with regional arrangements and institutions, not subordinated through obligations to the UN, nor managed by the UN, but at least acting in accordance with the provisions of the UN Charter and the generally accepted norms of international law. Such a vertical structure is not yet established, nor is it even properly theoretically elaborated. As a result, the international community is confronted with unresolved practical problems regarding the interaction of the UN with the CSCE, NATO, the Western European Union, the Commonwealth of Independent States, the Organization of African Unity, etc. These sensitive political problems should be treated very carefully.[11] But within this structure lies the possibility of addressing other current problems, among which are humanitarian assistance, UN decision enforcement, financing, social and economic activities, ecological protection, democratization of the UN system, and the protection of human rights.

One of the ways in which the UN can maintain international peace and security is through peace-keeping operations. These operations are established by the Security Council with the assistance of the Military Staff Committee and are directed by the Secretary-General. The Military Staff Committee was established to advise and to assist the Security Council on all questions relating to its military requirements. Having been influenced by the East-West confrontation, the general rules for such peace-keeping operations are such that they must have the consent of the host government and other parties involved. Peace-keeping contingents must play the role of an impartial third party in a conflict. An operation must not intervene in the internal affairs of the host country, and must not be used in any way to favour one party against another in internal conflicts. The soldiers of the UN peace-keeping forces should have only light weapons to be used solely in self-defense.

Old conflicts born in the epoch of East-West confrontation are losing their momentum and are gradually exhausting themselves. Some of them have been resolved successfully in the course of the last few years, such as German unification, and the creation of independent Namibia. One also can see the relaxation of tensions and trends towards peaceful settlements of conflicts in Indochina, Central America, Angola, Mozambique, the Middle East and South Africa. Simultaneously, new conflicts which had been contained by the East-West confrontation are emerging and receiving so-called "operational space". The demand for peace-keeping has increased dramatically, but the post-Cold War conflicts have assumed a new character. Consequently, the means of peace-keeping are also the subject of profound changes. For the time being, the temptation to cope with the new *types* of conflict, such as those in the former

Yugoslavia, in Moldova, Georgia and Nagorny Karabakh, by traditional military means remains quite strong. The outcome of the Gulf War promoted this inclination.

The fate of Iraqi aggression against Kuwait, however, was predetermined neither by smart weapons, nor by the professionalism of the generals, but by the unanimity of states opposing Iraq and their determination not to allow Saddam Hussein to benefit from his military action. The Security Council demonstrated that it will not tolerate the use of force by one state against another, and that its members are able to reach an agreement in a very sensitive area and to follow coordinated policies towards an aggressor, including military action. The Gulf war, where the lines of confrontation were clear-cut, has shown that an international police force can work. The international community should think over whether in this connection the Military Staff Committee of the UN has to be transformed into a viable organ.

On the basis of the experience gained in the resolution of conflicts in the post-Cold War era one comes naturally to the conclusion that the mechanisms of the UN Charter for strengthening international peace and security, and those of other global and regional IGOs and NGOs can be used efficiently in the post-Cold War era as well. Still, this does not mean that the Security Council is properly equipped to meet new challenges.

From 1988 to 1992, thirteen new peace-keeping operations were initiated by the Security Council, compared with thirteen such operations over the previous 40 years. In El Salvador, Cambodia, Nicaragua, Haiti, and Namibia these operations involved not only traditional military activities, but a whole range of civilian ones, including the reduction of armed forces, the creation of a new police force, the reform of the judicial and electoral systems, the protection of human rights, the promotion of social and economic issues, the control and supervision of various parts of the national administration, the organization and monitoring of national elections, the repatriation of refugees and displaced persons, ensuring the peaceful accession of a country to independence, and the distribution of relief supplies. About one in four UN peace-keepers are now assigned to civilian or police work.[12] But in contrast to the military operations of peace-keepers, the implementation of these civilian functions does not lean on an integrated UN machinery. The UN now needs procedures that are better suited to its increasing role in civilian peace-keeping.

Existing procedures make it difficult to mobilize peace-keeping contingents and to move them swiftly to operational areas. Furthermore, the absence of proper financial arrangements prevents the UN from maintaining sufficient stocks of equipment to organize a unified, well-coordinated contingent. It is obvious that regular peace-keeping training in military and civilian fields is badly needed and has to be organized.[13]

In January 1992 the Security Council met at the level of Heads of State, and adopted a declaration which called on the Secretary-General to recommend ways to improve the UN capacity for preventive diplomacy, peace-keeping, and peacemaking. In *An Agenda for Peace*, Dr. Boutros Boutros-Ghali recommended the increased use of confidence-building and fact-finding activities as well as the establishment of an early-warning system for assessing possible threats to peace to promote preventive diplomacy. He also suggested preventive deployment procedures to deter hostilities, to create demilitarized zones and to organize information-gathering on economic and social situations, such as mass migration, famine and ethnic unrest, which might pose a threat to international peace.

Within the framework of UN peacemaking activities, the Secretary-General pointed out an important role for the General Assembly to play in supporting efforts at mediation, negotiation or the arbitration of disputes. Dr. Boutros-Ghali also emphasized the need for a greater reliance on the International Court of Justice.

According to the Secretary-General, the creation of specially trained peace enforcement units has to be on the UN agenda. Dr. Boutros-Ghali appealed to states for information on the kind and number of personnel they were prepared to offer the UN for peace-keeping operation and proposed to finance such missions out of states' defense budgets. The Secretary-General recommended that the Security Council seriously consider collective measures that would come into effect if there were attacks on the UN's military or civilian staff members.

A wide range of peace-building activities are recommended for the post-conflict period, such as joint efforts by the parties to repatriate refugees, remove land-mines, improve transportation and utilize such resources as water and electricity. The importance of UN assistance in monitoring elections, rebuilding or strengthening governmental institutions and advancing efforts to protect human rights also was stressed. Finally, he proposed that Heads of States and Governments of the Security Council members meet every two years to stimulate ideas on how the UN might best serve to "steer change into peaceful courses".

The Secretary-General's *An Agenda for Peace* is widely recognized as a starting point for serious discussion on how to revitalize the collective security system envisaged in the UN Charter.[14] These important proposals do not exhaust the UN agenda of maintaining international peace and security, especially in respect to the changing understanding of security. For example, the establishment of international tribunals to punish all those responsible for war crimes is an important step towards the inviability of human rights under extreme circumstances of war and conflict.

As for enforcement measures, there are those who do not agree with the proposals contained in *An Agenda for Peace*. The arguments of Eugene Rostow are typical in this sense. He opposes Article 43 to Article 51 of the UN Charter, characterizing the interaction between these as "the essential dilemma of the Charter system" and recommends that the US government reject the model of Article 43, which, in his view, embodies a noble idea to be preserved as an aspiration, but not as a matter of practical politics. His conclusion runs as follows:

> Despite the high hopes invested by the world in the feasibility of UN enforcement actions carried out by the Security Council, the nations will have to continue indefinitely to rely for their security on actions of individual or collective self-defense, and not on the Security Council... as peacemaker and peacekeeper. [15]

During the Cold War the impotence of the Security Council originated in its inability to act on behalf of all its permanent members. The situation is now different. However, while the Security Council still should increase the effectiveness of its enforcement measures, this does not mean that its prerogatives should supplant the philosophy of individual or collective self-defense in the post-Cold War era.

There are many conflicts in the contemporary world where the principles of individual or collective self-defense cannot be referred to as an indisputable excuse for an action. For example, in Somalia the satisfaction of the humanitarian needs of Somalians could not be undertaken under the title of individual or collective self-defense of any state taking part in the UN peace-keeping operation in that country. In the resolution of many ethnic and national conflicts of the post-Cold War era the philosophy of individual or collective self-defense is also hardly applicable.

What kind of solution is there to the crisis in the former Yugoslavia? Rostow believes that the military and diplomatic institutions of NATO should be used against Serbia to enforce the rule against aggression in accordance with the principle of collective self-defense. NATO could play an important role in peace-keeping efforts, at least in the Euro-

Atlantic region, but these actions must be undertaken in accordance with the provisions of Article 53 of the UN Charter, which reads that, "[n]o enforcement action shall be taken under regional arrangements or by regional agencies without the authorization of the Security Council, with the exception of measures against any enemy state".

These provisions of Article 53 should not be perceived as a noble idea to be preserved as an aspiration but should be treated as a basis for practical politics. Arguing in favour of the collective self-defense philosophy exercised by NATO, Rostow insists that, "Great Britain, France and the United States ... are and must remain the core of any peace-keeping effort."[16]   Obviously, such efforts would not exclude action on the territory of the former USSR.   But does this mean that such actions could be taken by NATO in accordance with the principle of collective self-defense, without the authorization of the Security Council and all its permanent members, including Russia?   It is too dangerous to give an affirmative answer to this question.

The author does not recommend that the US government should take the lead, nor that it should accept the model of Article 43 in principle. This means, in fact, that the principles of the UN Charter should not be enforced at all outside the Euro-Atlantic area, where these tasks should be handled by NATO on the basis of the collective self-defense principle. But the UN Charter has global geographical applications and its principles must be applied throughout the world.

CONCLUSION

There are still many problems to be resolved with the transition from the Cold War to the cooperative security of the 21st century. We are not able to meet the new challenges by means which were effective under completely different conditions in world politics. Due to the unprecedented changes in the contemporary world, the political goals and aspirations of different states are the subject of considerable transformations which are being reflected in their military doctrines, concepts of national and international security, understanding of national interests, means of inter-governmental politics and in their perception of global problems. More cooperative concepts of security on global and regional levels are emerging and taking root. The concept of security in terms of military power and nuclear deterrence had pushed the world to the verge of self-destruction. The accumulation of military power, which promised to strengthen security, in reality undermined it in many respects. Now the role of military power in ensuring security requires a new approach.

The former global military threats to security are gradually being replaced by other global threats of a non-military nature in the ecological, economic, social and technological spheres, such as AIDS, global warming, environmental pollution, the energy supply, and demographic growth. The present understanding of security is becoming quite different in comparison to that which prevailed under the Cold War and will continue to change in the long-term.

During the election campaign of Bill Clinton a bipartisan commission of American government veterans, headed by Winston Lord, former US Ambassador to China and State Department planning chief, and sponsored by the Carnegie Endowment for International Peace, published a report demonstrating the gap between new security realities and US responses, and pointing to ways of closing this gap. The commission recommended spending on such priorities as population growth, refugees, peace-keeping and peacemaking, economic development, the environment, promoting economic growth, cutting military expenditures, and raising energy taxes. This package of proposals profoundly redefines US national security away from military concerns and towards a new agenda, which has become the official policy of President Clinton. There is a number of reasons to believe that a gap also exists between the new realities and the UN's, as well as the European responses, and that this gap also should be bridged.

If a new understanding of security is tending to include these other dimensions, is it still reasonable to consider that the Security Council, having the primary responsibility to maintain not only international peace, but also security, is properly equipped to meet these new challenges? Do its existing rules and procedures provide it with reliable means of resolving, say, ecological or demographic problems? Can the specific powers of the Security Council and the principle of unanimity of its permanent members be helpful in addressing not only conflicts, but also the global problems of civilization in an efficient manner? The answer to these questions can hardly be affirmative.

However, at the same time one can see tendencies within the UN to respond properly to this kind of problem. *Agenda for the 21st Century*, adopted by the UN Conference on Environment and Development in Rio de Janeiro was the first responsible attempt of member states to devise a code of behaviour for humanity for the next century, both in the ecological sphere and in the field of international relations. A special Commission for Sustainable Development as a functional commission of ECOSOC has been established in accordance with Article 68 of the UN

Charter and procedures for its functioning are being elaborated. A special session of the UN General Assembly, which will review an implementation of the *Agenda for the 21st Century* programme, is to be held not later than 1997.

Of course, the concept of sustainable development is still the subject of discussion, and most probably will involve issues of broader concern in respect to the UN reform in general, and ECOSOC and its commissions, in particular.[17] In the view of the present writer, the concept of sustainable development will be more suitable in the future to characterize a new understanding of security than the traditional one. This should also include the protection of human rights and freedoms in political, social and economic spheres as a core element and as an indicator of the sustainability of a security system.

It is reasonable to anticipate that discussions on the problems of sustainable development could result in, or at least contribute to the emergence of an updated conception of security that will be helpful in meeting the global challenges to humanity in the 21st century. If the understanding of security does develop in this direction, it might be useful to address problems of strengthening peace in accordance with *An Agenda for Peace*, quite differently organizationally and in substance from the problems of security (sustainable development), as they are indicated in *Agenda for the 21st Century* in terms of decision-making procedures, bodies, institutions, and structures.

NOTES

1. "Basic Facts About the United Nations", Department of Public Information, United Nations, New York, (1992), p.94. Italics added.
2. Gro Harlem Brundtland, "The Environment, Security, and Development", in *SIPRI Yearbook 1993, World Armaments and Disarmaments*, SIPRI (1993), p. 18.
3. "Basic Facts About the United Nations", note 1, pp. 94-95.
4. *Ibid.*, p. 95.
5. See Mihaly Simai, "The Five Decades of the United Nations: Accomplishments and Limitations", *Peace and the Sciences*, vol. XXIV, (September 1993).
6. Eugene V. Rostow "Should Article 43 of the United Nations Charter be Raised From the Dead?", *McNair Paper Nineteen*, Institute for National Strategic Studies, National Defense University, (July 1993), p. 21.

7. "UN Weekly", United Nations Information Service, Vienna, Vol. 10, Number 7, 15 February 1994, pp. 2-3.
8. *SIPRI Yearbook 1993*, note 2, p. 22.
9. "Peace and Disarmament News", Department of Foreign Affairs and Trade, (October 1993).
10. "Basic Facts About the United Nations", note 1, p.33.
11. See Luisa Vierucci, "WEU: A Regional Partner of the United Nations?", Institute for Security Studies, Western European Union, Paris, (December 1993), pp. 3-14.
12. "Financing an Effective United Nations", A Report of the Independent Advisory Group on UN Financing, a Ford Foundation Project, New York, (1993), p. 16.
13. *Ibid.*, p. 16.
14. *SIPRI Yearbook 1993*, note 2, p. 17.
15. Rostow, "Should Article 43 of the UN Charter be Raised From the Dead?", note 6, pp. 7, 10, 11.
16. *Ibid.*, p. 22.
17. This point is made by Professor Grigory Morozow, "Mirovaya economika i mezhdunarodniya otnosheniya", Number 11, 1993, p. 17.

2 The United Nations and the International Political System

R. J. Barry Jones

Today's United Nations warrants neither the naive idolatry nor the casual dismissiveness with which it is conventionally treated. The UN has achieved much of substance during the past fifty years, suffered serious setbacks and shortcomings, but remained fundamentally a creature of the international system within which it is located. An understanding of the nature of the prevailing international system, and its myriad implications for an organization that purports to order the affairs of humanity, is thus essential to a judicious view of the UN, its record and prospects.

Procedurally, the identification of the nature and effects of the prevailing international political order requires an alternation between an examination of the role of institutional efforts to construct a New World Order on the one hand, and an analysis of the constraints exerted by a world of states on the other. Such a procedure parallels the successive epistemological and methodological switch herein between reflective and rationalistic approaches to the study of international institutions.

METHODOLOGICAL CONSIDERATIONS

The contention that the prevailing international system remains, at heart, a politically constructed[1] club of states is the starting point of this discussion. This view corresponds closely to Anthony Giddens' interpretation of all complex social institutions as products of structuration processes amongst human beings[2], and permits a critical perspective upon contemporary realities that avoids the extremes of deconstructionist theory.[3] A consideration of the implications of a complex arena of jealously sovereign states, however, also demonstrates the need to go beyond the intersubjective focus of structuration theory and re-admit notions of system and structure that reflect realities that go beyond the

19

sum of the mutually reinforcing sets of beliefs, understandings and expectations of the members of any identifiable human society or system.

An analytical approach to the contemporary international system that starts on the reflective side of Robert Keohane's distinction between "reflective" and "rationalistic" approaches to the study of international institutions[4] may be highly illuminating but, as will be seen in the subsequent discussion, has to return to the rationalistic domain if it is to be able to deal effectively with an arena of dense and complex interactions.

The work of Max Weber exemplifies a major interpretation of the human condition with its central focus upon the meaningful foundations of such behaviour.[5] The residual contribution of the recent revival of critical theory[6] has been to cast a sceptical light upon much of the empirical social scientific agenda, revealing the normative bias inherent in much of this programme and the relative triviality of many of its findings. Such views reinforce a fundamental distinction between human activity and phenomena of the non-human realm (with some possible qualifications in the areas of the higher, and especially aquatic, mammals). The actions of the latter is held to be unaffected by ideas that agents have about themselves and the behaviour that is appropriate to various circumstances. Human behaviour, in direct contrast, is held to be largely governed by the ideas that human agents have about themselves, their circumstances, the probable behaviour of others with whom they interact and, most significantly, the values that govern their aspirations and normative judgements.

Much of that which is timeless and universal in human behaviour is relatively trivial. Enormous variation in the practices of human societies and considerable change over time and circumstance are to be detected within the human experience. In the explanation of variation and change, a central role must be attributed to the variability of human ideas about desirable and practicable forms of behaviour.

The core of the human condition may be seen as a "socially constructed reality"[7], in which the basic values, understandings and expectations of the members of any society generate corresponding patterns of behaviour. Social behaviour usually exhibits a level of consistency sufficient to establish a self-perpetuating "reality" for all members of any society. The socially constructed reality of any society is robust and enduring to the extent that the underlying set of values, understandings and expectations is widely shared and accepted throughout that society.

The language system of any society embodies and perpetuates sets of shared understandings and expectations. Facilitating basic capabilities for comprehension and communication, such language systems condition that which can be readily comprehended and that which may remain literally inconceivable. Language systems thus rest at the heart of the socially constructed reality of any common language based society. The acquisition of a shared language demonstrates the top-down influence of culture, institutions and social experiences. However, each individual's continuing contribution to interpersonal communication highlights the bottom-up role of the ideas and behaviour of individual human beings, in the classical cycle of "structuration".

There are two major weaknesses of such a perspective upon human activity. The first is that it generates an epistemological self-referential paradox: that the idea that social realities are intersubjectively constructed is itself a product of social construction and might, therefore, not be true. This can be resolved only through the adoption of an epistemology that permits a differentiation between first-order principles and second-order propositions about the human condition.[8] The second difficulty is that explanations of major changes in human conduct can only be explained in terms of apparently spontaneous changes in the systems of beliefs, understandings and expectations upon which that behaviour is based.[9] This difficulty underlies the need to move back into rationalistic approaches at critical stages in the development of any analysis.

THE POLITICAL CONSTRUCTION OF THE INTERNATIONAL POLITICAL ORDER OF STATES

Political life can be seen, at a first-order level of analysis, to be a special part of social life; political realities being a socially constructed component of the wider socially constructed reality of any community or arena of inter-social activity. Ultimately, the political component of the wider socially constructed reality of a society is concerned with the self-conscious effort to identify that society, the definition of the relationship between the social whole and its parts, and the regulation of the behaviour of the members of society towards one another. The differentiation of the political from the wider realm of the social will be clarified in the subsequent discussion of appropriate definitions of politics.

Normative components thus assume a central role in the construction of social and political realities. Core values direct much of human behaviour and provide a foundation upon which understandings and expectations of the behaviour of others is based. This conception of the nature of political activity weakens the conventional distinction between empirical and normative theory in the study of human affairs, for the study of empirical realities within the social and political realms must involve an examination of the normative foundations of that behaviour, unless the analysis is to be confined to what are often the relatively trivial *consequences* of conditioning forces. Equally, the study of normative social and political theory cannot be conceived as a marginal activity, of interest only for appreciative purposes, for normative theory becomes central to the realm of critical examination of the actual foundations of empirical social and political activity.

Such a perspective suggests a complex role for political analysts, being potentially both analysts and activists in their public pronouncements. The agendas and languages of the political orders that they study can be accepted, with a conditioning effect upon the priorities and practices consequentially adopted, or they can be resisted and a necessarily critical perspective incorporated into all subsequent study and statements. This is a complication that has characterized thought about inter-national relations from its inception.

POLITICS: DEFINITION AND CONTENT

The politics that is inherent in, and constitutive of, the prevailing international order is that of sovereign states and their inter-relations. A political order of states, lacking any simple analogue of an authoritative central government, creates difficulties for many established definitions of politics which are either too abstract for ready application or overly oriented towards well-established systems of government at the state and sub-state level. David Easton's "authoritative allocation of values"[10] remains too elusive and elastic. Harold Lasswell's "who gets what, when and how"[11] slides from a distributional connotation into a vague catch-all notion. Bernard Crick's emphasis upon pluralism within a political order that provides for the orderly (and peaceful?) conciliation of diverse interests and aspirations requires a stable governmental system.[12] This appears to preclude the application of the term "politics" to the realm of interstate relations for, as Crick himself argues, "the dilemma of international relations is actually the need to try to practise politics without the basic conditions for political order".[13]

A multi-layered notion of politics and political order that operates at three analytically distinct, but empirically inter-related and overlapping levels can provide a clarification. Each level embraces potential, and actual, disputation and carries the possibility of discord with one or more of the other levels of political life.

At the *foundational level*, politics is about the definition of the collectivity for which the political order exists, the acknowledged members of that collectivity, and the fundamental principles that will direct the relationships both between the collectivity and its individual members and amongst its individual members. At the *institutional level*, politics concerns the institutional expression of the fundamental principles that have been widely agreed, or imposed by dominant actors or groups. Finally, politics at the *day-to-day level* is concerned with the consequences of the institutional (and constitutional) arrangements that prevail within any political collectivity, in terms of electoral outcomes, the less fundamental of governmental policy decisions, distributional effects, voting in representative bodies of various types.

The basic identification of a political collectivity, the definition of its acknowledged (and legitimate) members, and the establishment of basic principles for the general regulation of the relationships between the collectivity and its individual members and, as a lesser issue, the relationships amongst those individual members is the foundation of all political orders. The foundational level may be addressed only occasionally within daily political life. Where well-established and widely accepted political systems are absent, or under challenge, however, the centrality of political fundamentals becomes all-to-apparent.

The foundational principles of any political order may evolve over time, finding full recognition only at times of new, formal political settlements or, more gradually, by divination from changing institutional arrangements and practices, or from day-to-day political actions and outcomes. Profound value preferences and contestable practical judgements, however, will be inherent in any order and the arguments that sustain its existence.

The foundational principles of the contemporary international political order are essentially statist. Statism is enshrined in the Charter of the United Nations and in international law. With only a few notable exceptions, conflicts between states and all other candidates for global recognition — individuals, non-state groupings of people — have been resolved in favour of states. Continuous disputation turns around the claims of such individuals, non-state groups or trans-national affiliations to equal, if not superior, treatment as compared to states.

The essentially contested character of foundational politics may be lost sight of as reflection upon fundamental principles slips from daily discussion and even consciousness. Dominant definitions of essentially contestable concepts [14] are likely to emerge, reflecting the foundational principles of the prevailing political order, interstate or national. Such covert dominance does not make such principles any less political or open to conscious reflection and contestation.

The fundamental principles of any political order will find expression in the framework of arrangements and practices that constitute that order. Such arrangements and practices may arise informally and be crystallized in conventional patterns of behaviour, or be institutionalized in constitutions, treaties, or other formal arrangements. In international relations, such second-level politics embrace formal international organizations, the operation of international regimes,[15] and the diplomatic practices and arrangements that are sustained by states and their representatives.

Second level politics may also incorporate many arrangements that reflect the realities that draw their greatest significance from the context generated by prevailing foundational principles. Thus, the establishment within the United Nations of a Security Council with a core of permanent members reflected the realities of differential *state* power and influence in the immediate post-war world.

While foundational principles may often remain latent and even obscure, the members of a political order will be aware of the functioning nature of that order, whether it be born of informal or formal processes. Political orders are thus differentiable from less formal social mechanisms of control by constituting self-conscious mechanisms for the regulation of explicitly defined units (some real individual human beings, some composite actors and some essentially legal entities) across a clearly specified, and usually limited range of activity.

The foundational principles of the modern international system have been persistently statist, and its institutional and operational manifestations consistently hierarchical. The question for students of international organization is the extent to which it may be possible, in principle and practice, to construct a viable international order based upon cosmopolitan ethics and universalistic procedures. The nature and limits of an institutionalist approach to international order thus have to be evaluated against the constraints, if not imperatives, of a system of sovereign states.

THE INSTITUTIONALIST APPROACH TO WORLD ORDER

The rationale of the United Nations, as of many other international organizations, lay in the hope that the foundations of a new and more propitious international political order could be constructed through, and on the basis of, an appropriate institution.[16] Such an institution might both enshrine new principles of behaviour and, by promoting appropriate action in significant situations, provide confidence-building experience of effective, collaborative international conduct. However, the issue has been the extent to which the declaratory institutional aspirations of the UN have been compatible with the statist foundational principles of the prevailing international order.

The Collective Security systems of both the inter-war League of Nations and the post-war United Nations were invested with much institutionalist optimism. However, such aspirations and expectations collided with the inherent difficulties facing effective collaborations amongst otherwise uncoordinated, sovereign actors and ran counter to the realities of the prevailing distributions of power, influence and dispositions towards effective action amongst the membership of the international system.

The institutionalist approach to international order immediately encounters the problem inherent in an international political order based upon statist foundational principles, which are the source of many dilemmas for the management of human affairs at the global level. Two problem areas are particularly prominent: the potential clash between cosmopolitan values and the needs and interests of states; and the general problem of preserving order and collective well-being in a system fragmented into a myriad of jealously sovereign states. The difficulties of securing such principles as universal human rights exemplifies the former problem, while the difficulties of operating effective Collective Security systems illustrate the latter. Moreover, the limited success of universalistic ethical notions and the deficiencies of many experiments in Collective Security also illustrate the capacity for structural features to constrain constructionist initiatives in the arena of international conduct.

THE UN AS CLUB OF STATES

The early history of the UN demonstrates the profound and persisting normative conflict at its heart between genuine human universalism and a narrower statist philosophy in which the interests and sensitivities of *states* were deemed to be paramount.[17] Thus, a contradiction existed from the outset between such universalistic pronouncements as the declaration of human rights and the enunciation of the principle of self-determination in Article 1 (2) of the Charter, on the one hand, and the preservation of states' domestic jurisdiction as enshrined by Article 2 (7) on the other. Fine sentiments notwithstanding, there was clear early evidence that what was being created was not the institutional basis of a new world, or global, society but a forum for a quite different, and ultimately minimalist, inter-state society: this was to be a society *of states,* created *by states, for states.* This self-regarding statism was a recipe for the crude power politics practised by the United States and its closer allies during the organization's first decade.[18] A statist philosophy thus fused with the ideological preoccupations of the evolving Cold War both to shape, and give substance to the apparent imperatives of power politics and, ultimately, to corrupt the UN's universalistic principles.

The Trials of Collective Security

The idea of Collective Security expands the principle of "one for all and all for one" to the global level. In the event of aggression, all the members of the Collective Security system are supposed to take appropriate action to protect the victim of the aggression, if necessary with coercive measures. The threat of overwhelming opposition would, it was hoped, constitute a massive preponderance of power sufficient to deter would-be aggressors. Should such collective deterrence fail, however, the victim would be preserved and the aggressor convincingly punished by the combined efforts of the rest of the international community.[19]

The effectiveness of Collective Security systems, in both theory and practice, have been discussed widely by students of international relations[20] and international history.[21] Such traditional studies laid great emphasis upon such factors as a relatively even distribution of military capability throughout the system, and the confidence that all members would have in the certainty of the support of their fellows against aggressive states. The problem is that the development of such a Collective Security system amounts to an attempt to provide a *collective good* for the international system, under the demanding conditions of voluntary contributions, the semi-visibility of those contributions, ideological diversity and even division, a large collectivity, some divisibility of the good itself, and massive disparities of wealth and strength amongst the potential contributors. The necessary levels of mutual commitment and confidence have been difficult to create under such circumstances.

The persistent danger in any arrangement made for mutual protection and defense is the possibility that one or more members will attempt to "free-ride" on the efforts and sacrifices of the other alliance members; a special case of defection in a prisoners' dilemma game amongst supposed friends or potential allies. Such free-riding might assume one of two forms. A state might fail to fulfil its obligations when the Collective Security system is called into operation by a challenge to the security of one or more of its members. Such defection in the face of the enemy is a possibility that often has reduced the confidence that states are prepared to place in the alliances that they have joined.[22]

More common are instances of free-riding states seeking to shelter behind the security shield provided by others, or to gain disproportionately from membership of a Collective Security system. Seminal discussions of the problems of free-riding and the provision of collective goods have identified mechanisms by which potential free-riders can be brought into line and persuaded to make some contribution to the provision of a desired collective good, such as an effective Collective Security system. Mancur Olson's initial list of such mechanisms emphasized the force of common ideological commitments in the alliances of the post-war world.[23] Firm and possibly compelling action by alliance leader(s) has also proved significant to the preservation of many alliances throughout history[24], from the Peloponnesian War[25] to the Cold War. However, disproportionate burden sharing is all too common where the participants in an alliance differ significantly in size, wealth, military capability, or commitment to the system.[26] The Collective Security system that results from the deployment of such cohesion-maintenance devices amongst a disparate collection of states is likely to embrace a range of striking, and noticeably asymmetrical interdependencies and to contradict many of the expectations and prognoses of the early theorists of effective Collective Security systems.

Practical expressions of collective security operations thus have been limited to operations of three types. Peace-keeping operations of relatively modest cost and which can be sustained by contributions from states of a range of size and strength have been launched in the aftermath of a number of international and civil disputes.[27] There also have been a number of attempts to reverse military aggression, or unacceptable political behaviour, through the imposition of economic sanctions under the League of Nations and the United Nations. Most rarely, major military operations have been launched to reverse acts of international aggression through physical force. The special circumstances under which operations of the last kind have been initiated will be a matter to which the discussion will return subsequently.

Institutionalist Echoes

International relations are not as unchanging in their fundamentals as the cruder theorists of power-politics have sometimes appeared to suggest. The objectives, as well as the means, of international activity evolve with changing circumstances, both material and normative. The history of the second decade of the United Nations clearly illustrates such evolution and, in parentheses, the plasticity of the normative principles that influence international conduct.

The growing bloc of Third World states within the UN was able to exploit the organization's declared principles and the sensibilities of world opinion to press for accelerated decolonization within the decade 1955 to 1965. A norm of anticolonialism was gradually crystallized and established as a dominant norm for subsequent international conduct. It would undermine the ability of colonial powers to justify their continued control of foreign territories and thence alter the bases upon which states could, and would, justify intervention in the affairs of other societies.

However, the propagation of new international norms and the preservation of peace and orderliness in the international arena has continued to be affected by its political fragmentation into sovereign states. In the pursuit of collective goods and cosmopolitan values, all states are dependent upon one another's fidelity to the principles of Collective Security, the practices of mutual support and the ethics of universal community, but remain vulnerable to the free-riding tendencies and self-interested impulses towards which their fellows are all too prone.

The fragmentary impulse at the heart of a system of sovereign states thus reasserted itself and proved its durability in the face of challenging political principles. A range of experiences with a full-blown system of Collective Security has further emphasized the persistence of such constraints upon universalistic norms and behaviour.

Hegemonies, Hierarchies, Regimes, and the United Nations

Traditional teaching on Collective Security has stressed the desirability of a reasonably even distribution of strength and capability throughout the international system. However, recent work on the most favourable conditions for international cooperation and collaboration has identified the advantages of a relative preponderance of strength in the hands of those states that are prepared to "underwrite" cooperative arrangements and hence re-emphasize the significance of the stronger members of the international system.

The problems confronting effective Collective Security systems thus parallel those encountered by the development and preservation of an international free trade system and other areas of collaboration within the international political economy that bring costs as well as benefits to participants. These problems have long attracted the attention of analysts of the international political economy and stimulated a burgeoning literature on the significance and role of hegemons, hierarchies and "regimes" in the international system.

Students of international relations have long argued that the effective management of a fragmented international system is not automatic, but not impossible either. The central problematic is to construct the appropriate structures and institutions within which the actions of individual actors on the international stage can be coordinated effectively. The origins of such structures and institutions may be varied.[28] Hegemonic management, with one or a small number of the strongest states effectively writing and enforcing rules of conduct for all other members of the international system, offers one of the simplest means to such an end.[29] Hegemonic dominance, if such a condition can be defined with precision, thus would furnish one path to a form of international order, and thereby fulfil the expectations of those who emphasize the role of structures of power and influence within international relations. However, such hegemonic management is vulnerable to exploitation by the strong and to dissolution in the wake of any substantial dilution of hegemony, as will be considered at a later stage in this discussion.

The longer-term management of the system may be ensured, however, if enduring *regimes* can be developed. Regimes may emerge in a number of ways. Voluntary negotiation might create the basis for the institutionalized management of international relations[30], possibly encouraged, if not driven, by like-minded groupings of international specialists.[31] Leadership, whether hegemonic or more distributed in character, may be sufficient for the generation of suitable international regimes.[32] The resultant international regimes can find expression through formal regulatory institutions or less formal sets of rules, sustained by a suitable pattern of inter-subjectivity amongst pertinent actors. Either type of regime, if effective, can offer a solution to the problems of effective co-ordination within a politically fragmented international system. Politics, of a wide and less adversarial character than that envisaged by political Realism, may be at the heart of international collaboration and management if developments follow a more *institutionalist* path.

The benign effect of hierarchical influence, and/or institutional learning, is the creation of a regime for the management of some areas of international interaction, including that of Collective Security. The concept of the international regime has been extensively used in contemporary studies of international relations. Indeed, its very breadth of application has stimulated serious doubts about its analytical efficacy. In his introduction to the seminal survey, Stephen Krasner defines regimes as, "principles, norms, rules, and decision-making procedures around which actor expectations converge in a given issue-area."[33] The existence of discrete issue-areas within international relations is itself problematical. The definition of regimes is so wide as to happily encompass a wide diversity of empirical conditions, from highly formalized, treaty-based organizations, such as the United Nations and associated agencies, to situations wholly lacking formal recognition or regulation, but with widely acknowledged principles.

The optimism of institutionalists and international idealists does not remain unchallenged, however, even in the realms of regime analysis. Realists, and those who reflect upon the problems of supplying collective goods, concluded that the development and maintenance of valuable regimes in areas of costly international interaction continues to rest upon the efforts of the states that are dominant economically and/or militarily, depending upon the arena within which the regime operates. A condition of "hegemonic stability" may thus arise and serve the needs of the entire membership of the international system, as in the hey-day of British economic dominance in the late nineteenth century and the dominance of the United States throughout the non-Soviet world for two or three decades following the Second World War.[34] Indeed, any condition of hegemonic stability is likely to generate a number of regimes in areas of interest to the hegemon.

Three questions arise about the role of hegemonic powers in the international system. The first concerns the influence actually exercised by the supposed hegemon, given the ease within which it can be exaggerated by enthusiasts. Detailed studies of Great Britain's role in the nineteenth century suggest that her role in the international financial system of that time was less that of a straightforward hegemon than sometimes has been claimed.[35] Similar doubts have been expressed by the ultimate extent of the political-military power at the disposal of Great Britain beyond the maritime sphere.

Should a measure of hegemony exist, however, there is still the question, secondly, as to whether all members of the international system benefit equally. The danger is that the prime beneficiary of any international regime, or set of regimes, established under the influence of a hegemon will be the hegemon itself. Great Britain and the group of core industrial economies was able to transmit the greater share of the costs of adjusting to trade imbalances to weaker economies through the operation of the Gold Standard during the later nineteenth century. The United States benefited considerably from the liberalization of trade during the era of her economic dominance after the Second World War. In the international political realm, the operation of the UN was dominated by the US and her Western allies during the initial decades of that institution's life.[36] In the extreme, a hegemony might contribute to the exploitative dominance of the international system by a small number of states and/or their economic and political leadership groups. Such a critical perspective is offered by the neo-Gramscian approach that has become popular in recent years, which identifies an insidious form of intellectual and ideological hegemony that has been generated by dominant capitalist interests and sympathetic state actors and that subordinates the peoples of much of the world, mentally as well as materially.[37]

The third central question about hegemony, and its effects, concerns the durability of the conditions generated by it when the material basis of that condition begin to dissolve. Two possibilities provide the specific regimes and the general stability generated by the previous hegemon with some prospects for survival.

Regimes may be sustained as a result of experience of those regimes themselves.[38] In game-theoretical terms, the cost-benefit schedules faced by individual states when considering behaviour that might sabotage an established regime will differ in significant ways from that facing a state considering participation in the creation of a new one. The diplomatic costs of destroying a valued regime will be far heavier than those of merely failing to join a new venture. Moreover, the understandings and expectations of political decision-makers, military planners, business leaders, and citizens may all have been changed significantly by past participation in the regime. Finally, material changes to production patterns, trade flows, defence plans and military deployments might have followed from participation in the regime. Real costs might therefore follow from any disruption or destruction of the regime by withdrawal. Self-interested behaviour may still prevail in an essentially Hobbesian world, but calculations of self-interest may have been modified substantially by changing institutional conditions and experiences.

The cumulative effects of hegemonic leadership upon the international system and the generation of a range of inter-locking regimes may also provide a basis for sustained general stability. It is possible that expectations, practices, and patterns of interaction will have been altered progressively by a world in which stability and co-ordination were underwritten by hegemon(s), or the cumulative influence of effective regimes. One possible result of such a situation might be the gradual emergence of a world of "complex interdependence"[39], if such a phenomenon is held to be a real-world condition rather than a heuristic model.[40]   The emergence of such a world, with multiple channels of association amongst societies and their peoples, an absence of a simple hierarchy amongst the issues of political and economic decision-making, and the diminished utility of force in the relations amongst states[41] would have been generated by a period of stability and confidence in world affairs and would, in turn, demonstrate a deepening and widening of prevailing international interdependences.   An enhanced role for the UN, and a firmer foundation for Collective Security, could be the product of the further deepening of any such empirical condition of complex interdependence and the associated consolidation of numerous regimes in areas of important international interaction.

Such are the intellectual foundations of hopes in, and expectations of, the cumulative construction of a new international or global political order through the auspices of the UN and similar international agencies. Serious questions remain, however, about the prospects for any new international order that is not promoted, and subsequently sustained, by one or more dominant states.

THE PERSISTENCE OF "BIG POWER" INFLUENCE WITHIN THE CONTEMPORARY INTERNATIONAL ORDER

A re-reading of a number of seminal experiences of the League of Nations and the United Nations may suggest the persisting role and influence of the major states within a politically fragmented system of sovereign states. Such disproportionate significance can be identified in the contrasting fates of the principle of decolonization during the UN's second decade, and the success of UN forces in reversing aggression in Korea and Kuwait, with the failure of the League of Nations in its actions to reverse Italy's invasion of Ethiopia in the mid-1930s, and the dismal record of vacillation during the early, critical phases of the cataclysm in Bosnia-Herzegovina.

Decolonization Revisited

The universal adoption of the principle of decolonization in the UN during its second decade can be presented as a marked triumph for cosmopolitan principles constructed by a coalition of the enlightened and the colonially oppressed. Central to the force and persuasiveness of the arguments against the perpetuation of colonialism, however, was the fact that this was one of the few major issues of the post-war world upon which the two dominant, but otherwise adversarial, states could agree and act in accord. The histories and foundational principles of both the Soviet Union and the United States enshrined anti-colonialism, and both states promoted this principle with enthusiasm and effect in the post-war world. Those who sought independence from colonial control and the enunciation of anti-colonial principles were thus pushing against an open door as far as the world's major powers were concerned during that critical era.

Moreover, the norm of anticolonialism remained tainted by the statist philosophy prevalent within the UN. The more fundamental principle of self-determination was thus neglected as states, on far too many occasions, placed *their* interests before those of the populations of the territories for which decolonization was being sought, or became equally repressive towards the rights to self-determination of minority peoples once the initial decolonization struggle had been won.

Korea and Kuwait

The UN's actions to reverse aggression in Korea and Kuwait aroused expectations of a new, and more universalistic international order but served, in the end, merely some basic lessons about the prevailing international order, for both took place under the clear leadership of the United States.

The North Korean invasion of its Southern neighbour in 1950, evoked the rapid and forceful response of the US.[42] It was, moreover, only the tactical absence of the Soviet Union from the UN's Security Council that permitted the response to be mobilized through, and under the formal auspices of the UN. The preponderance of the US in the subsequent military operation reinforced the central significance of a dominant, or hegemonic state in such operations. This was to be re-emphasized in the response to Iraq's invasion of Kuwait some forty years later.

Mobilizing the UN's Collective Security system against Iraqi aggression highlighted interesting features of prevailing conditions.[43]   The ending of the Cold War and the growing amity between East and West created an unique international configuration of power and purpose. Underwriting Collective Security against Iraq's aggression involved acceptance of the economic costs of compensating the weaker states that were most adversely affected by the imposition of sanctions and the military costs of ejecting Iraq from Kuwait. In the longer term, the costs of underwriting a revitalized Collective Security system would have to be shared rather more evenly amongst the world's stronger and wealthier states. The gradual institutionalization of a durable system of Collective Security would then have to await the general adoption of the principles and practices of Collective Security.

The League's Failure During the Italo-Ethiopian War and the United Nation's Weakness in Bosnia

Mobilizing the League of Nations against Italy's invasion of Ethiopia in 1935 was deemed both to be unavoidable and to offer an ideal opportunity to revitalize the Collective Security system as a deterrent against future German aggression.[44]   Unfortunately, British and French leaders were overly alarmed, not by the weakness of League sanctions against Italy (as in popular mythology), but by a growing fear that the planned oil sanction would prove so effective as to precipitate damaging armed Italian retaliation against British and French forces in the Mediterranean. Moreover, increasing pressure could well alienate Mussolini from the common front against Hitler's Germany. The disreputable Hoare-Laval Pact of January 1936 resulted, with the subsequent destruction of the League of Nations as an effective force in world affairs. British and French policy-makers had summoned up the genie of Collective Security only to cast it down in apprehension of its possible military costs and fear of its diplomatic consequences!

The Italo-Ethiopian conflict demonstrated the problems of effective response to determined challenges to the established international order. The stakes are raised massively once political leaders define an international action as a fundamental challenge. Irresolution subsequently encouraged others with aggressive impulses. Unfortunately, the need for a resolute response did not ensure the availability of suitable policies. Weakness amongst the leading League member states, under such circumstances, fatally compromised the resolution and effectiveness of collective action and subsequently inflicted terminal damage upon the League and its Collective Security system.

Indecision and disharmony amongst a number of the leading members of the UN and the North Atlantic Treaty Organization had a similarly damaging effect upon the clarity and forcefulness of the international response to the breakdown of order and inter-communal harmony within the former Yugoslavia, and within Bosnia-Herzegovina in particular. Diplomatic initiatives were launched by a variety of international actors. Persuasive pressure, however, required the credible threat of physical coercion. Prevarication by those states that would provide the bulk of the necessary armed forces ensured, however, that credible compulsion did not materialize in the critical period during which peace and order were disintegrating. Until, and unless, the major military underwriters were prepared to act forcefully, collective action on Bosnia, however worthy in intent, would be of strictly limited practical effect.

The Congo Crisis and the Institutional Reassertion of States' Interests

The period of decolonization was not, however, entirely lacking in challenges to the statist foundations of the *inter-state* order. During the early phase of the Congo crisis of the early 1960s, UN officials secured a relatively high level of autonomy in their conduct of peace-keeping operations within that troubled land. This level of autonomy threatened, albeit temporarily, to supersede the rule of states by a novel form of supranational authority and thus offered a hint of the potentiality of a new, genuinely global political authority. The restrictions placed upon Dag Hammarskjöld's successors as UN General Secretary, however, marked the re-affirmation of the primacy of states' interests.[45]

CONCLUSIONS

The political order of the post-war international system has remained resolutely statist at the foundational level and this has been the source of the greatest problems confronted in generating the necessary collective goods for the international community. The system also has remained profoundly hierarchical at the institutional and day-to-day levels and, hence, in its response to the problems confronting the provision of required collective goods. Practices of big-power management, weighted voting in many international organizations, the manner of the establishment of international regimes, the character of multilateral and bilateral diplomacy, occasional recourse to Collective Security procedures and the limited acknowledgement of international (inter-state) law have all attested to such features of the prevailing order.

The experience of the UN in the post-war international political system does not demonstrate that the structural and systemic constraints of such a state system are either universal or timeless. Rather, the problems besetting cosmopolitan principles and the effective supply of collective goods demonstrate the power of the constraints encountered when attempts are made to pursue purposes, or adopt practices, that clash implicitly or explicitly with the foundational principles of the international order that previously has been constructed.

Foundational principles define many of the characteristic problems that will arise within any political order and the constraints that will operate in any solutions or institutional and behavioural innovations that may be sought. Any order may permit, and even prompt, developments that appear to challenge that order, while also inhibiting the adoption of specific solutions to those challenges. A statist order thus permits states to challenge the security of other states whilst inhibiting, thus far at least, responses from the international community that challenge the inherent sanctity of state sovereignty. A statist order also endows many non-state actors, from terrorist groups to multinational corporations, with strategic advantages in their dealings with states while limiting the range of actions that states can take legitimately to constrain such advantages. All orders, whether political, economic or social, are likely to embrace such paradoxes. The problem for the international political system, and for the United Nations within it, is that such paradoxes have often assumed a deadly mantle.

NOTES

1. For the original idea of the "social construction of reality", see Peter L. Berger and Thomas Luckmann, *The Social Construction of Reality: A Treatise in the Sociology of Knowledge,* (Harmondsworth: Allen Lane, Penguin Press, 1966).
2. Anthony Giddens, *The Constitution of Society: Outline of the Theory of Structuration*, (Cambridge: Polity Press, 1984).

3. On which see David Wood (ed.), *Derrida: A Critical Reader*, (Oxford: Basil Blackwell, 1992); and Christopher Norris, *Derrida*, (London: Fontana, 1987).

4. Robert O. Keohane, "International Institutions: Two Approaches", *International Organization*, vol. 32 (1989), pp. 379-96.

5. See, for example, the discussions in Peter Winch, *The Idea of a Social Science and its Relation to Philosophy*, (London: Routledge and Kegan Paul, 1958); and M. Hollis and S. Smith, *Explaining and Understanding International Relations*, (Oxford: Oxford University Press, 1990) esp. Chs. 3 and 4.

6. On which, in particular, see M.T. Gibbons (ed.), *Interpreting Politics*, (Oxford: Basil Blackwell, 1987); Mark Hoffman, "Critical Theory and the Inter-Paradigm Debate", *Millennium: Journal of International Relations*, vol. 16, no. 2, (1987), pp. 231-49; and see also: R.J. Barry Jones, *Anti-Statism and Critical Theories in International Relations*, Reading Papers in Politics, No.4, March, 1991, Dept. of Politics, University of Reading, England.

7. See, in particular, Peter L. Berger and Thomas Luckmann, *The Social Construction of Reality*, (Harmondsworth: Penguin, 1967).

8. On which see R.J. Barry Jones, "The English School and the Political Construction of International Society" in B.A. Roberson (ed.), *The English School of International Relations Revisited* (forthcoming).

9. M.S. Archer, *Culture and Agency*, (Cambridge: Cambridge University Press, 1988).

10. David Easton, *The Political System* (New York: Alfred Knopf, 1953).

11. Harold Lasswell, *Politics: Who Gets What, When, How*, (NY: McGraw-Hill, 1936).

12. Bernard Crick, *In Defence of Politics* 2nd ed., (Harmondsworth: Penguin, 1982), p. 21.

13. *Ibid.*, p. 29.

14. See W.B. Gallie, "Essentially Contested Concepts" in Max Black (ed.), *The Importance of Language*, (Englewood Cliffs, NJ: Prentice Hall, 1972) pp. 121-168; and Richard Little, "Ideology and Change", in B. Buzan and R.J. Barry Jones (ed.), *Change and the Study of International Relations*, (London: Frances Pinter, 1981), pp. 30-45.

15. For a review of the "regime" concept and its difficulties see S.D. Krasner, *International Regimes*, (Ithaca, NY: Cornell University Press, 1983).

16. A perspective that informs J.C. Plano and R.E. Riggs' classic *Forging World Order: The Politics of International Organization*, (New York: Macmillan, 1967).

17. Evan Luard, *A History of the United Nations: Volume 1, The Years of Western Domination, 1945-1955,* (London: Macmillan, 1982), and *A History of the United Nations: Volume 2, The Age of Decolonization, 1955-1965,* (London: Macmillan, 1989).

18. Luard, *ibid.,* vol. 1.

19. For the classical statement of the theory of Collective Security see: Inis Claude, *Swords into Ploughshares* 3rd ed., (New York: Random House, 1964); and see also Plano and Riggs, *Forging World Order,* note 16, Ch. 10.

20. See, for example, Otto Pick and J. Critchley, *Collective Security,* (London: Macmillan, 1974); and Claude, *ibid.*

21. See, for example, F.P. Walters, *A History of the League of Nations,* (Oxford: Oxford University Press, 1953); and Evan Luard, *A History of the League of Nations,* note 17.

22. For illuminating discussions of the problems of maintaining confidence in the Anglo-French alliance before the outbreak of the Second World War see Arnold Wolfers, *Britain and France between Two Wars* (New York: Harcourt Brace and Co., 1940), reprinted (New York: W.W. Norton and Co, 1966); and R.J. Barry Jones, *Challenge and Response in International Politics: An Analysis of the Development of British Policy Towards Germany During 1935 and early 1936,* (Unpublished D.Phil thesis, University of Sussex, England, 1975).

23. See Mancur Olson, *The Logic of Collective Action: Public Goods and the Theory of Groups,* (Cambridge: Cambridge University Press, 1965).

24. On the theoretical significance of which see N. Frohlich, J.A. Oppenheimer, and O.R. Young, *Political Leadership and Collective Goods,* (Princeton: Princeton University Press, 1971).

25. Thucydides, *The Peloponnesian War* (trans. Rex Warner) (Harmondsworth: Penguin Books, 1954).

26. On which see Mancur Olson Jr. and Richard Zeckhauser, "An Economic Theory of Alliances", *The Review of Economics and Statistics,* vol. 48, no. 3 (August, 1966), pp. 266-279.

27. On which see Alan James, *Peacekeeping in International Politics,* (London: Macmillan/IISS, 1990).

28. See in particular Robert O. Keohane, "The Analysis of International Regimes", in V. Rittberger (with P. Mayer) (ed.), *Regime Theory and International Relations,* (Oxford: Clarendon Press, 1993), pp. 23-45.

29. For the now standard exposition of this approach see Robert Gilpin, *The Political Economy of International Relations,* (Princeton: Princeton University Press, 1987), esp. pp.75-80; and for a judicious review of this argument see Andrew Walter, *World Power and World Money: The*

Role of Hegemony and International Monetary Order, (Hemel Hempstead: Harvester/Wheatsheaf, 1991).

30. See in particular Stephen D. Krasner (ed.), *International Regimes*, (Ithaca: Cornell University Press, 1983); Robert O. Keohane, *After Hegemony: Cooperation and Discord in the World Political Economy*, (Princeton: Princeton University Press, 1984); and V. Rittberger with P. Mayer, *Regime Theory and International Relations*, note 28.

31. See Peter M. Haas, "Epistemic Communities and the Dynamics of International Environmental Co-operation", in Rittberger, *ibid.*, pp. 168-201.

32. Oran R. Young and Gail Osherenko, "Testing Theories of Regime Formation: Findings from a Large Collaborative Research Project", in V. Rittberger *Regime Theory*, note 28.

33. Stephen D. Krasner, "Structural Causes and Regime Consequences: Regimes as Intervening Variables" in Krasner, *International Regimes*, note 30, p. 1.

34. On Hegemonic Stability theory see: Charles P. Kindleberger, *The World in Depression, 1929-1939*, (Berkeley: University of California Press, 1973); Kindleberger, "Hierarchy versus Inertial Cooperation", *International Organization* vol. 40 (Autumn, 1986). But on the limitations of the role of the hegemon, see Timothy J. KcKeown, "Hegemonic Stability Theory and 19th Century Tariff Levels in Europe", *International Organization* vol. 37 (Spring, 1983), pp.73-91; and on its continuing analytical difficulties see: David A. Lake, "Leadership, Hegemony and the International Economy: Naked Emperor or Tattered Monarch with Potential", *International Studies Quarterly*, vol. 37, no. 4 (1993) pp. 459-89.

35. See Andrew Walter, *World Power and World Money*, note 29.

36. See Luard, *History of the United Nations, vol. 1*, note 17.

37. For a full account of this perspective see S. Gill and D. Law, *The Global Political Economy: Perspectives, Problems and Policies*, (Brighton: Harvester/Wheatsheaf, 1988) esp. Chs. 5, 6 and 7.

38. Keohane, *After Hegemony*, note 30.

39. R.O. Keohane and J.S. Nye Jr., *Power and Interdependence: World Politics In Transition*, (Boston: Little, Brown, 1977).

40. Keohane and Nye themselves later suggest that complex interdependence was intended to be no more than a heuristic model. See R.O. Keohane and J.S. Nye, "*Power and Interdependence* Revisited", *International Organization*, vol. 41, no. 4 (Autumn, 1987), pp. 725-53.

41. *Ibid.*, pp. 245.

42. See Glenn D. Paige, *The Korean Decision, June 24-30, 1950*, (New York: Free Press, 1968).

43. For a general account see Ken Mathews, *The Gulf Conflict and International Relations*, (London: Routledge, 1993).

44. For an account of the Italo-Ethiopian crisis see Walters, *A History of the League of Nations*, note 21, ch. 53.

45. Luard, *A History of the United Nations, vol. 2*, note 17, esp. ch. 10.

3 Leadership, the United Nations, and the New World Order

Jarrod Wiener

The concept of international leadership has become almost central to discourse about United States foreign policy, and about the effectiveness of the United Nations in the New World Order. The concept was used in 1990 and 1991 by some politicians, journalists, and academics to denote an activity that promotes action, a role that promulgates vision and purpose, and a force that maintains stability in the post-Cold War international system. Then-US President George Bush stated before Congress on 11 September 1990 that, "we are now in sight of a United Nations that performs as envisioned by its founders"[1], and exclaimed in January 1991 that, "we are the only nation on this earth that could assemble the forces of peace. This is the burden of leadership."[2] The rhetoric of the administration during its attempt to build the Coalition against Iraq seemed to suggest that the bipolar stability of the Cold War would be replaced by a great-power consensus supported by American leadership. During the Gulf War, *The Guardian* sounded a typical comment, that: "The Allies embarked, under dominant American leadership, upon the first testing of a New World Order, with the United Nations at its heart".[3] Advocates of the "renewalists" thesis on US hegemony, such as Joseph Nye, argued that the US, with its unique combination of military and economic power, its political culture, and experience in realpolitik, was *Bound to Lead*.[4]

But, the euphoria that accompanied the supposed new system of collective security during the Gulf War soon was replaced by the "gloom of early 1992".[5] In stark contrast to the overwhelming commitment of the US to the Gulf War − both politically and in terms of resources − the Clinton administration defined US foreign policy in terms of "assertive multilateralism", which proved not to be very assertive. References to US leadership became associated with lamentations of an apparent disinclination of the US to lead.[6] As the news of death camps

41

in Bosnia was brought to world attention in August 1992, *Time International* noted that, "like it or not, the world looks to the US to lead an international response".[7] As late as February 1994, a senior US State Department official reportedly stated that Europe was "calling, even pleading for US leadership"[8] over the Bosnian crisis, while members of the administration publicly contradicted each other over the possibility of NATO air-strikes. There remained a vexed political inertia over a solution to the conflict, and the commander of the UN — the organiz-ation that only a year earlier was at the "heart" of the New World Order — was empowered with only his ball-point pen to prevent UN peace-keepers from coming under attack. The "New World Disorder" that ensued became characterized by a lack of vision and direction, and the seeming primacy of interests over morality. The US withdrawal from Somalia effectively resulted in the country reverting to the control of warlords; and the slow, disjointed response to the humanitarian crisis in Rwanda either mocked Bush's moral triumphalism, or exposed it as the circumstantial politically expedient rhetoric that it was. What can explain this apparent pendulum swing of US leadership activity, and what are the consequences for the stability of the United Nations are the subjects of this chapter.

MACRO-UNILATERAL AND MICRO-MULTILATERAL LEADER-SHIP IN INTERNATIONAL RELATIONS THEORY

Despite popular usage of the term, what is meant by "international leadership" is almost as vague as the "New World Order". There is no paradigm on the concept of leadership generally in political science; in fact, one scholar's review of the literature found 130 definitions.[9] In International Relations, there is added confusion due to differing levels of analysis, which leads to disagreement over the functions that a state assumes in a leadership role, and consequently also over the attributes that a state needs to lead and to legitimate such a role over sovereign states. In the interest of clarity, this section presents a classification of leadership theories according to levels of analysis, "macro-unilateral" and "micro-multilateral".

Macro-leadership

Macro-level analyses are concerned mainly with three unilateral leadership activities at the global level. The first is providing intellectual leadership in espousing principles on which to base international order. The second, and related to this, is providing the initiative and impetus towards creating authoritative structures within an anarchical system based upon these ideas. The third is securing the international system from the threat of a challenger, thereby providing all states in the international community with the public good of security. Macro-unilateral leadership is generally associated with the period of US hegemony in the West after the Second World War, and is articulated theoretically by George Modelski's "long cycle school of world leadership".[10]

This theory suggests the occurrence of fairly well defined one hundred year cycles in the international system. Each cycle, of which there have been six, historically has been "led" by a state that was more powerful than all others in the system. At the conclusion of the last major-power war, the US emerged with a military ascendancy of a monopoly character, and an economy that produced and traded techno-logically advanced products. Like preceding preponderant states, the US favoured the status-quo and had the power and willingness to project its own vision of order onto the international system. Whereas the principles favoured by the major powers historically had been embodied in the peace treaties of hegemonic wars, the US institutionalized an order in the United Nations. It is this shaping of the overall character of the system, or making rules that govern the manner in which states relate to the dominant power and to each other, which Modelski termed "global leadership". In this sense, leadership relates to a political activity in shaping international structures to suit the ascendant state's interests.

A world leader also meets the challenger to the system, which in the case of the US was the USSR. This aspect of macro-leadership rests on putative resources as the lead state bases this global defense on its military "global reach". In other words, the leader legitimates itself by providing a collective good of security to the other states in the system. Other leadership activities include stimulating the world economy, "enforcing the rules of international trade", and "exploiting the possibil-ities for common interest and minimizing the areas of conflict".[11]

It is important to recognize that Modelski does not elaborate a precise concept of leadership, meaning that he does not explain precisely what a state does when it is leading. Rather, his theory delineates broad categories in which leadership takes place. The closest that this theory comes to a definition is that leadership occurs "when a state acts in the public interest and its actions are thought legitimate".[12] This is very broad, and can easily encompass any action taken by the lead state on which other states consent. In the long-cycle theory, leadership is an explanation for the theory's main concern – the occurrence and maintenance of a rule-oriented and norm-governed system. It therefore cannot be faulted for this imprecision. But for present purposes its explanatory power ends there; the concept of leadership serves this theory as an explanation, rather than being explained by it.

Micro-leadership

By contrast, micro-multilateral leadership refers to a relationship between leaders and followers within a well-defined normative order, such as in an international regime, and refers to a process of multilateral policy coordination whereby a leader gains a followership behind its agenda through persuasion, negotiation, and brokering the concerns of others to induce them to follow. Micro-leadership rests upon a behavioural concept of power because it stresses the skills that a leader activates in a relationship with followers, rather than putative resources.

This conception has been articulated in political science by James MacGregor-Burns, among others, who defined it as, "leaders inducing followers to act for certain goals that represent the values and the motivations – the wants and the needs, the aspirations and the expectations – of both leaders and followers."[13]   For MacGregor-Burns, leadership relates to a legitimate, cooperative relationship that is "linked to a common purpose".[14] A leader persuades, guides, cajoles, and coaxes to "mobilize and arouse" others to engage in a certain behaviour, and is therefore a means to promote cooperation. For MacGregor-Burns, "leadership is exercised in a condition of conflict or competition in which leaders contend in appealing to the motive-bases of potential followers....in pursuit of common, or at least joint purposes."[15] While no coherent theory of micro-leadership has been formulated in International Relations, recent work by Oran Young has articulated a conception of "entrepreneurial leadership" in regimes which involves "leaders making use of negotiating skills to influence the manner in which issues are presented, and to fashion acceptable deals bringing willing parties together".[16]

The Theory of Hegemonic Leadership

The Theory of Hegemonic Leadership incorporates both macro and micro levels of analysis. It explains the creation of authoritative normative structures as well as the stability of its component international regimes as a result of leadership. However, this theory confuses the two levels by assuming that putative resources are necessary for both types of leadership. It is important to recognize this error, as, although this theory has been elaborated most extensively in the context of the post-Second World War Bretton Woods international economic regimes, it informs the discussion of US international leadership more generally.

The original formulation of the theory presumes that only a state that is preponderant, in terms of material resources, can "lead" in the international system. Robert Keohane listed such attributes as, "control of raw materials, sources of capital, markets, competitive advantage in the production of highly valued goods, finance capital, technologies, natural resources, [and a] large home market" as bases of hegemonic power.[17] This emphasis on resources is due to the theory's use of public-goods arguments to define the motivations of states to "lead", and to "follow". These terms are presented in inverted commas because they relate more properly to a process of "provision" and of "usage", respectively, when the theory discusses leadership at the macro-level.

Macro-leadership in this theory relates to the act of a preponderant state furnishing, meaning singly paying for, international public goods, among which are such things as a stable international currency, fixed exchange rates, and free trade.[18] These goods involve a cost, either materially or in forgone opportunities, and it is assumed that egoistic states will prefer to allow another state to pay for them and to "free-ride", or to enjoy their benefits without contributing. Given this dilemma, the theory argues that international public goods tend to be underproduced unless a wealthy state that has an overwhelming interest in having such goods provides them for itself. As Charles Kindleberger, who originated the public-goods approach stated, "for the world economy to be stabilized, there has to be a stabilizer, one stabilizer... a country which is prepared... to set standards of conduct for other countries and... to take on an undue share of the burdens".[19] Revisions to the theory have argued that public goods can be provided by a privileged "K-group", meaning a wealthy collectivity, and not only by a single hegemonic leader.[20] This presents an advance upon the theory, for it accepts that collective action is not always precluded by coordination difficulties such as prisoners' dilemmas in the absence of a single predominant state. However, like the original formulation, such revisions also refer to "leadership" in terms of a provision.

Both the original formulation of the theory and subsequent revisions have been concerned with the manner in which the cost of public goods is met in an anarchical system. The central concern is who pays for them. Kindleberger seems to imply that a beneficent hegemon "leads" the system by paying for the goods, and that others "follow" by free riding, or using the goods. But usage is very different from followership, as the former can occur without leaders and followers engaging in a relationship. For example, a state's ships theoretically can enjoy the freedom from pirates on the high seas, which is a public good, and be oblivious of the fact that the hegemonic state's navy is actively engaged in policing them. The revised version of the theory seems to imply that collective goods can be provided without "leadership" — where leadership means a single hegemon paying for the goods. The research programme of the revisions has been to demonstrate that a demand for a public good can be an incentives to contribute to it, and has not regarded the means of coordinating collective action. But, leadership may be a feature of the bargaining within the K-groups themselves. Whereas a single hegemon deems what goods are necessary *a priori*, the members of the K-group must agree amongst themselves what they will spend their resources and energies on, and within this context there is an opportunity for micro-leadership to occur. Indeed, there is a high likelihood that members of the group will attempt to gain acceptance for their own preferences, to convince others that its ideas are beneficial to all and therefore the best course of action for the group, and to mobilize a followership.

The Theory of Hegemonic Leadership conceives of leadership at the micro-level as relating to the act of organizing acceptance of the rules governing the use of public goods. In Kindleberger's words, after having set the standards, leadership involves seeking "to get others to follow them".[21] At this level, the theory is divided into two viewpoints. Regime stability, meaning the maintenance of a set of norms and rules that is relatively well-obeyed, can be maintained either by other states free-riding on the goods provided by the hegemon, in other words going-along, which is characteristic of a "beneficent hegemony" of the neoliberal perspective, or by the preponderant state forcing other states to adhere to certain rules, which is a coercive, but benevolent hegemony typical of the neorealist variant.[22]

But, again, free riding is not a description of followership. In Kindleberger's list of public goods, the freedom of shipping routes is perhaps the only good that the hegemon can provide unilaterally. Fixed exchange rates and lower tariff levels not only require cooperation, but often can entail opportunity costs. Gaining acceptance for such rules can require inducing, or coercing others to cooperate. Moreover, the hegemon cannot solely pay for a free trade regime as by definition this is a collectivity, and standards, such as fixed exchange rates, are useless unless all follow the same rules.[23] It is therefore difficult to see how the neoliberal variant differs from its neorealist cousin in this respect. Robert Gilpin, the main exponent of the neorealist variant, suggested that regime stability is sustained by the "initiative, bargaining, [and] sanctions", of the dominant power.[24] And, Kindleberger suggests a type of leadership by "persuasion" which may involve a certain degree of "arm-twisting and bribery".[25] It is therefore apparent that it is not only Gilpin's "coercive" neorealist hegemon that must "tax" others, but that the "beneficent" hegemon of the neoliberal variant must also be coercive. In fact, the neoliberal hegemonic leader would be abrogating its "responsibility" to maintain order if it failed to maintain the public good, which could entail coercing states to cooperate against their will.[26]

But hegemonic micro-leadership is not exploitative. For, the hegemonic leader does not rely primarily on negative sanction for inducing cooperation, but resolves opportunity cost through positive inducements. At the micro-level, the Theory of Hegemonic Leadership believes that preponderant resources are used, in effect, to *pay* others to cooperate. This permits the hegemonic leader to maintain sufficient legitimacy for sovereign states to accept its coercive behaviour at times. But this emphasis on resources leaves the theory effectively with only one mechanism of legitimation, a hegemonic payment, and, crucially, this is what leads it to the conclusion that only a predominant state with such resources can lead internationally.

Like the long-cycle school, the Theory of Hegemonic Leadership is ambiguous about the precise nature of international leadership. The conflation between the material resources that are required to pay for public goods and the act of leadership leads this theory to confuse governance, or management, with leadership. Hegemonic leadership does operate at both the macro- and the micro-level, and resources may very well be required to legitimate a newly-created order. In the 1940s, the US had both legitimated its role of leader and the series of regimes that it instituted. It had gained the acceptance of principles by using its resources to grant more concessions to others than it received in return, which legitimated the order. But it was the manner in which the US carried out the negotiations for this order, by taking on board the concerns of others, that legitimated its own role.

This distinction between the legitimation of a normative framework on one hand and the legitimation of a leadership role on the other is crucial, but the Theory of Hegemonic Leadership assumes that the two processes always take place at the same time. In domestic politics one normally does not confuse the legitimacy that is accorded to a particular system of governance, such as party politics, or to particular principles, such as those relating to representative democracy, with the legitimacy that is accorded to a particular government or administration. The former can endure despite the flagging popularity, and successive changes, of the latter. The initiation of structure by a hegemonic leader − the normative or ideological underpinnings of a regime − may confer legitimacy to the hegemonic system, but it is in the leadership situation − that is, the coordinating of policies for a mutually advantageous outcome − which legitimates a particular leader. This dichotomous legitimation suggests two things. The first, as some scholars already have pointed out, is that a regime can retain its legitimacy and become self sustaining even after the power that brought it into being wanes. The second, which builds upon this, is that a state does not need hegemonic resources to lead within a regime where the norms are already internalized.

The utilitarian-contractarian contribution to the debate over the stability of hegemonic regimes once the power that created them declines places central importance upon the continuation of mutual advantage. Robert Keohane has argued that long term, enlightened self-interest and an expectation of future reciprocity − "even if there is no convincing evidence to that effect"[27] − can explain how regimes can be sustained "after hegemony"; in other words, how the obligations required for participation in the regime can be secured without relying on continual hegemonic resources as compensation.[28]

It follows from this that micro-leadership can take place within a regime, and that if the leader appeals to norms that are already accepted, its initiative can be strengthened by them, and hence can be less expensive, and have a greater chance of success, than the leadership that created the regime. While the norms of the regime reflect a particular will, or order, they also define the structure of international authority wherein leadership may take place. The substantive norms of regimes are the residue of US hegemony, and constitute the "structure of the internationalization of political authority".[29] Recall that MacGregor-Burns' conception of legitimacy was based not upon a Weberian rational-legal mechanism that rests on authorized coercion, such as in the form of the police and other forms of organized state violence, but from mutual benefits, the attainment of goals that are shared between leaders and followers. A leader can appeal to the accepted principles of the regime, which perhaps approximates more J.S. Mill's "moral coercion" than a legal compulsion[30], but implies that a legitimate political system can exact duties, or the performance of obligations from its constituents.[31] This means that a leader's behaviour can be legitimated by the fact that the norms, principles, and decision-making procedures to which it appeals have prior acceptance.

Thus, what the Theory of Hegemonic Leadership regards as micro-leadership is really the provision of incentives for followership, a mechanism of legitimation for leadership rather than the act of leading, and it overlooks the fact that in a multilateral regime such incentives can emanate from sources other than directly from the leader. Leaders and followers within a stable political order have congruent value-hierarchies, otherwise there would not be an order, and they agree in principle that an agenda of the leader which reflects those values is desirable. This would explain, for example, the willingness of contracting parties to the GATT to undertake the arduous negotiations of the Uruguay round from 1986 to 1994 despite some very strong reservations with various aspects of the negotiating agenda on the part of a number of participants.[32] The outcome of the negotiations in principle reflects the original desires of the hegemonic leader, as a "residual hegemony". This is similar to Gramscian hegemony, which refers to the universalization of an ideology, which, once accepted, determines which issues are politicized onto the international agenda, the fora in which they are treated, and the manner in which they are resolved.[33]

The conclusions to be drawn from this is that leadership at the micro-level must be a coercive activity, in that it manipulates the actions of others. But, crucially, leadership can remain legitimate even if this coercion involves extracting a payment from others. For, rather than offering a payment as a source of legitimation, a leader can initiate and guide a situation with reference to extant norms, rules, and decision-making procedures of the relevant community in which the leadership takes place. A leader in a multilateral framework can manipulate interdependences strategically such that issues are linked to one another and that the payoffs are exchanged in a complex fashion, rather than emanating solely from the leader.

LEADERSHIP IN THE NEW WORLD ORDER

Theories of leadership in International Relations have difficulty in explaining US leadership activity in the New World Order. This is partly because the conditions under which the theories explain leadership no longer pertain, and partly because the theories themselves are confused. However, the greatest difficulty in explaining the variation in the intensity of leadership, from a high level in the case of the Gulf War to near political inertia in the case of the former Yugoslavia and a disjointed and incremental involvement in Rwanda, stems from the fact that popular perceptions of what the US should lead about differs from the motives that have prompted the US to assume a leadership role in the past. The extent to which the US leads appears to be judged popularly on moral criteria, rather than on the level of state interest, and on this the theories of international leadership are illustrative.

The conditions under which a state can exercise macro-leadership, in the sense of imbuing the system with authoritative principles, do not pertain in the New World Order. The post-Cold War system has inherited the United Nations. With some practical modifications, the principles of the UN were based on the moral leadership of Woodrow Wilson's Fourteen Points and driven by his insistence in 1918 on the incorporation of the Covenant of the League of Nations into the peace treaties of the First World War. Franklin D. Roosevelt invited Great Britain, China and the Soviet Union to Dumbarton Oaks in 1944, and the remainder of the original members of the UN to San Francisco in 1945. The post-Cold War system began with this framework of principles for maintaining security, however dysfunctional they had been during the Cold War, that reflected the US political culture of promoting order through legislation. In the interim, the US had made no effort to disguise the fact that it had become "disillusioned" and that it had "failed to take the UN seriously".[34] What President Bush had done in espousing the principles of the New World Order at Andrews Air Force Base in April 1991 was not to create a new organization, but to signal the US re-engagement in it, and the renewal of the original assumption of the UN that the great powers would cooperate. But Bush introduced, explicitly, an entirely new element: that the system would work under US leadership. Rather than leading at the macro-level to create order, he implied that US micro-level leadership in organizing action would activate the Collective Security apparatus of the UN in order to uphold it.

The New World Order is therefore a continuation of the previous system, rather than an entirely new one in this respect. What is new is that Collective Security, in theory, can operate as envisioned. Moreover, the threat of a global challenger has receded. Whereas American hegemonic leadership was motivated by "enlightened self-interest", where the costs of assuming a disproportionate burden in the short-term were offset by the longer term strategic interest of maintaining the European and Japanese pillars of Cold War security, the post-Cold War system lacks a single threat which could motivate a state to commit the resources necessary for this sort of global leadership. Therefore, the New World Order is not conducive to macro-leadership, both in the sense of a state creating authoritative normative structures and using its global reach to provide security unilaterally for the system. Any discussion of leadership in the New World Order must therefore relate to micro-leadership.

Yet, at this level, the theories are confused, and can lead to vastly divergent views of US leadership in the New World Order. Scholars ascribing to the "declinist" thesis argue that the US has declined in material terms, and invoke the concept of "overstretch" to explain why the US no longer has the financial capability to underwrite its leadership.[35] They argue that there is a disjuncture between the goals of US foreign policy and its resources to achieve them, and point to the fact that the US required multilateral funding for the Gulf War.[36] This perspective implicitly accepts the assumption of the Theory of Hegemonic Leadership, which makes a state's ability to lead at the micro-level contingent on its material capabilities, which was shown above to be confused. Interestingly, those contesting the view that the US has declined, the "renewalists", also explicitly ascribe to this assumption of the theory, only they argue that the US maintains attributes for leadership which Europe and Japan lack.[37] The assumption that resources are required for leadership remains.

Certainly, economic considerations have had an important place in determining US foreign policy. *The Economist* quite rightly stated in June 1993 that "after four decades of leading the free world, Americans are increasingly wondering whether they still want, or need, the job".[38] In terms of policy, this finds expression in the concept of "burden-sharing". As recently as May 1994, the House of Representatives voted on an amendment to reduce the number of US personnel stationed in Europe by 75,000 if its allies did not pay 75% of their non-salary costs. A statement by Thomas H. Andrews is typical of the "diminished giant syndrome": "Since they [America's European allies] do not have to pay their fair share for their own defense, they invest their dollars in taking our jobs".[39] And, this burden-sharing was seen in practice after the Gulf War, when the US pressured its allies, particularly Germany and Japan, quite strongly to compensate it monetarily for its efforts.

But while the fact of the US obtaining contributions from coalition allies against Iraq can not be denied, it can be interpreted in a different way. Rather than indicating that the US was forced by its economic circumstances to go around with a begging-bowl, this could suggest that there is a greater likelihood that the US will exercise micro-leadership if it does not have the resources to undertake actions unilaterally, or if it is not inclined to pay solely for them. Ironically as far as the Theory of Hegemonic Stability is concerned, decline can mean a greater engagement in leadership. This implies not only a greater role for the UN, but a more effective one. Clinton stated that "it is time for our friends to bear more of the burden" in "a wider coalition of nations of which America will be a part", such as "NATO and a new, voluntary UN Rapid Deployment Force"[40]. In the context of Somalia, he stated that the US would continue "its unique role of leadership in the world... through multilateral means, such as the UN, which spread the costs and express the unified will of the international community".[41] The consequence for the UN is that the US would become, in Clinton's words, "the catalyst for a collective stand against aggression".[42]

If "catalyzing" action is to be interpreted as micro-leadership, then US leadership and a central role for the UN are inextricable. In fact, one could argue that the US was not only leading by organizing action and collecting payment for the Gulf War, but that this behaviour constituted a type of governance as well. Since the purpose of the Coalition was to uphold the principles of non-aggression and territorial integrity enshrined in the UN Charter, the US was performing a policing role, not dissimilar to that of the police in the domestic context, which is a facet of a government's efforts to maintain law and order.

But this assessment may be overstated, particularly if it is taken to imply that the US was motivated by some altruistic, moral sense of its purpose in the world to defend the UN Charter. For, it has also been suggested that the Gulf War, the shining moment of the UN Collective Security in the post-Cold War era, was in reality a display of US "headship" rather than leadership, and "going-alongism" on the part of the Coalition members instead of followership. Andrew Fenton Cooper, Richard Higgott and Kim Nossal have suggested that the enterprise is more properly conceived as a US-dominated action, with the other members of the Security Council either going along or reserving comment. These authors concluded that "no one could quite figure out how to prevent leadership turning into headship, where decisions for the group are arrived at unilaterally by a leader whose overweening power ensures that subordinates will have few other options than to comply".[43] They are not alone in this view. Barry M. Blechman argued that the Gulf War was "essentially a US operation... undertaken without benefit of the mechanisms for enforcing collective security that are enshrined in the UN Charter".[44] Indeed, this may say something about the US approach to resolving a problem in which it perceives a relatively large interest. In August 1991 *The Guardian* suggested that "the US.... favours genuine multilateral command, which in practice means American leadership"[45]; one should read "control" instead of "leadership". And, this was echoed in the attitude of at least one official in the Clinton administration in the context of the crisis in Bosnia as he stated that, "we know from experience that the allies will fall in line if we toughly set out what we're going to do. This business of the President saying we can't lead if the allies won't follow ignores the lessons of the past 40 years. They'll follow if we lead.... For a democratic superpower, consultation is important, but it should always be essentially cosmetic."[46]

If this is so, the implication of having hailed the dawning of a new era of collective management in the UN as being due to leadership is a confusion of leadership with US control − or unilateralism, although that may be going too far − in one unique circumstance, which means that Collective Security is a smoke-screen. For, if the Security Council is so effective only if driven by the US "calling the shots", as it were, and using the UN only for purposes of legitimation, the UN can risk being relegated to a convenience, a set of principles that can be activated on command. This is not to suggest that the UN would not continue to have an increasingly greater role in peace-keeping operations, as indeed it has, but that it would have spectacular effectiveness only when a great power utilises it for purposes that supersede its commitment to the organization, which in reality would be rhetorical only. After all, that a set of principles can become such a tool is not new; as one observer noted at the dawning of the previous "new" international order, "like all utopias that are institutionalized, the post-war utopia became the tool of the vested interests".[47]

Conversely, if commitment to the UN is rhetorical only, the organization's processes of multilateralism could be used to obscure shying away from leadership when vital national interests are not directly at stake, and could become a scapegoat on which to blame inertia. Indeed, the US has been criticized for deferring to the UN, *instead of* taking the lead. Senator Robert Dole stated in September 1993 that a greater reliance on the UN is an "abdication of American leadership".[48] Senator Richard Lugar asserted that, "multilateralism has become a cover for US retrenchment and abandonment of leadership to the vagaries of international events".[49] Others, while not denying this, agree that this approach has tactical advantage. While Richard Nixon believed that the concept of "assertive multilateralism being advanced by some supporters of the United Nations can only be described as diplomatic gobbledy-gook", he argued that "we should follow President Bush's example in the Persian Gulf War, using the UN, not being used by it".[50]

That there can be two such diametrically opposed, and equally legitimate, views on whether the US led or controlled the Gulf War, and whether a role of catalyst for collective action in the UN is leadership or an abdication of leadership is due to the fact that the theories in International Relations are collectively responsible for failing to define precisely what leadership is. As stated above, the long-cycle theory uses the concept of leadership to explain stability, rather than explaining what is meant by it, and the Theory of Hegemonic Stability has not explained precisely what dynamics are involved in mobilising states to follow a particular agenda save for "arm twisting", and using "a certain amount of persuasion". As Arthur Stein has observed, both variants of the theory, "mention that a hegemon uses inducements and force... but none provides a sense of how this occurs".[51]

It is not within the scope of this chapter to take on such an herculean task of formulating a stipulative definition of international leadership, and it is doubtful whether any one would be universally accepted. But even without such a definition, the foregoing discussion would lead us to conclude that by getting the Coalition members on board a particular agenda *and* by coercing them to pay for the outcome, *and* by legitimating this action by appealing to the embedded norms of an accepted framework the US did lead in the Gulf War. But the question remains why, after having demonstrated such activity in 1990 and 1991, the US is now perceived not to be leading.

To answer this question, it is important to identify the contexts in which the US is perceived not to be leading. A lack of "leadership" has been used most often as the explanation for the disjointed action in response to the conflict in the former Yugoslavia. For example, *The Guardian* suggested in August 1993 that the US allies were wondering "what happened to US leadership".[52] Also, the term "leadership" has helped some Congressmen to define their particular preference for US intervention in that conflict within the larger, traditional US foreign policy agenda to help build political support for it. For example, Senator Joe Biden stated that "the US must lead the West in a decisive response to Serbian aggression"[53]; Senator Richard Lugar stated that, "the vigorous, robust quality of leadership just isn't there like it ought to be"; and Dan Glickman stated that, "you just can't be a leader at home, you have to be a leader abroad as well".[54] Thus, the term was utilized as a means for some Congressmen to admonish Clinton for what *they* perceived as his failings in foreign policy. In fact, both media commentary and political rhetoric have accused the US of not leading in preventing genocide, human rights abuses, and other humanitarian disaster, an accusation which is based on moral criteria.

The reason why it is important to recognize this is because, traditionally, international leadership has related to the creation of order and the maintenance of stability, not to making the world just. And, all of the theories of international leadership recognized that national interest had a central position in determining a state's motivation to lead. The long-cycle school reasoned that the predominant power, which benefits the most from the status quo, will have an interest in protecting the system. The Theory of Hegemonic Stability argued that the largest actor in a collectivity will have the most to lose from not having a particular good, and will therefore set about providing it for itself. In practice, there is little doubt of the US motivations for leadership following the Second World War. The need to maintain free democratic, capitalist states within a military alliance was, at bottom, the motivation behind US political and economic leadership.[55] While there is some debate about the motivations of the US in the Gulf War, maintaining a regional balance of power, safeguarding oil supplies, and indeed jobs, were declared war aims. Thus at both the macro- and micro-levels during and after the Cold War, respectively, the record of US leadership shows that when the US has led, it has been to serve its own particular interests.

The reasons why the term should come to be used in a moral context remains a matter for speculation. Perhaps Bush's rhetoric in motivating his domestic public opinion to support him in the Gulf War unwittingly built a lingering popular expectation of what is possible in the post-Cold War period, and somehow implied that US leadership would be related to humanitarian intervention. After all, there was a moral overtone to his rhetoric, as upholding human rights was among the four principles around which Bush framed his New World Order in addition to the peaceful resolution of disputes, collective action against aggression, and arms control.[56] His references to upholding not only international law, but also such value-laden terms as "freedom" and "justice" in almost the same breath as espousing the "burden of American leadership" perhaps elevated popular expectations that US leadership would relate not only to coordinating action, but to pursuing justice.[57] Having said that, Bush subsequently demonstrated a pragmatic caution about intervening in Iraq to depose Saddam Hussein after the UN cease-fire, and was slow to respond to the plight of the Kurds. Perhaps it was Clinton, who in the course of the presidential campaign criticized Bush for failing to see that Slobodan Milosevic was emerging as a "tyrant" and promised to take a more proactive approach who added this dimension to popular expectations of US leadership.[58]

Whatever the reason, the fact remains that the issues over which the US is accused of not leading in the post-Gulf War world do not satisfy the test of interest. However, it is interesting to note that the confusion between hegemony and leadership that had permeated the academic discussion of international leadership seems now to be replaced by a popular confusion between cosmopolitan ethics informed by the vagaries of public opinion, and the real state interests that motivate leadership. None of this alters the fact that the US is not leading; but it does help to explain why it is not. The international system lacks an overarching mission which requires leadership, and lacks a threat which can motivate a state to assume it.

The New World Order is characterized by small, isolated, and often internal conflicts, which, besides presenting logistical difficulties for intervention, imply piecemeal actions. The conflict in the former Yugoslavia is only one of a number of its kind, yet it is the one that has received the most media attention. And, with the possible, but remote, exception of the conflicts spilling over into Macedonia and Bulgaria, it, like most others, does not imply an immediate threat to US security. As Richard Boucher of the State Department said, the conflict in the former Yugoslavia is "a European matter", or at least is not of direct consequence to the US.[59] A potent pressure for the US to intervene has been domestic public opinion. The so-called "CNN-factor" that projects powerful scenes of suffering that morally outrage has stirred a real, but by no means universal or constant demand for action. In fact, Congressmen reproached ABC News anchor Ted Koppel and CNN Vice-President Ted Turner for depicting humanitarian tragedies in graphic detail. As House Foreign Affairs Committee Chairman Lee H. Hamilton stated, "pictures in Sarajevo get us more involved".[60] However, as the US experience in Somalia illustrates, this humanitarian concern is likely to change, or to be overcome by the opinions of others when US soldiers begin to be killed in a battle that is remote from immediate US security interests.

This is not to suggest that there are no threats to US security. Nuclear proliferation and the export of sensitive technologies is a danger, and the smuggling of plutonium from Russia, allegedly, which first came to light in May 1994 illustrates that it is a very real one. But this, and other such threats, while not precluding some kind of action on the part of the US, are such that they are not conducive to international leadership. The US could play a major role, for instance, in assisting transitional democracies with safeguards procedures, both intellectually and monetarily. However, it is difficult to assert effectual leadership over a situation where the illegal activities of certain individuals undermine the commitments made by political leaders.

Therefore, the reason why the US is perceived not to be leading could be, quite simply, because it is not. But it is of utmost importance to recognize that the reason why it is not is issue-specific, and related to its willingness, rather than something chronic, or worse, structural and related to its ability. Whereas international leadership during the Cold War was a strategic manoeuvre, abstaining from leadership in the post-Cold War system can be equally prudent. Disjointed steps guided by public opinion are not well advised. But, whether a state chooses to lead or not to lead, the decision must be a conscious one. For, to lead internationally requires domestic leadership in building a consensus on foreign policy, and to chose not to lead requires managing pressure. That the Clinton administration has failed in the latter − Somalia is a case in point - could be responsible for the perception of a vacillation in US leadership. From the point of view of an interest-based approach to leadership, the vacillation is more apparent that real; it relates not so much to international leadership, but to managing domestic pressures.

It is interesting that there is a strong argument that US leadership is *necessary* for the effective functioning of the UN. Roger A. Coate, speaking for the contributors to a recent volume on US policy towards the UN, argued that, "US leadership will be required to revitalize the United Nations".[61] But if the US is unwilling, rather than unable, to lead, as has been argued here, there remains some reason for optimism about the role of the UN in the New World Order. It means that the US very well could lead, when it has an interest to do so. And when it does, as in the Gulf War, there is every likelihood that it will wish to channel its efforts through the UN both for international legitimacy and for the purpose of forging favourable public opinion at home. This also means that when the US chooses not to lead, the organization will continue to have a greater role. The multilateralism of the UN is well suited to the diffuse conflicts that are characteristic of the New World Order. It is not surprising, therefore, that the Clinton administration asked Congress for an increased peace-keeping budget − and this within an atmosphere of a "bottom-up" review of defense spending − and made a, albeit qualified, statement in support of UN peace-keeping: that the US will say "yes" to UN peace-keeping operations, with the proviso that the UN can learn to say "no" and get involved only selectively in conflicts rather than in every one of them. This qualification is understandable. As Cyrus Vance, the Representative of the Secretary General to Yugoslavia recognized, peace-keeping forces cannot keep a peace where there is no political willingness on the part of the parties to the conflict to make one. The UN should ensure a clear "escape scenario" prior to any engage-ment, for it certainly would burden the peace-keeping budget and damage the organization's credibility if it were to multiply its commitment to protracted cases such as Cyprus or the Golan Heights.

The bottom line, therefore, is that with or without US leadership, the UN will continue to have a greater role. However, it is premature to speculate about a shift to UN leadership, as the financing of its oper-ations is still very much dependent on its member states. But where there is no need for macro-leadership, international stability will remain, arguably as it always has remained, the result of a proper balance between national interest and the respect for legal order. But where the element of national interest diminishes, rather than signalling a with-drawal of the US into "quasi-isolationism", as has been proffered, there can be a greater reliance upon the coercive apparatus of the legal order. It could be that, as the UN passes its fiftieth anniversary, it enters a far more dangerous world to be sure, but one over which it will be delegated more control — so long as it respects the interests of its most powerful states.

ACKNOWLEDGEMENTS

The author is most appreciative of an "impromptu seminar" on this paper with Dominic Powell and John Kennair, and of the useful suggestions made by Amanda Linter, Dan Hiester and Adrian Roper. The author remains solely responsible for the views expressed here.

NOTES

1. "I Can Call Spirits from the Vastly Deep", *The Economist*, 15 Septem-ber 1990, p. 43.
2. "Gulf War Defining Moment for Nation", *The Guardian*, 30 January 1991, p. 1.

3. "The First Days of Euphoria", *The Guardian* (London), 25 February 1991, p. 22.

4. Joseph Nye, *Bound to Lead: The Changing Nature of American Power*, (New York: Basic Books, 1991).

5. So-called by *The Economist*, "When Cold Warriors Quit", 8 February 1992, p. 15.

6. And, noticeably, the term has been used with increased frequency. These trends are perceptible with the benefit of CD-ROM technology.

7. "Atrocity and Outrage", *Time International*, 17 August 1992, p. 21.

8. "This Time We Mean It", *Time International*, 21 February 1994, p. 15.

9. James MacGregor-Burns, *Leadership*, (New York: Harper & Row, 1978), p. 2.

10. George Modelski, *Long Cycles in World Politics*, (London: Macmillan, 1987); and Modelski (ed.), *Exploring Long Cycles*, (London: Pinter, 1987).

11. Modelski, "Long Cycles of World Leadership", in W.R. Thompson (ed.), *Contending Approaches to World Systems Analysis*, (Beverly Hills: Sage, 1983), p. 138; and Modelski, *Long Cycles in World Politics, ibid.*, p. 17.

12. Modelski, "Long Cycles of World Leadership", in Modelski (ed.), *Exploring Long Cycles*, note 10, p. 122.

13. MacGregor-Burns, *Leadership*, note 9, p. 19.

14. *Ibid.*, p. 2.

15. *Ibid.*, pp. 18-19.

16. Young, "Political Leadership and Regime Formation: On the Development of Institutions in International Society", *International Organization*, vol. 45, no. 3, (1991), pp. 281-308 (288). For an application of these insights, see Richard Higgott and Andrew Fenton Cooper, "Middle Power Leadership and Coalition Building: Australia, the Cairns Group, and the Uruguay Round of Trade Negotiations", *International Organization*, vol. 44, no. 4, (1990), pp. 589-632. For an interesting discussion of leadership within the European Union, see Wayne Sandholtz, "Esprit and the Politics of International Collective Action", *Journal of Common Market Studies*, vol. XXX, (1992), pp. 1-21.

17. Robert Keohane, *After Hegemony: Cooperation and Discord in the World Political Economy*, (Princeton N.J: Princeton University Press, 1984), pp. 32-33. See also Robert Gilpin, *The Political Economy of International Relations*, (Princeton, N.J: Princeton University Press, 1987), p. 76.

18. What precisely constitutes an international public good has been the subject of intense debate. See John A.C. Conybeare, *Trade Wars: The Theory and Practice of International Commercial Rivalry*, (New York: Columbia University Press, 1981); Duncan Snidal, "The Limits of Hegemonic Stability Theory", *International Organization*, vol. 39, no. 4, (1985), pp. 579-614; and Joanne Gowa, "Rational Hegemons, Excludable Goods and Small Groups: An Epitaph for Hegemonic Stability Theory", *World Politics*, vol. 41, no. 4, (1989), pp. 307-342.

19. Kindleberger, *The World in Depression, 1929-1939*, (London: Allen Lane & Penguin Press, 1973), pp. 28 & 305.

20. On "K-groups", see David Lake, "International Economic Structures and American Foreign Economic Policy", *World Politics*, vol. 35, (1983), pp. 510-543; and Lake, "Hegemonic Leadership: Naked Emperor or Tattered Monarch With Potential?", *International Studies Quarterly*, vol. 37, (1993), pp. 459-489.

21. Kindleberger, *The World in Depression*, note 19.

22. On this distinction, see Snidal, "The Limits of Hegemonic Stability Theory", note 18. The hegemon can also be coercive-exploitative if it forces others to adhere to rules that are not in their interest.

23. Conybeare explained that there are two problematiques involved in international trade, a public goods problem and a prisoner's dilemma. However, it remains difficult to see how contributing to the public good of free trade is different from refraining from raising trade barriers. See Conybeare, "Public Goods, Prisoners' Dilemmas and the International Political Economy", *International Studies Quarterly*, vol. 28, no. 1, (1984), p. 20.

24. Gilpin, *U.S. Power and the Multinational Corporation: The Political Economy of Foreign Direct Investment*, (New York: Basic Books, 1975), p. 85.

25. Kindleberger, *The World in Depression*, note 19, and: "Dominance and Leadership in the International Economy: Exploitation, Public Goods, and Free Rides", *International Studies Quarterly*, vol. 25, no. 2, (1981), p. 245; "International Public Goods Without International Government", *American Economic Review*, vol. 76, no. 1, pp. 1-13; "System of International Economic Organization", in David P. Calleo (ed.), *Money and the Coming World Order*, (New York: New York University Press, 1976), pp. 15-39; and, "U.S Foreign Economic Policy, 1776-1976, *Foreign Affairs*, vol. 55, (1977), pp. 395-417.

26. This is deliberately overstated. For example, in the late 1960s states were not "coerced" by the US to support the dollar over and above the extent to which they were willing to support the monetary system

because of a subjective belief in their own interest in doing so. See Barry Eichengreen, "Hegemonic Stability Theories of the International Monetary System", in Richard N. Cooper, Barry Eichengreen, and Robert D. Putnam (eds), *Can Nations Agree? Issues in International Economic Cooperation*, (Washington, D.C: The Brookings Institution, 1989), esp. pp. 277-278.

27. Keohane, "The Demand for International Regimes", in Keohane (ed.) *International institutions and State Power: Essays in International Relations Theory*, (London: Westview, 1989), p. 158.

28. Keohane, *After Hegemony*, note 17, p. 258. Normative behaviour can also persist due to the demand of the regimes' participants for stable channels of interaction, to their desire for information, and to their institutional recollection of the disarray before the regime was created.

29. Ruggie, "International Regimes, Transactions and Change" in Krasner (ed), *International Regimes*, (Ithaca: NY: Cornell, 1983), p. 196. See also Finlayson and Zacher, "The GATT and the Regulation of Trade Barriers", in Krasner, *ibid.*, pp.276-282; and Hans Kelsen, *The Pure Theory of Law*, (Translated by Max Knight), (Berkeley: University of California Press, 1970), p. 10.

30. J.S. Mill, *On Liberty*, (London: Penguin, 1974), esp. p. 68.

31. Keohane, "Reciprocity in International Relations", in Keohane (ed.), *International Institutions and State Power*, note 27, p. 146-147; See also Axlerod, *The Evolution of Cooperation*, (New York: Basic Books, 1984).

32. For an application of these thoughts on leadership in the Uruguay round, see Jarrod Wiener, *Making Rules in the Uruguay Round of the GATT: A Study in International Leadership*, (forthcoming).

33. See Robert Cox, "Gramsci, Hegemony, and International Relations: An Essay in Method", *Millennium: Journal of International Relations*, vol.12, no.2, (1983), p. 172; and Stephen Gill, *American Hegemony and the Trilateral Commission*, (Cambridge: Cambridge University Press, 1990).

34. Secretary of State George Shultz, "The United Nations After Forty Years: Idealism and Realism", *State Department Bulletin*, 85, 2101, August 1985, p. 20.

35. On this, see Paul Kennedy, *The Rise and Fall of the Great Powers: Economic and Military Conflict from 1500-2000*, (London: Fontana Press, 1989); and Gilpin, *The Political Economy of International Relations*, note 17.

36. Henry S. Bienen invokes the image of the US going "around with the begging bowl". "America: The Firsters, the Decliners, and the Searchers for a New American Foreign Policy", in Richard Leaver and James L. Richardson, *The Post-Cold War Order: Diagnoses and Prognoses*, (Australia: Allen & Unwin, 1993), p. 160.

37. See Nye, *Bound to Lead*, note 4; and Henry R. Nau, *The Myth of America's Decline: Leading the World Economy into the 1990s*, (Oxford: Oxford University Press, 1990).

38. "The Reluctant Sheriff", *The Economist*, 9 June 1993, p. 13.

39. "House Coalition Repels Efforts to Cut Military Further", *Congressional Quarterly*, 21 May 1994, pp. 1320-1325. The vote was rejected 268-144.

40. Clinton/Gore National Security Position Paper. Internet Gopher Information: gopher marvel.loc.gov, Clinton-speeches.src.

41. "In the Name of the UN, Stop It", *The Guardian*, 14 June 1993.

42. "Foreign Affairs: Remarks of Governor Bill Clinton to the World Affairs Council", Los Angeles, CA, 13 August 1992. Internet Gopher Information: gopher marvel.loc.gov, Clinton-speeches.src.

43. "Bound to Follow? Leadership and Followership in the Gulf Conflict", *Political Science Quarterly*, vol. 106, (Fall, 1991).

44. Barry M. Blechman, "The Military Dimensions of Collective Security", in Roger A. Coate (ed.), *US Policy and the Future of the United Nations*, (New York: Twentieth Century Fund, 1994), p. 68.

45. "Allies May Send Ground Troops to Bolster Gulf Force", *The Guardian*, 11 August 1991, p. 20.

46. "Clinton's Feelgood Strategy", *Time International*, 17 May 1993, p. 36.

47. E.H Carr, *The Twenty Years' Crisis*, (London: Macmillan, 1939), p. 289.

48. "Clinton Fudges Plans for Peace Troops", *The Guardian*, 25 September 1993.

49. "Foreign Policy: Is Congress Still Keeping Watch?", *Congressional Quarterly*, 21 August 1993, pp. 2267-2269.

50. Richard M. Nixon, *Beyond Peace*, (New York: Random House, 1994).

51. Arthur M. Stein, "The Hegemon's Dilemma: Great Britain, the United States, and the International Economic Order", *International Organization*, vol. 38, no. 2, (1984), pp. 356-386, p. 357.

52. "Bumbling While Bosnia Burns", *The Guardian*, 14 August 1993.

53. "Do Something... Anything", *Time International*, 3 May 1993, pp. 44-45.

54. "Defining the National Interest: A Process of Trial and Error", *Congressional Quarterly*, 26 March 1994, pp. 750-754.

55. See Gilpin, "The Politics of Transnational Economic Relations", *International Organization*, vol. 25, no. 3, (1971), pp. 349-419.

56. See "Address by the President to the Air University", Maxwell Air Force Base, Montgomery, AL, Office of the Press Secretary, White House Press Office, Washington DC, 13 April 1991.

57. This chapter can not do justice to the normative implications of the New World Order, and certainly not with the authority that Molly Cochran has done in her contribution to the special issue on international ethics of *Paradigms*. See Cochran, "The New World Order and International Political Theory", *Paradigms: The Kent Journal of International Relations*, vol. 8, no. 1, (1994), pp. 106-122.

58. Governor Clinton, "New Covenant Speech", 12 December 1991. Internet Gopher Information: gopher marvel.loc.gov, Clinton-speeches.src.

59. "America is Going Home", *The Guardian*, 25 May 1993, p. 20.

60. "When Pictures Make Policy", *Congressional Quarterly*, 30 April 1994, p. 1078.

61. Roger A. Coate, "The Future of the United Nations", in Coate (ed.), *US Policy and the Future of the United Nations*, note 44, p. 21.

4 UN Reform: The Post-Cold War World Organization

Georgios Kostakos

The end of each of the two World Wars which occurred in the course of the 20th century was marked by the creation of a world organization as guarantor of the post-war status quo and harbinger of a peaceful future. The League of Nations and the United Nations which succeeded it expressed the hopes of their creators that the great evil which brought them into existence would never happen again. In the case of the former, such hopes proved completely wrong. In the case of the UN, things are somewhat more complicated. It is true that no global war has occurred since 1945. But it is also true that the Cold War, which lasted for several decades, often brought international cooperation to a standstill and humanity to the brink of annihilation.

The end of this prolonged period of cold terror and mutual deterrence sparked significant changes in international affairs, and opened up new opportunities, but at the same time allowed many limited, but hot conflicts to erupt around the globe. The UN, clearly not having failed, did not need to be abolished and rediscovered under some other name. It remained alive and was assigned new, enlarged tasks, in the framework of renewed cooperation between its member states, especially the great powers.

Although it is often said, with perhaps an excessive degree of optimism, that the spirit of the Charter has been revived and that the purposes of the UN founders finally can be realized, this is not the 1940s. A serious effort must be made by the organization and its membership to adjust to new international circumstances. In this respect, a new world organization has to be built, and is being built on the foundations - not the ashes - of the former, keeping the name but changing many of its standard operating procedures and its guiding concepts. This "New United Nations" has not taken its final shape as yet, for the New World Order has not yet taken *its* final shape. The dual transformation is still under way and will probably continue for at least a few more years to come.

This chapter aims to examine the various steps taken in the direction of enabling the organization to deal with new international circumstances and to maximise its contribution to the world, and to its lords - the member states and the peoples they represent — especially in the field of international peace and security. The approach adopted herein attempts to be comprehensive in that it examines several levels of UN transformation, including new political considerations, structural and administrative reform, and economic readjustment, as well as the overarching conceptual framework guiding thought and action.[1] However, the analysis is limited to reform relating to the peace and security field and does not include an examination of the attempts to effect reforms in economic and social areas.[2]

THE CHANGED POST-COLD WAR SETTING AND THE UNITED NATIONS

The Political Aspects

The end of the Cold War brought about an air of unity and rediscovered cooperation among the UN members, especially the five permanent members of the Security Council. The right of veto which was used by the one side or the other to block decisions in the past (it was used 279 times from the inception of the organization until May 1990) is being left aside in a period of substantive consultations and consensus decision-making.[3] The Gulf War was the first very clear instance of close great power cooperation, to such an extent that it raised fears of a great power directorate in international affairs.[4] The first ever Security Council Summit Meeting which took place in New York on 31 January 1992 sealed this new partnership and gave a further impetus to the UN and to its then newly elected Secretary-General, Dr. Boutros Boutros-Ghali.[5]

Significant change in the UN General Assembly has occurred in recent years with the addition of several new members. These new states have emerged mainly from the break up of the Soviet Union, the bloody dissolution of the former Yugoslavia, and the peaceful split of the former Czechoslovakia. With the addition of a few more states, usually minuscule ones, UN membership today has become virtually universal. Switzerland remains a notable exception as it refuses to join (partially only, as far as the political organs are concerned), while Taiwan (or the

"Republic of China on Taiwan" as it calls itself) is kept out by its big brother who replaced it as UN member in the early 1970s. There has been only a single instance of UN membership contraction, which was brought about by the unification of the two German states in late 1990. In early 1994, UN membership stands at 184 and could grow even further if the trend toward ethnic self-determination continues to hold strong.

The world of the 1990s continues to be one of nominally equal states, all of which have one vote in the UN General Assembly. However, the distribution of effective power is asymmetrical in the international arena. The high society of states has its corporate barons, dukes, princes and kings, with the "Emperor" residing in Washington DC, and the "Pope", the world organization, in New York. It is the "Holy Global Empire" of the late 20th century AD, not less messy than its predecessor of the Middle Ages.

Within the world body and its organs, the end of the East-West division has brought about a significant increase in the number of formal meetings and informal consultations. Moreover, qualitatively speaking, the percentage of decisions adopted without a vote or by consensus has increased significantly.[6]

Peace and security related activities are experiencing a tremendous growth. While in the period from 1945 to 1987, 13 peace-keeping operations were established to deal with conflicts around the world, this number has been exceeded in the few years since 1987. A total of more than 70,000 men and women, military and civilian personnel, serve in the on-going operations, the cost of which in 1993 was estimated at US$3.5 billion.[7]

The great emphasis put on security and the concomitant upgrading of the Security Council, however, is not met with enthusiasm from all sides. The countries of Third World are suspicious of this rediscovered great power consensus and see in it an attempt at global condominium. They feel that the UN body of which they have the upper hand, the General Assembly, is being limited to a secondary role, as is the Economic and Social Council (ECOSOC) and other "democratic" and broadly representative organs, while the great power controlled Security Council is gradually enlarging its sphere of competence, for example by including humanitarian intervention in its list of priorities. This emphasis on security distracts the international community from an area of at least equal global importance, that is the area of development and economic assistance, which is vital to the South's survival and progress. Another fear shared by Third World countries is that the enhancement of the authority of the organs dealing with peace and security issues, mainly the Security Council and the Secretary-General, will sooner or later jeopardise the sovereign rights of states and of their ruling elites. As international intervention for humanitarian and related purposes becomes the norm, the way opens for international interference in the internal affairs of states, formerly a sacrosanct territory.[8]

The Structural and Administrative Aspects

The UN structure at the intergovernmental level has undergone no changes in recent years; in fact, the principal organs remain the same as in 1945. Even the Trusteeship Council is still there, although its agenda has shrunk practically to zero.[9] A recent instance of secondary reform came about as a result of the revitalization of the work of the General Assembly and consisted in the merging of the Fourth (Decolonization) Committee with the Special Political Committee; the number of the General Assembly Main Committees was reduced thus from seven to six.[10]

The membership of limited membership bodies has also remained stable for quite some time. An increase in the Security Council membership, from 11 to 15, not affecting the Permanent Five, came about by a Charter amendment which was adopted by the General Assembly on 17 December 1963 and came into force on 31 August 1965. ECOSOC's membership was simultaneously increased from 18 to 27; it was later increased to 54 by a Charter amendment adopted by the General Assembly on 20 December 1971, which came into force on 24 September 1973.[11] These amendments may have satisfied the demands for better representation of new members of the United Nations, many of which had just emerged from the decolonization process. However, while UN membership has increased substantially since, this has not been reflected in the membership of limited membership bodies which are perceived to have become more elitist and unrepresentative.

The increased importance of the peace and security field in recent years again has drawn attention to Security Council membership. Proposals to elevate Japan and Germany to permanent membership are seemingly welcome, especially by the developed countries and particularly the United States which is interested in burden sharing. However, it is not clear what should happen to the veto prerogative: should it be extended to the new permanent members or not? Should it be activated by more than one permanent member or should each one of them individually continue to possess this right?[12] Should the veto be abolished altogether? If the "Pandora's box" of Charter amendment and Security Council membership revision opens up, many contenders will appear, especially from large Third World countries such as India, Nigeria and Brazil.[13]

It remains to be seen whether the General Assembly Open-Ended Working Group on the Question of Equitable Representation on and Increase in the Membership of the Security Council will make any steps in the direction of formulating a broad consensus on these issues. An overview of the positions of the member states expressed in writing, at the invitation of the Secretary-General, or orally, during the 48th session of the General Assembly, indicates that, "[v]irtually all Member States of the United Nations favour an increase in the membership of the Security Council", as they want "the Security Council to reflect the radical changes in the world and the increase in the Organization's overall Membership, in order to make it more representative and democratic". However, views vary widely when it comes to the criteria to be used to revise the Council's composition, its total membership, the categories of membership, and the accompanying privileges.[14]

At the level of the international civil service, the issue of Secretariat reform has been a recurring one. It acquired great urgency following the adoption of the Kassebaum Amendment by the US Congress in 1985, according to which, the US contribution to UN bodies would be partly withheld unless greater say in the process of budget formulation was given to large contributors. As a result of this and other pressure, broad reforms were introduced into the UN structures and managerial practices. *Inter alia*, a new budgetary procedure was adopted based on consensus decision-making at the intergovernmental level (thus giving the major contributors an informal but effective veto). Several Secretariat departments were abolished or consolidated and a freeze was imposed on recruitment, in line with the Group of 18 (G-18) proposals and relevant General Assembly resolutions.[15]

As he had promised in his speech to the General Assembly upon his formal designation to succeed Javier Pérez de Cuéllar, Boutros Boutros-Ghali took on the task to "eliminat[e] what is wasteful or obsolete".[16] He started by eliminating high-level posts and concentrating the work of the Secretariat in a few key departments. By late 1992 the trend of abolishing or merging departments was reversed and three new departments were created to deal with development and economic and social issues, thus partly redressing the imbalance between the peace and security sector and the economic and social sector and appeasing the Third World.[17] Throughout this period, senior staff were moved from one position to another at short intervals. The question remains whether there is a plan behind the attempted reforms or whether they are ad hoc and improvised in response to changing political, financial, managerial and even person-related considerations.[18]

The fact that two Americans, Richard Thornburg and Melissa Wells, successively have held the post of Under-Secretary-General for Administration and Management in the last couple of years demonstrates, on the one hand, the emphasis put on improving the managerial aspects of the United Nations and on appeasing the US, by far the largest contributor to the UN budget and, on the other hand, the high mobility associated with this tough and controversial post.[19] Moreover, an external management consultant was reported to be examining the "efficiency and cost-effectiveness" of the Secretariat – "sending tremors through an already demoralized staff".[20] As a result, the Secretariat personnel shows no increase in numbers, despite the significant increase in the tasks entrusted to it.[21] Regular long-term recruitment has been suspended "owing to the requirements of restructuring and streamlining" except for the filling of junior professional positions through national competitive examinations.[22] Paradoxically, the conditions of service and the salaries of the staff employed by UN organizations have been steadily deteriorating in comparison to the broader labour market (including the Bretton Woods institutions and other international organizations outside the UN system), something that the Secretary-General allegedly is determined to redress in the near future.[23]

Coordination among the various organizations of the UN system is purportedly improving through the restructured Administrative Committee on Coordination (ACC) and the new spirit prevailing among the executive heads of the UN organizations participating in it. However, as the Secretary-General indicated, a great responsibility in this direction lies with governments, which "must develop system-wide strategies and policies and provide effective guidelines for the work of the secretariats represented in the Administrative Committee on Coordination" and "must take coherent and consistent positions in the governing bodies of the various organizations".[24]

Economic Aspects

The United Nations has no independent sources of finance. It must rely on the goodwill of its member states to provide it with the money to carry out its various mandates. The regular budget is approved by the General Assembly biennially and the expenses of the organization are divided among its member states, according to each one's "real capacity to pay".[25] As a rule, the permanent members of the Security Council are asked to carry a somewhat larger share of the financial burden for peace-keeping operations, thus relieving the contributions of the economically less developed states.[26] The field of peace-keeping, as stated above, has experienced a tremendous growth; the 1993 expenditure of US$3.6 billion increased sharply from the US$1.4 billion of 1992. By comparison, the increase in the regular budget is modest, from about US$2.19 billion in the biennium 1990-1991 to some US$2.47 billion in the biennium 1992-1993.[27]

Over the years, member states' arrears have accumulated. As of 31 January 1994, unpaid assessed contributions totalled more than US$2.7 billion, of which about US$1.3 billion was owed for the regular budget and US$1.4 billion for peace-keeping operations. The list of debtors was headed by two of the most important states, which are Security Council permanent members and major contributors, namely the United States (owing about US$530 million for the regular budget and US$288 million for peace-keeping) and the Russian Federation (owing about US$68 million for the regular budget and US$507 million for peace-keeping).[28] According to Article 19 of the UN Charter, a state "which is in arrears in the payment of its financial contributions to the Organization shall have no vote in the General Assembly if the amount of its arrears equals or exceeds the amount of the contributions due from it for the preceding two full years". Still, the same article includes a "safety valve" providing that "[t]he General Assembly may, nevertheless, permit such a Member to vote if it is satisfied that the failure to pay is due to conditions beyond the control of the Member".

Following a request by the Secretary-General, an Independent Advisory Group on United Nations Financing consisting of personalities of world stature in the economic field was convened by the Ford Foundation in September 1992 to "examine the problems associated with financing the United Nations and its affiliated programs". In its report presented to Boutros Boutros-Ghali in February 1993 the Group made a number of recommendations regarding the regular UN budget, the financing of peace-keeping operations as well as some other related issues.[29]

The group recommended that UN expenditures should continue to be divided into three categories "with the regular budget financed by assessed contributions, peace-keeping financed by a separate assessment, and humanitarian and development activities financed largely by voluntary contributions".[30] The regular budget should continue to be approved by the established consensus procedure.[31] Member states should pay their dues fully and on time, otherwise interest should be charged on their arrears. The level of the Working Capital Fund should be raised by US$100 million to US$200 million, but the UN should not be given authority to borrow commercially or otherwise to meet its obligations.

In the area of peace-keeping, governments should be prepared to pay significantly increased sums in the years to come. "Because peace-keeping is an investment in security", consideration should be given to getting those increased sums out of national defense budgets. A revolving reserve fund of US$400 million should be created for peace-keeping (the current Peace-keeping Reserve Fund created by the General Assembly in December 1992 was set at US$150 million),[32] while the merits of having an annual unified peace-keeping budget instead of a separate budget per operation should be examined. A regular appropriation at an adequate level should be devoted to training UN staff and military contingents from various member states for them to deal successfully with increasingly complex activities related to peace-keeping.

Finally, the Advisory Group recommended that the UN should continue to be financed exclusively by assessed and voluntary contributions of its member states. This would "maintain proper control over the UN's budget and its agenda". It also believed that existing proposals "for additional, nongovernmental sources of financing the UN are neither practical nor desirable".[33]

The Secretary-General's response to these proposals is contained in his report of 2 November 1993 to the General Assembly.[34] In it, Dr. Boutros-Ghali endorsed most of the proposals of the Group which often reflected similar views expressed by himself or by his predecessor.[35] Moreover, the Secretary-General strongly maintained that the Working Capital Fund "should represent 25 per cent of the net annual level of the regular budget", that is US$300 million (rounded) in 1994. However, the Secretary-General stood by his position that the UN should be authorized to borrow commercially, as a last resort, whenever no funds are available. The interest to be paid on such loans should be matched by the interest charged to member states in arrears, the behaviour which makes borrowing necessary.[36] The Secretary-General proposed to finance the UN partly from non-governmental sources, such as through the establishment of a United Nations Peace Endowment Fund, with the initial target of US$1 billion. He did not consider there to be any problem with such proposals "so long as the activities to be financed are consistent with the established objectives and mandates of the Organization".[37] Of course, the body able to act upon these and other relevant proposals is the General Assembly (and its subsidiary bodies), the principal organ which has the ultimate control over financial and administrative affairs, according to the Charter.

The Conceptual Framework

In the field of peace and security the Secretary-General's *An Agenda for Peace* issued in mid-1992 attempted to clarify the concepts and operational methods which should govern action by the world body under the new, post-Cold War conditions. Through this report, Dr. Boutros-Ghali gave his own version of "the new world order", a popular term still awaiting definition. The proposals contained in *An Agenda for Peace* are discussed by other contributions to this volume and elsewhere.[38] This discussion will be limited to some key concepts.

The Secretary-General considers preventive diplomacy, peacemaking, peace-keeping and post-conflict peace-building as the main categories under which action for the maintenance or restoration of international peace and security falls. Preventive diplomacy aims to deal with an emerging dispute before it breaks out; peacemaking aims to restore peace once breached, through diplomatic and other means; peace-keeping refers to the traditional UN function of interposing international troops between the adversaries in order to stop the fighting, to guarantee a cease-fire and to buy time for diplomacy; and post-conflict peace-building encompasses attempts to rehabilitate the people(s) and territory(ies) affected by a conflict, at restoring indispensable utilities and at establishing a lasting peace. To this list "peace enforcement" was added later[39] to refer to enforcement measures taken by the UN to restore peace, under the provisions of Chapter VII of the Charter. In *An Agenda for Peace*, this was uncomfortably included in "peacemaking" together with the peaceful measures of Chapter VI.

Although many of these ideas were received favourably by the representative UN organs and the member states[40], suspicion arose among Third World countries in view of the one-sided emphasis put on peace and security, while the issue of development, which is closer to their interests, was perceived to be left out of the mainstream. Also, dangers to state sovereignty were discerned emanating from a rejuvenated UN led by a small group of powerful states acting in tandem, along with a very active and ambitious Secretary-General. [41] An "Agenda for Development" was specifically requested from Dr. Boutros-Ghali[42] who promised to submit promptly such a ground-breaking report.[43]

A BROADER DISCUSSION

It is evident that reform has occurred in the UN framework in several respects. This wave of change to some extent was imposed on the organization by structural changes in the international system. Attempts at adjusting the world body to the new circumstances also have been made wilfully by the intergovernmental organs as well as by the Secretariat. However, the extent to which purposeful reform actually has affected the UN's inner processes remains to be seen. The years to come will show whether a new United Nations has been built on solid foundations and is ready to handle significantly altered circumstances or whether the old edifice has just been patched up and has started to crack under the pressure of developments. Some further thoughts on strengthening the organization will be put forward below.

At the Secretariat level, the Secretary-General should remain a strong, authoritative international actor, side by side with states and their governments. However, more responsibilities in the running of daily affairs could be delegated to the various Under-Secretaries-General, Assistant Secretaries-General, and Directors. This latent international cabinet could establish individual and collective responsibility and bring more people into the decision-making process. In this respect, it is worth paying attention to proposals about having a small number of Deputy Secretaries-General appointed to assist the Chief Executive with the coordination of the various departments and services falling together under certain key areas of activity, such as: (i) political affairs, peace and security; (ii) economic, social and development affairs; (iii) humanitarian and human rights affairs; and (iv) administration, management and conference services.[44] Overall, the Secretariat should be allowed to become really independent. System-wide coordination definitely is required to avoid duplication and to make the system more rational, with a more efficient use of limited resources. At a later stage, the high-level executives of the various agencies and programs could also be incorporated more explicitly into an overall functional UN hierarchy.

With regard to peace-keeping and peace enforcement, serious attention should be paid to developing standard operating procedures and holding joint exercises for troops designated for UN service. Gradually, arrangements with troop-contributing countries should be formalized, in the framework of Article 43 of the Charter as suggested in *An Agenda for Peace*, thus creating some sort of standby international force with pre-designated facilities around the world. Finally, a "UN Officers' College" should be created to give the officers of prospective multinational forces a better grasp of the UN principles and processes, to acquaint them with the special ways of conflict management employed by the UN and to teach them how to cooperate harmoniously and effectively with each other.[45]

The measures which have been adopted or seriously considered up to now regarding the financial situation of the United Nations seem to deal only with immediate needs related to solvency. Both the Working Capital Fund and the Peace-keeping Reserve Fund may enable the organization to deal with money due to it in the short-term, but do not provide a secure financial basis which would allow for long-term planning. The determination not to allow the organization to go bankrupt is there, but at the same time there is a tendency to keep it under tight control, in a "lame duck" situation. New sources of finance should be tapped gradually, including non-governmental ones, although the final appropriation authority should remain with the General Assembly. Proposals which would stimulate states to be more responsible with their UN obligations, such as the charging of interest upon unpaid contributions to the regular budget or peace-keeping operations, should be adopted under the provisions of Article 19 of the Charter.

The UN no longer suffers from a lack of relevance. Instead of being bypassed, as was often the case in the past, it is now being asked to intervene in virtually every dispute around the globe. A breakdown because of overstretch may be imminent. A more selective approach is required, one that will include "No" as a possible answer to the various requests for action. A quantitatively decreased but qualitatively much stronger and more authoritative presence at various trouble spots could be a prudent way to proceed. To do this, the UN has to develop, most of all, its moral authority. To that end, much hard work, resoluteness and consistency are required from world leaders and the organization's staff, as well as a lot of moral and material support from governments and individuals alike.

The fiftieth anniversary of the United Nations is expected, from many quarters, to be a watershed for the future of the world organization and its development in many fields. However, the most important field, the one which directly or indirectly guides action in all others, the conceptual one, is usually left out of this. If an amendment to the Charter *is* finally agreed upon, it is not expected to bring about a substantive qualitative change. Whether or not more states will be brought into the global elite of permanent Security Council membership is not the crucial question at this level. What the organization needs most is a reinterpretation of its role under the new circumstances and the challenges facing it in view of the coming 21st century. *An Agenda for Peace* is a good first step towards dealing with the new environment in the area of peace and security by using the potential enshrined in the Charter to a greater extent than before. However, a further breakthrough is needed, a more bold and imaginative approach.

Will the promised *Agenda for Development* bring new meaning to the world body? Perhaps, if it is not restricted to development, economic, and social issues. Otherwise, it will be dismissed as yet another effort by the Third World to increase the pressure on the developed countries and to leave aside the fundamental issues of peace and security. A broader theme often repeated by the Secretary-General is that of the interrelation between peace and security, democratization and human rights, and development. These terms describe the objectives of the organization; as the Secretary-General points out, "[t]hey are interlocking and mutually reinforcing". None of these can exist for long without the other two, at the global or the regional level.[46] Perhaps this tripolar approach could provide the UN with an adequate conceptual framework to lead action and to balance interests between North and South - although the North could still get more out of it.

CONCLUDING REMARKS

The United Nations is experiencing a "second youth" following the termination of East-West confrontation. The UN did not succeed, but it did not fail completely in the years since its inception. It now has a second chance to show what it is worth. But, it must do it quickly and establish itself as a credible agent at the highest global level before controversies and differing approaches, especially between its major member states, start marring the global consensus once again.

Things are not yet clear. It is quite difficult to keep up with change, especially when it appears to be anarchical and fuzzy, as is usually the case. Nevertheless, attempts at adjustment do take place, willingly - such as through *An Agenda for Peace* - or unwillingly, under the pressure of events. The question is not how to keep an organization, a bureaucratic structure, alive. The question is how the broadly acknowledged interdependence and interconnection at the world level can better be served to the benefit of as many as possible. Although this has not been decided upon definitively, it is the global well-being or global interest which should inspire any attempt at institution-building or institution-adjustment at the global level.

NOTES

1. In this sense, this chapter builds on the analytical framework used by the author in his PhD thesis: Georgios Kostakos, *Reforming the United Nations: 1985 - 1989*, University of Kent at Canterbury, 1989.
2. For a presentation of attempts at reform in the economic and social area see Nancy Seufert-Barr, "Towards a New Clarity for UN Work", *UN Chronicle*, vol. XXX, no. 4 (December 1993), pp. 38-47.
3. See Boutros Boutros-Ghali, *An Agenda for Peace: Preventive Diplomacy, Peacemaking and Peace-keeping*, (New York: United Nations, 1992), paras. 14-15. Recently, Russia is reported to have cast a veto against a draft resolution making contributions towards the expenses of a UN Peace-keeping Force in Cyprus (UNFICYP) mandatory. Russia made clear that the negative vote was due solely to practical economic considerations. See *United Nations News* (United Nations Information Centre, Athens, Greece, PR 72/93, 12 May 1993), and the Greek newspaper *Eleftherotypia*, 12 May 1993, p. 11 and *ibid.*, 13 May 1993, p. 3. See also James C.O. Jonah, *Differing State Perspectives on the United Nations in the Post-Cold War World*, (Providence RI: The Academic Council on the United Nations System, ACUNS Reports and Papers 1993 No. 4, 1993), esp. pp. 14-15.
4. Paul Taylor & A.J.R. Groom, *The United Nations and the Gulf War, 1990-91: Back to the Future?* (London: The Royal Institute of International Affairs, RIIA Discussion Paper No. 38, 1992), esp. pp. 3-4, 8-11 & 43-44.
5. "Security Council Meets at Head of State and Government Level", "Secretary-General's Statement at Security Council Summit Meeting" and "Joint Statement by the Security Council on Maintenance of International Peace and Security", in *United Nations News*, 1 February 1992, PR 20/92, PR 21/92 and PR 22/92, respectively.
6. See Boutros Boutros-Ghali, *Report on the Work of the Organization from the Forty-sixth to the Forty-seventh Session of the General Assembly* [hereafter "GA Report 1992"] (New York: United Nations, September 1992), para. 16 and Figures 1 & 2; Boutros Boutros-Ghali, *Report on the Work of the Organization from the Forty-seventh to the Forty-eighth Session of the General Assembly* [hereafter "GA Report 1993"] (New York: United Nations, September 1993), paras. 30-31, 37 and Figures 1-3; and *United Nations News*, PR 1/94, 10 January 1994.

7. Boutros Boutros-Ghali, *An Agenda for Peace*, note 3, para. 47; *United Nations Peace-keeping*, (New York: United Nations, 1993), pp. 3 and 11-12; *United Nations News*, PR 1/94, 10 January 1994; and Boutros Boutros-Ghali, "GA Report 1993", note 6, paras. 108 & 296.

8. Robert O. Matthews, "United Nations Reform in the 1990s: North - South Dimensions", in Gerald Dirks *et. al.*, *The State of the United Nations, 1993: North - South Perspectives*, (Providence RI: The Academic Council on the United Nations System, ACUNS Reports and Papers 1993 No. 5, 1993), pp. 28-30 & 34-37 and Mats R. Berdal, *Whither UN Peacekeeping?* (London: IISS/Brassey's, Adelphi Paper 281, October 1993), pp. 74-75.

9. Only Palau remains a Trust Territory administered by the US. See *United Nations News*, INF 1/94 (January 1994).

10. GA resolution 47/233, 17 August 1993.

11. "Introductory Note", *Charter of the United Nations and Statute of the International Court of Justice*, (New York: United Nations, 1987).

12. The case for a "three-vote-veto" is made by Keith Handell, "The UN Security Council I: Filling the Gaps", *The World Today*, vol. 46, no. 12 (December 1990), pp. 216-217.

13. See Robert O. Matthews, "United Nations Reform in the 1990s: North - South Dimensions", in Gerald Dirks, *The State of the United Nations*, note 8, pp. 30-31.

14. *United Nations News*, PR 14/94, 21 January 1994.

15. Douglas Williams, *The Specialized Agencies and the United Nations: The System in Crisis*, (London: C. Hurst & Company, in association with the David Davies Memorial Institute of International Studies, 1987); Paul Taylor, "Reforming the System: Getting the Money to Talk", in Paul Taylor & A.J.R. Groom (eds.), *International Institutions at Work* (London: Pinter Publishers, 1988); and Georgios Kostakos, *Reforming the United Nations: 1985-1989*, note 1.

16. See *The Diplomatic World Bulletin*, vol. 22, no. 15 (December 9 - 16, 1991), pp. 2-3.

17. Nancy Seufert-Barr, "Towards a New Clarity for UN Work", note 2, pp. 43 and 45; *The Diplomatic World Bulletin*, vol. 23, no. 6 (8-15 June 1992), p. 2 and vol. 23, no. 12 (December 7 - 14, 1992), p. 1 ; and *United Nations News*, PR 27/92, 10 February 1992, PR 205/92, 8 December 1992, PR 16/93, 3 February 1993.

18. See Georgios Kostakos, *Boutros Boutros-Ghali's First Year at the Helm of the United Nations*, (Athens: Hellenic Foundation for Defense and Foreign Policy (ELIAMEP), Defense and Foreign Policy Studies No. 12, 1993), pp. 5-7. The Advisory Committee on Administrative and

Budgetary Questions (ACABQ) and the Joint Inspection Unit (JIU) also expressed concern. See Nancy Seufert-Barr, "Towards a New Clarity for UN Work", note 2, p. 43. For an exposition of the Secretary-General's reasoning, see GA Report 1993, note 6, paras. 88-91.

19. "Transcript of Press Conference by Secretary-General Boutros Boutros-Ghali held at Headquarters on 1 February 1994", UN Press Release SG/SM/5216, 1 February 1994, pp. 9-10.
20. *The Diplomatic World Bulletin*, vol. 23, No. 5 (May 18 - 25, 1992), p. 10; *ibid.*, vol. 23, no. 6 (June 8 - 15, 1992), pp. 2-5; *United Nations News*, PR 35/93, 12 March 1993.
21. UN Press Release SG/SM/5216, 1 February 1994, p. 12.
22. GA Report 1993, note 6, para. 73. The military and civilian personnel used for field operations, which is mostly offered by member states on a case by case basis, has increased dramatically. The number of ad hoc appointments of Special Representatives or Envoys for specific missions from outside the career Secretariat structures does not seem to have decreased either.
23. *Ibid.*, paras. 77 and 101.
24. *Ibid.*, paras. 95-101.
25. *Basic Facts About the United Nations* (New York: United Nations Department of Public Information, 1993), p. 22.
26. Shijuro Ogata, Paul Volcker, et. al., *Financing an Effective United Nations: A Report of the Independent Advisory Group on UN Financing* (New York: Ford Foundation, 1993), p. 21.
27. GA Report 1993, note 6, para.108; UN Doc. A/48/565, 2 November 1993, para. 37; Shijuro Ogata, Paul Volcker, et al., *Financing an Effective UN*, note 26, Figure II (p. 29); and *United Nations News*, PR 70/93, 7 May 1993.
28. "Summary of Contributions to Regular Budget and Peace-keeping Budgets: 31 January 1994", Contributions Section, 14 February 1994 and "Wednesday Highlights", Central News, DH/1584, 16 February 1994 (both provided by the United Nations Information Centre in Athens).
29. See Shijuro Ogata, Paul Volcker, et al., *Financing an Effective UN*, note 26. For a summary of the recommendations, see *ibid.*, pp. 25-27.
30. *Ibid.*, pp. 6 and 25.
31. This procedure was established under the pressure of the Kassebaum Amendment in the mid-1980s. See above and Georgios Kostakos, *Reforming the United Nations: 1985 - 1989*, note 1, pp. 19-30.
32. Shijuro Ogata, Paul Volcker, et al., note 26, pp. 16 & 26; and UN Doc. A/48/565, 2 November 1993, paras. 40-42.

33. Shijuro Ogata, Paul Volcker, et al., *Financing an Effective UN*, note 26, pp. 24 and 27.
34. UN Doc. A/48/565, 2 November 1993.
35. See, *inter alia*, Boutros-Ghali, *An Agenda for Peace*, note 3, paras. 48 & 69-74; GA Report 1992, note 6, paras. 50-54; and UN Doc. A/48/565, 2 November 1993.
36. UN Doc. A/48/565, 2 November 1994, paras. 30 & 33.
37. See, *inter alia*, *An Agenda for Peace*, note 3, paras. 69-74; GA Report 1992, note 6, paras. 50-54; and UN Doc. A/48/565, 2 November 1993, para. 55.
38. Adam Roberts, "The United Nations and International Security", *Survival*, vol. 35, no. 2 (Summer 1993); Tapio Kanninen, "Die Agenda fuer den Frieden", *Der Ueberblick*, (April 1992); Nigel Gould-Davies, *The Evolving World Order: The State of Deliberations*, (Washington, D.C.: The Hitachi Foundation, 1993), pp. 14-15; Roberto Toscano, "Peacekeeping in the New International Situation", *The International Spectator*, vol. XXVIII, no. 1 (January - March 1993).
39. GA Report 1993, note 6, para. 278.
40. Report of the Secretary-General on the "Implementation of Recommendations Contained in *An Agenda for Peace*", UN Doc. A/47/965 - S/25944, 15 June 1993; and GA Report 1993, note 6, paras 276-277.
41. Robert O. Matthews, "United Nations Reform in the 1990s: North - South Dimensions", in Gerald Dirks, et. al., *The State of the United Nations*, note 8, pp. 28-31.
42. See the General Assembly speeches of the representatives of Argentina, Indonesia and Iran, in UN Docs. A/47/PV.31 (pp. 26-35), A/47/PV.37 (pp. 29-41) and A/47/PV.38 (pp. 33-43), respectively; and Robert O. Matthews, *ibid.*, pp. 29-30.
43. GA Report 1993, note 6, para. 120.
44. See Erskine Childers and Brian Urquhart, "Towards a More Effective United Nations", *Development Dialogue*, vol. 1, no. 2 (1991), pp. 11-40 and Figure 2 (p. 13). Also Georgios Kostakos, *Reforming the United Nations: 1985 - 1989*, note 1, Appendix V (pp. 220-221).
45. *An Agenda for Peace*, note 3, paras. 42-45; Jeffrey Laurenti, *The Common Defense: Peace and Security in a Changing World*, (New York: The United Nations Association of the United States of America, 1992), pp. 18-32; and Paul Taylor & A.J.R. Groom, *International Institutions at Work*, note 15, pp. 43-47. For a sceptical approach to UN "administer[ing] a multilateral culturally varied army" see Kevin M. Cahill, "A Necessary Balance", *The Brown Journal of Foreign Affairs*, vol. 1, issue 1 (Winter 1993-1994), esp. p. 11.

46. Public speeches by the Secretary-General, *United Nations News* PR 86/92, 25 May 1992, PR 37/93, 17 March 1993 and PR 40/93, 26 March 1993. Boutros Boutros-Ghali, "The United Nations at the Crossroads", *The Brown Journal of Foreign Affairs*, vol. 1, Issue 1 (Winter 1993-1994), pp. 2-3.

5 The UN Secretary-Generalship at Fifty

Benjamin Rivlin

> To appreciate correctly the role of the Secretary-General is to appreciate the whole mission of the United Nations ... [which] in turn, is central to the way international life is organized.
> — Javier Pérez de Cuéllar[1]

Where does the Secretary-General fit in the scheme of world affairs after nearly fifty years of the United Nations' existence? As this jubilee commemoration approaches, a close observer of the UN scene offered the opinion that "The Office of the Secretary-General ... has suffered something of a quantum shift ever since the end of the Cold War spun it into a high-energy international orbit. It is no longer the predictable centre of a system immobilized by rival superpowers, but something of an enigma at the centre of interlinked conundrums in the political, economic and social spheres."[2] At about the same time, an op-ed article in the *New York Times* carried the headline, "The Secretary-General Should Revert to Chief Clerk."[3]

If these two opinions agree on anything, it is on the fact that the role of the UN Secretary-Generalship has been changed by events since the end of the Cold War. Implicit in both is that the Secretary-General has assumed a broader role in world affairs than he had played in the past. However, the implication that the Secretary-General was ever merely a "chief clerk" is quite erroneous as would be any contention that the Secretary-General is a wholly independent actor in the international arena.[4] Has the role changed?

THE SECRETARY-GENERAL'S CONSTITUTIONAL BASE

Constitutionally, according to the UN Charter, the Secretary-General is envisaged as playing a dual role. One is as "chief administrative officer"

81

in which he acts as the world's top international civil servant. In this capacity, he directs the Secretariat and performs services at the behest of the policy making organs of the United Nations, primarily the Security Council and the General Assembly. The other is a more autonomous political role which emerges from the establishment by Article 7 of the Secretariat as a principal organ of the United Nations along with the Security Council, General Assembly, the Economic and Social Council, the Trusteeship Council and the International Court of Justice. This does not mean that all these organs are equal. Certainly, the Security Council and the General Assembly are more important than the Economic and Social and Trusteeship Councils. But, being designated as a "principal organ" in its own right gives the Secretariat and its head added significance and a degree of autonomy. Moreover, the Charter charges the Secretary-General with the responsibility "to make an annual report on the work of the organization" and with specific authority "to bring to the attention of the Security Council any matter which in *his opinion* may threaten the maintenance of international peace and security."[5] These powers are clearly not those of a clerk. On the contrary, it has been suggested that the power to call matters to the attention of an international organization is usually a prerogative reserved to a government.[6]

The provisions of the UN Charter regarding the Secretary-General deliberately endowed the office with autonomous political and diplomatic prerogatives, in marked contrast to the League of Nations Covenant, which prescribed a role for its Secretary-General strictly limited to administrative and management functions. The Secretary-General of the United Nations is the symbolic leader of the world, and as the Preparatory Commission noted in 1945, "more than anyone else, will stand for the United Nations as a whole" and "in the eyes of the world... must embody the principles and ideals of the Charter."[7]

In broadening the role of the Secretary-General in this way, the Charter set the stage for a recurring tug-of-war between the Secretary-General and the member states for control of the policy-making principal organs, the Security Council and the General Assembly. As understood by one occupant of the office, Pérez de Cuéllar, the Secretary-General is "co-responsible with the other organs (the General Assembly, the Security Council and so on) for achieving the organization's aims and purposes."[8] In political life, domestic or international, sharing of responsibility is an invitation to disputation even though it may be intended to produce cooperation.

Although the Charter provisions concerning the Secretary-General have not been amended one iota since originally adopted, the nature of the office has certainly not been static. Because these provisions are not particularly explicit or detailed, the functions of the office have evolved over the course of the past half-century, elaborated by interpretation and practice. The Charter does not endow the Secretary-General with any specific authority as third-party mediator, negotiator, coordinator, conciliator, or extender of good offices. Yet, over the years these functions have become identified as fundamental attributes of the office. The good offices functions, covering a broad range of interventions by the Secretary-General acting as a third-party, "derive from four different kinds of authorization: from resolutions of the Security Council or General Assembly, or as an emanation of his inherent powers, or by agreement of disputatious parties."[9]

It would be a mistake to assume that there has been a linear expansion upward of the role of the Secretary-General. A more accurate depiction would be one of ups and downs. What largely determines the fluctuations is the overall state of the United Nations, which is a function of the changing international political climate.

CONTINUITY OF THE ROLE

Over the course of nearly fifty years, much has been written about this singular position in the world – the Secretary-Generalship of the United Nations. Six individuals, including the present incumbent, have held the office, and each of them – Trygve Lie of Norway, Dag Hammarskjöld of Sweden, U Thant of Burma, Kurt Waldheim of Austria, Javier Pérez de Cuéllar of Peru, and Boutros Boutros-Ghali of Egypt – has brought to the position a distinct personality, cultural background, professional experience, style of work and set of ideas. Each has approached the position in his own fashion.

Chronic issues and problems, some of which date back to the early years of the United Nations or even predate it, have beset each Secretary-General. These include such regional issues as those in South Africa, Palestine, Kashmir, Cyprus, Namibia, Western Sahara, and global issues such as the process and aftermath of decolonization, disarmament, economic and social development, and the lack of adequate human and financial resources. In addition, each had to deal with differing crises of their time: Lie with the partition of Palestine, the first Arab-Israel War, and Korea; Hammarskjöld with Suez and the Congo; U Thant with the Six Day War, Vietnam, the Cuban Missile Crisis and the Bay of Pigs; Waldheim with the Yom Kippur War and the American hostages in Iran;

Pérez de Cuéllar with Central America, Afghanistan, the Iran-Iraq War, and the Gulf War; and Boutros-Ghali with Cambodia, Somalia, and Yugoslavia. Running through this diversity of crises and issues faced by six different Secretaries-General are a set of uniformities and constants:

1. Role ambiguity.
2. Overburdened office.
3. Ambivalent relations with the Security Council and the General Assembly.
4. Constraints as head of the Secretariat.
5. Minimal authority to coordinate heads of specialized agencies.
6. Limited means to lead resulting from a lack of a political base and constituency; lack of human and financial resources; and dependence upon outside sources of information.
7. Changing international political climate.

These constants overlap. Overall, they reflect the basic reality that the United Nations, although involved in world governance, is not a government, and that its personification, the Secretary-General, does not head an independent sovereign entity but rather an organization that is controlled by its member states. There is little indication that sovereign states are prepared to defer to the leadership of the UN Secretary-General when high politics are involved. But, this does not mean that the Secretary-General is merely a puppet devoid of any display of independence.[10] Does the individual occupying the position make any appreciable difference in the role played by the Secretary-General? While former Secretary-General Pérez de Cuéllar contended "Men come and go but institutions remain"[11], the individual's performance also counts. Effectiveness is the combined product of the limitations imposed on the Secretary-General by the nature of the international system and the personal qualities of the office-holder. Surely the differing styles and personalities of each of the six men who have held the position, while not leaving a lasting stamp on the office, in some ways affected their effectiveness in it.

THE OVERBURDENED "IMPOSSIBLE" JOB

When the first UN Secretary-General, Trygve Lie, described his position as "The Most Impossible Job in the World," he did not supply chapter and verse for his assessment. Even without specifics, it is not difficult to surmise that the frustrations and exasperations experienced by Lie and all his successors are at the root of this judgement. However, if we examine the experience of the current Secretary-General, Boutros Boutros-Ghali, a clearer picture of the "impossibility" of the UN Secretary-Generalship emerges. Frustration sets in when, despite the obvious interdependence of the world, the UN member states, particularly its most powerful members, recognize this condition rhetorically but fail to follow through with commensurate action. Exasperation sets in when the Secretary-General is called upon to undertake complex and sensitive operations but is denied the financial and human resources to carry them out.

The "impossibility" of the job can also be attributed to the many hats the Secretary-General has to wear. In 1990, a study listed the following nine functions assigned to the Secretary-General:

1. Administration and management of the Secretariat.
2. Official representation of the United Nations worldwide.
3. Constant contact with member states.
4. Representation and interpretation of the United Nations to the public, and to the non-governmental and private sector.
5. Coordination of the UN system.
6. Maintenance of a global watch on major developments.
7. Generating ideas and strategies.
8. Use of good offices and crisis management (peacemaking and peace-keeping).
9. Good offices on humanitarian rights and humanitarian matters.[12]

This study notes that the "job, at present, constitutes three or four more or less full-time jobs."[13] It would be difficult to carve up these responsibilities since they are all interconnected and require a single individual at the top to pull them all together. During the search for a successor to Pérez de Cuéllar, the prominent Finnish diplomat, Max Jakobson, called for the appointment of a Secretary-General who is "a communicator like Reagan, a reformer like Gorbachev, a diplomat like Kissinger, and a manager like Iacocca."[14] In a similar vein, it was suggested that "the Secretary-General should have the administrative skills of a Robert MacNamara" and that the task of effectively coping with the economic and social structure of the United Nations, in which some 70 percent of UN resources are expended, would be beyond the grasp of even a John Maynard Keynes.[15]

The "impossibility" of the job has been magnified in the four years since this list was compiled by the explosion of peace-keeping operations and humanitarian interventions which in 1994 has put the Secretary-General in command of 70,000 peacekeepers in 17 operations throughout the world at a cost of $3.5 billion a year. The enormity and complexity of this aspect of the Secretary-Generalship cannot be exaggerated. The modalities of each operation – terms of reference and engagement, acquisition of personnel, logistical support, coordination with other UN agencies and private organizations, usually in the humanitarian field – must be individually negotiated. Each operation must then be supervised, sustained and backed-up from UN headquarters in New York.[16]

RELATIONS WITH THE SECURITY COUNCIL AND GENERAL ASSEMBLY

In 1945, the UN Preparatory Commission envisaged a harmonious relationship between the Secretariat, headed by the Secretary-General, and the other principal organs. It noted that "while the responsibility for the framing of agreed international policies rests with the organs representative of the members ... the essential tasks of preparing the ground for the decisions and of executing them... will devolve largely upon the Secretariat". In the ensuing years, much of the work of the Secretary-General has come in response to directives and requests from these inter-governmental organs to undertake a wide diversity of assignments. Examples of these tasks are organizing a peace-keeping operation, analysing or monitoring a particular situation, recommending alternative courses of action that may be pursued regarding an agenda item, establishing specific units to implement the decisions of the Security Council and General Assembly, or supervising the far-flung peace-keeping operations authorized by the Security Council.

Pursuing these directives has often brought the Secretary-General into conflict with the Security Council, usually on matters pertaining to peace-keeping, and with the General Assembly, especially on budgetary matters. The basic decision to establish peace-keeping operations is made by the Security Council. Details as to the composition, command, and deployment of the forces are usually delegated to the Secretary-General. In one instance, the establishment of the United Nations Emergency Force (UNEF I) to meet the Suez War crisis in 1956, it was the General Assembly that requested the Secretary-General to submit a plan within 48 hours for the establishment of this force while authorizing him to negotiate a cease-fire and secure a withdrawal of all foreign forces from Egypt.[17]

The delegation of operational responsibility for peace-keeping to the Secretary-General has at times provoked differences of opinion as to how he should carry out his role. An example of this is the establishment of the Cyprus peace-keeping operation (UNFICYP) in 1964. According to the Security Council resolution, the composition and size of the force was left to the Secretary-General in consultation with the governments of Cyprus, Greece, Turkey and the United Kingdom; the force commander and the mediator were to be appointed by the Secretary-General and to report to him; and the Secretary-General was given the responsibility for accepting voluntary financial contributions for the operation.[18] A number of misgivings were expressed about this formulation. The Soviet Union, while not vetoing the resolution, together with the Czechoslovakian delegate expressed dissatisfaction with the paragraph that specified the Secretary-General's responsibilities in the deployment and function of the UN Cyprus force. The Czech delegate argued that this provision, "transfers to the Secretary-General a responsibility that, under the letter of the Charter, belongs exclusively to the Security Council itself."[19] France also expressed some reservations regarding the Council's action which it saw as "divesting itself of responsibilities which belong to it but which would clearly be difficult to discharge."[20]

This tension between the Secretary-General as an autonomous actor and his subservience to the other UN principal organs is evident in the words of the second Secretary-General Dag Hammarskjöld. The Secretary-General, he said, must, in addition to being a servant of the major organs, "also be a servant of the principles of the Charter, and its aims must ultimately determine what for him is right or wrong."[21] Earlier, as noted above, Hammarskjöld's predecessor, Trygve Lie, was rebuffed or criticized when he manifested an independent role for the Secretary-General. As the first Secretary-General, everything he undertook was in a sense unprecedented and each of his actions helped establish the role of Secretary-General and the parameters of the office. One thing is clear: he did not envisage his position as that of a chief clerk. His interpretation of the Secretary-General's authority was that of a world leader with the responsibility to provide direction for achieving the goals of the United Nations. Thus, at the outset of the Cold War he tried to defuse tension by proposing a comprehensive twenty-year peace plan for which there were no takers. Lie also tried to enhance the UN's role in maintaining peace when he urged the creation of a small permanent international guard force which he saw as a way of "strengthening directly the authority and prestige of the United Nations as an institution."[22]   Lastly, Lie's conception of a politically autonomous Secretary-General was evidenced when he condemned the North Korean invasion of South Korea.

THE COLD WAR CONTEXT

During most of the first four decades of the United Nations' existence, the Cold War dominated the world scene. The behaviour in the office of each Secretary-General from Trygve Lie to Pérez de Cuéllar was largely affected by the Cold War. Only in his second term was Pérez de Cuéllar able to function in an abating Cold War atmosphere. The current occupant of the position, Boutros Boutros-Ghali, may not be discharging his office within the Cold War setting, but, it may not be far-fetched to note that his official life has been made infinitely more difficult because of the absence of the Cold War. The uncertainties and turbulence of the post-Cold War world are reflected in the many challenges to the UN and hence to the Secretary-General.

The Cold War established parameters for the role of the UN in world affairs. Concomitantly, it defined the role of the Secretary-General. While the United Nations could be seen as "a diplomatic system immobilized by rival Super-Powers", it had become, in the General Assembly, the instrument of the Third World's "revolution against the status quo". On the one hand, it meant that conflicts and situations directly involving any of the superpowers could not as a practical matter be acted upon by the UN, as in the Guatemala coup of 1954, the Hungarian revolt of 1956, the Czech uprising of 1968, and the Vietnam War. On the other hand, local and regional conflicts such as between the Arabs and Israel, and in Cyprus, Western Sahara, Namibia, Angola, Mozambique, Afghanistan, Nicaragua and El Salvador were stymied in the United Nations until the relaxation and eventual end of the Cold War.

Trygve Lie felt the impact of the early days of the Cold War. He learned that it was difficult or impossible to satisfy the major antagonists. At first, he drew the disdain of the United States, which suspected him of pro-Soviet tendencies. Later, he became *persona non grata* to the USSR for his stance on the Korean War. Dag Hammarskjöld so infuriated the Soviet Union because his initiatives in the Congo were deemed by them to have been too pro-West that they proposed a radical transmutation of the office of Secretary-General, replacing the single occupant with a *troika*. U Thant, groping for a mediating role for the

United Nations in the Vietnam war, was categorically rebuffed by the United States.

It would be a mistake to assume that because the UN, particularly the Security Council, was stymied in the discharge of its responsibilities in the areas of maintaining and enforcing international peace, the entire organization came to a halt and the Secretary-General's office became useless. In fact, it was during the Cold War that the UN membership more than tripled from the original 51 as a result of the decolonization process in which the UN played a significant role. This growth in membership in turn changed the nature of the General Assembly, which became the venue of the underprivileged, underdeveloped majority of the world. These changes affected the office of the Secretary-General who, most notably, increasingly was involved in bridging the North-South divide.

The Cold War lent itself to a practice of turning to the Secretary-General to obviate the deadlock in the Security Council. Several years ago, Thomas Franck suggested that,

... the office of the Secretary-General has become the black box of the United Nations, into which, for lack of agreement on any particular course of action, the members deposit their most pressing and intractable problems, in the hope that, through the operation of some ineffable but ineluctable process, a solution will emerge.[23]

Although the practice went back to the days of Trygve Lie when the Security Council authorized the Secretary-General to work out an armistice between Israel and its Arab neighbours, it achieved notoriety in the days of Hammarskjöld as the "Leave it to Dag" syndrome. In a way it seemed as if, in turning to the Secretary-General, the deliberative organs of the UN, the Security Council and the General Assembly, regarded him as a sort of chief executive, giving him considerable leeway in implementing broad policy directives. These types of responsibilities are hardly bestowed upon "a chief clerk". They called for a considerable assertion of initiative by the Secretary-General and his staff. But this does not mean that he was transformed into a truly independent actor. It indicates that during the Cold War, the Secretary-General emerged as an actor in his own right on the world stage, despite the constraints established on the UN in dealing with the world's most pressing conflicts and problems.

THE POST-COLD WAR CONTEXT

With the end of the Cold War, tensions and conflicts that had been reined in by the Cold War were unshackled. The legitimacy of state borders and the very existence of many states configured during the Cold War became a prime cause of disequilibrium in the world – in Yugoslavia, Somalia, Haiti, Nagorny-Karabakh and elsewhere. It appeared, then, that a new and leading role was emerging for the United Nations, and by extension for the Secretary-General. As the US Ambassador to the United Nations, Madeleine K. Albright, reasoned as late as June 1993,

> ...the Cold War's end has removed the restraining, stabilizing effect of the East-West nuclear stand-off. Pent up, often violent, pressures for change have been released – *placing the United Nations in the centre of the effort to guide and safeguard a suddenly chaotic world.*[24]

The East-West confrontation that had all but paralyzed the UN was history. The successful authorized use of force under Chapter VII of the Charter in the face of Iraq's aggression against Kuwait gave credence to the general feeling that the world was at the threshold of a new era with the United Nations playing a central role in maintaining international peace. The humanitarian intervention on behalf of the Kurds in the north and the Shiites in the south of Iraq plus the continued UN observance of nuclear sites in Iraq gave further credibility to this notion. Moreover, international conflicts that had hitherto defied resolution were now moving towards resolution in Namibia, Afghanistan, Cambodia, El Salvador, Nicaragua, Mozambique, and Angola under the guidance of the United Nations. Talk of a "revitalized," "relevant," and "effective" United Nations was prevalent among scholars, practitioners, and the media.

In January 1992, seeking to capitalize on the UN's new visibility and successes, an unprecedented summit meeting of the Security Council was convened with one agenda item, "The Responsibility of the Security Council in the Maintenance of International Peace and Security". The president of the Council that month, Prime Minister John Major of the United Kingdom, declared that, "this extraordinary meeting ... marks a turning-point in the world and at the United Nations." A new era of international cooperation in collective security and the maintenance of international peace through the United Nations was envisaged. Held one month after Boutros-Ghali took office, the summit signalled an enhanced role for the Secretary-General: "We are here not only to wish ... Dr. Boutros Boutros-Ghali well, but to give him our full backing in carrying out his mandate. A new situation in the world needs new ideas and new impetus." In a demonstration of high regard for the office of Secretary-General and its new incumbent, the Security Council commissioned Boutros-Ghali to prepare, in less than six months, "his analysis and recommendations on ways of strengthening and making more efficient within the framework of the Charter the capacity of the United Nations for preventive diplomacy, for peacemaking and peace-keeping." [25] In the recommendations, the Security Council suggested that the Secretary-General could:

1. Cover the role of the United Nations in identifying potential crises and areas of instability as well as contributions to be made by regional organizations ... in helping the work of the Council.
2. Cover the need for adequate resources, both material and financial.
3. Draw on lessons learned in recent peace-keeping missions to recommend ways of making more effective Secretariat planning and operations.
4. Consider how greater use might be made of his good offices, and his other functions under the Charter.[26]

The Security Council's request implied that its members were intent on going beyond traditional peace-keeping and that they looked to the Secretary-General to provide leadership in this undertaking. Prime Minister Major declared the role of the Secretary-General "vital" in considering "how we can enhance the ability of the United Nations to respond effectively and ensure that it has the necessary resources, both financial and material, to enable it to do so."

When the summit met, elements of strain in UN peace-keeping activities arising from inadequate financing, the escalation in the number of operations and their increased complexity were already evident; but the situation had not attained crisis proportions as it would within the year over Somalia and Bosnia. It appeared that the Security Council working with the advice and leadership of the Secretary-General was expected to bring the United Nations into a new period of effectiveness in containing and resolving conflicts. It should be noted that this summit broadened the concept of international peace and security to include "non-military sources of instability in the economic, social, humanitarian and ecological fields" which it declared to "have become threats to peace and security." Consequently, it asserted that, "the United Nations as a whole, working through the appropriate bodies, needs to give the highest priority to the solution of those matters."[27]

While there were significant points of disagreement at the Security Council summit, notably over human rights, the prevailing air was one of optimism regarding a positive and central role for the UN and its Secretary-General to meet the peace and security needs of the international community. Several months earlier, the General Assembly exhibited similar optimism in its call on the Secretary-General "to monitor the state of international peace and security regularly and systematically in order to provide early warning" and "*on his own initiative* to consider undertaking a fact-finding mission when a dispute or situation exists."[28]

The Security Council and General Assembly moves were part of an effort to take advantage of the conciliatory international post-Cold War climate and to place the UN and the Secretary-General at the centre of an effort to establish a strengthened international system for dealing with problems of international peace and security. In doing so, they seemed to be moving towards the realization of Pérez de Cuéllar's counsel offered some years ago that a "conscious decision" be taken "on the part of the member states to strengthen the role of the Secretary-General and to provide him with better means to keep watch over actual and potential points of conflict."[29]

In a sense, the summit meeting was truly a "turning-point" insofar as the role of the Secretary-General is concerned. In calling upon the Secretary-General for the comprehensive analysis and recommendations as it did, the Security Council was breaking new ground. At no time in the past had the Security Council turned to a Secretary-General with such a broad mandate on matters within its domain. The idea of the Security Council extending such a request to the Secretary-General during the days of the Cold War is unthinkable. But this was a new era. The Security Council, no longer bogged down by the East-West confrontation, was reaching out to the Secretary-General for leadership. He was being challenged to lead with ideas on how the Security Council's peace-keeping, peace enforcement and peacemaking functions could be strengthened. Not only did this represent an important step in the direction of better collaboration between the Security Council and the Secretary-General; "implicit ... [in it] was encouragement to the new Secretary-General to assert his authority as the leader of the United

Nations, and as an influential international public figure."[30]

In suggesting to the Secretary-General that the issues covered could include the role of the UN in identifying potential crises and areas of instability, as well as the need for adequate resources, both material and financial, the Council imposed a challenging responsibility on the Secretary-General. The mandate lent itself to conflicting interpretations over the scope of analysis and recommendations the Secretary-General is to make. For example, a narrow interpretation of peacemaking would restrict it to situations arising under Chapters VI and VII of the Charter; a liberal one would broaden it to include "the creation of conditions of stability and well-being which are necessary for peaceful and friendly relations among nations" as called for in Article 55 of Chapter IX.

Secretary-General Boutros-Ghali responded in June 1992 with his report, *An Agenda for Peace.*[31] Our concern here is not a detailed examination of that report, but rather how the request for its preparation, its substance and the reception it received impact on the post-Cold War role of the Secretary-General.

Drafted by a high-level group of experienced UN officials, the report bore the imprint of the newly appointed Secretary-General. He was closely involved in its development and its final formulation. Clearly the Secretary-General took the Security Council's unprecedented request seriously with the expectation that out of the process started by the Council important changes enhancing the future role of the UN and its Secretary-General would ensue. Towards the end of *An Agenda for Peace,* Boutros-Ghali wrote, "[w]e must be guided not by precedents alone ... but by the needs of the future and by the shape and content that we wish to give it" and he advanced his vision that "this Organization may emerge as greater than the sum of its parts."

It must be recognized that Boutros-Ghali was not given a *carte blanche* but was instructed to make his recommendations "within the framework and provisions of the Charter" and to draw "on lessons learned in recent United Nations peace-keeping operations". The Secretary-General was charged to lead but within prescribed limits. In effect, he was asked to give the Security Council the benefit of his wisdom on how the issues of peace are to be dealt with by the Council but not to concern himself with what has become a contentious issue within the United Nations – the Council's structure and *modus operandi.* On the whole, the analysis and recommendations represent a balanced approach based on past experience. A key virtue of the report is its comprehensive and systematic approach. Out of the complex record of past and current United Nations' largely improvised involvement in the maintenance of peace over forty years, Boutros-Ghali and his associates presented a logical step-by-step conception of the UN conflict controlling mechanisms:

1. Preventive diplomacy seeks to resolve disputes before violence breaks out.
2. Peacemaking is the effort to bring hostile parties together by peaceful means as those foreseen in Chapter VI of the Charter.
3. Peace-keeping is the deployment of a UN presence in the field to halt conflicts and preserve peace once it is attained.
4. Peace-building is a post-conflict undertaking designed to prevent the recurrence of violence by identifying and supporting structures which will tend to strengthen and solidify peace.

The report also contains a number of more innovative and daring recommendations that go beyond the traditional pattern of peace-keeping. Thus, Boutros-Ghali has suggested the relaxation, under certain circumstances, of the long accepted principle of consent of the conflicting parties before a peace-keeping operation could be mounted. Also, reminiscent of Trygve Lie's 1948 proposal for a UN Guard Force, he called for the establishment of rapid deployment "peace enforcement units" on a permanent basis "under the command of the Secretary-General" to "respond to outright aggression, imminent or actual."[32]

The substance of this much heralded report has been subject to considerable analysis and criticism. Dealing, as it does, with the very essence of the United Nations — how it is to cope with the growing number of conflict situations in the unstable post-Cold War world — this was to be expected. Reaction in the General Assembly and Security Council has been cautious. Some of the strongest reservations came from Third World states, apprehensive over the potential limitations on sovereignty and the non-representative character of the Security Council. The Secretary-General's recommendations have been judged across a broad spectrum ranging from "bold" to "soggy", from "far reaching yet politically achievable" to "intriguing ... but not of an entirely practical nature."[33] The report also has been evaluated not only on its contents but also on what, its critics feel, has been left out. Thus, the Secretary-General has been called to task for not addressing the question of structural revision of the Security Council, the promotion of human rights, the UN response to civil strife within states, the international arms trade, and for focusing too restrictively on short-term crisis management and not enough on long-term social and economic problems.

When the Secretary-General was asked to focus his attention primarily on preventive diplomacy, peace-keeping and peacemaking, he was becoming involved in the thorny issue of how the Security Council, freed of the Cold War stranglehold, was discharging its responsibilities. Since the exceptional performance of the Security Council that marked its reaction to Iraq's invasion and thwarted annexation of Kuwait, there ensued a vigorous debate over the proper role of the Security Council and of the prevailing political dynamics within it. There were those who argued that the Security Council was finally fulfilling its Charter mandate. On the other extreme was the contention that the five permanent members, led by the United States, had "hijacked" the Council. In between there were those who did not actually object to the forceful action taken by the Security Council against Iraq, but who felt squeamish about the lack of open debate at Council meetings as the practice of closed informal consultations became the accepted pattern for Council deliberations.

When *An Agenda for Peace* appeared there was wide expectation that the Secretary-General's report would lead to a more sharply defined and strengthened role for the United Nations and the Secretary-General in the business of securing peace in the post-Cold War years. This expectation never materialized. The world did not come to a halt as the slow-moving UN process pondered the Secretary-General's recommendations. The fact that the United Nations was engaged in a debate over *An Agenda for Peace* did not prevent the burgeoning conflicts in Yugoslavia, Somalia and elsewhere from intensifying. The accelerated pace of war, wanton destruction and humanitarian disaster in Yugoslavia and Somalia hardly provided a calm atmosphere for the meticulous review and careful study of the Secretary-General's analysis and recommendations for reform and improvement of the UN role in the maintenance of international peace and security. Instead of working its way through the plodding UN process, reform of the capacity of the UN for preventive diplomacy, peacemaking and peace-keeping was now being determined by events. The optimism exhibited at the time of the summit was dissipated and replaced by an acrimonious debate over how the tragedies in Bosnia and Somalia could be contained through UN peacekeeping operations. In the centre was Secretary-General Boutros-Ghali, faulted, at times deservedly but mostly undeservedly, for the shortcomings of the United Nations field operations.

From the very outset of his assuming office, Boutros-Ghali gave evidence that he was going to be an active and more outspoken Secretary-General. It was not long before he emerged as a controversial world figure. A little more than a year after assuming office, Boutros-Ghali was hailed as someone "uniquely suited to help bring the UN into a different kind of structure" which can begin to deal with the problem of policing the world, even though he "has gotten a lot of people unhappy because he has his own views."[34] At about the same time, he was portrayed as "an intellectual and a politician but not a diplomat and not a master of UN complexities" due to his "abrasive, arrogant, confrontational and worse, often imprudent methods."[35] Clearly, there was no uniform assessment of Boutros-Ghali, except possibly on his being the most outspoken and independent-minded Secretary-General since Hammarskjöld. A notable example of his outspokenness, which made him suspect in some quarters and a hero in others, was his criticism of the Security Council's neglect of the famine in Somalia while focusing its attention on "the rich man's war" in Bosnia. In Somalia itself, Boutros-Ghali proved controversial in some quarters, largely for his determination to disarm the warring factions and his role in the UN's putting a price on the warlord Mohammed Farah Aidid but also because of his pre-UN identity with Egypt's policy in the horn of Africa.[36] He was resented at various times by the leading Western powers in the Security Council for having "'repeatedly told the Security Council 'what it should or should not do' about Bosnia, Somalia and Israel."[37] At the same time, a sense of disappointment was felt among Third World countries that Boutros-Ghali, elected to the Secretary-Generalship because it was Africa's turn to fill the post, has not been attuned to their needs while being preoccupied with the Security Council and its western members. Clearly, Boutros-Ghali was a controversial figure.

With the collapse of the post-Cold War expectations, the UN was in the throes of a crisis over peace-keeping. With the peace-keeping operations in Bosnia and Somalia bogging down and proving incapable of containing violence and brutality, bickering between leading members of the Security Council and the Secretary-General intensified. Most unsettling, the Secretary-General was at odds with the United States not only over tactics in Somalia and Bosnia but also over basic concepts such as the scope of UN peace-keeping activities. US President Bill Clinton, addressing the United Nations General Assembly, cautioned the world that "if the American people are to say yes to UN peace-keeping, the United Nations must know when to say no."[38] In marked contrast to this admonition is Boutros-Ghali's denial that "some peace-keeping operations [are] more important than others" and his assertion that "The United Nations attaches equal importance to all conflicts."[39]

The firestorm that erupted in the US Congress and the media over the loss of American lives following the failed attempt to capture General Aidid brought relations between Boutros-Ghali and the United States to a low point. Trying to distance itself from the failed US Ranger action, the Clinton Administration pointed a finger at the UN. While Boutros-Ghali begrudgingly accepted the role of scapegoat for himself and the United Nations, it became clear that the role of the UN and of Secretary-General in the post-Cold War was being redefined in a manner not envisaged at the summit. Because the situations in Somalia and Bosnia had become more intractable and new conflicts were being dumped into the lap of the world body, the new post-Cold War climate did not lend itself to reasoned discourse over how the UN could be "strengthened" and made more "effective" in dealing with threats to the peace, as called for by the summit.

Two factors defined this new post-Cold War climate for the UN. The first was its overloading. New conflicts calling for international peace-keeping were being added to the Security Council's agenda even as the cost of existing operations mounted; but the commensurate funding was not provided. Speaking in Tokyo, Boutros-Ghali noted that "funds are decreasingly available for peace operations and conflicts escalate as resources and willpower are in short supply" at the moment that taxpayers in every country are suffering from "donor fatigue".[40] This situation created a new role for the Secretary-General – that of scrounger for funds.

The second defining factor is the changing nature of peace-keeping. The classic approach to peace-keeping – the interposition of an impartial UN force between two disputants to preserve a cease-fire or an armistice – was hardly applicable to the multi-sided conflicts in Bosnia and in Somalia. The neutrality of the initial humanitarian intervention could not easily be maintained and the limited UN aid forces came under fire. At this point, the logical extension would be forceful UN intervention to protect the humanitarian effort and, if necessary, military action against the perpetrator. This is what happened in Somalia with such disastrous results when Pakistani and then US troops came into harm's way. The thought of intervening militarily in Bosnia was ruled out because no Western power was prepared to undertake such action on the ground for fear of the impact casualties would have at home.

This newly-defined international political climate established a set of parameters for the role of the United Nations and its Secretary-General far more restrictive than was envisaged at the summit. The crisis that befell UN peace-keeping was not anticipated at that historic meeting.

The Secretary-General was given mandates of extraordinary complexity in highly unstable areas, without getting adequate support from member states.

As the UN faltered under the overload, there was a tendency to lay much blame on Boutros-Ghali not only for his outspokenness and political judgement, but also for his deficiencies as administrator. Dissatisfaction with the Secretary-General's management of the Secretariat long preceded Boutros-Ghali. The issue of effective management of the Secretariat has always been closely related to the chronic squabbles over UN finances. The contention is that the UN's inveterate financial crisis is in large part due to the bloated and inept Secretariat, rife with political cronyism, feather-bedding practices, and fraud. The United States, as the largest contributor to the UN budget, has been particularly critical of the Secretariat bureaucracy, as Congressman Tom Lantos of the House Foreign Affairs Committee noted, "...the support of the American people, and I can say the American Congress, for the United Nations is contingent upon our conviction that the organization is lean, trim, efficient and well-managed."[41]

Boutros-Ghali's track record as head of the Secretariat has not improved the situation. As the managerial role of the Secretary-General has increased commensurately with the growth in the number and complexity of UN peace-keeping operations, so has the incidence of mismanagement and inefficiency of these field operations. However, management is not one of Boutros-Ghali's strengths. More at ease in dealing with the political and legal complexities of international politics, he has exhibited a heavy-handed style as chief administrative officer that has contributed to low morale and disarray in the Secretariat.

As the fiftieth anniversary of the UN approaches, both it and Boutros-Ghali have been operating in a highly unstable political climate. This climate has put unusual demands on all the key actors in the UN drama of peace-keeping, the Security Council member states individually, the Security Council as a collective entity, and the Secretary-General. Largely due to domestic pressures, there is a marked reluctance on the part of the more powerful states who control the Security Council to provide adequate funding for peace-keeping operations and to undertake new, costly and at times dangerous operations. This attitude is reflected in the decisions of the Security Council which, although usually couched in lofty principled terms, are often vague and indecisive. This, in turn, puts a burden on the Secretary-General in trying to implement the Security Council's directives.

Due to the difficulties encountered by the UN in Bosnia and Somalia, the prestige and credibility of the organization has plummeted. Some would lay this at the feet of Secretary-General Boutros-Ghali for his impetuous and overzealous behaviour. Yet, in reflecting on what brought on the UN reversals, it is clear it was not by Boutros-Ghali's actions and efforts, but rather the constraints under which he was operating and the unrealistic expectations. To critics who have accused him of over-extending his authority, Boutros-Ghali responded:

> In cases such as Bosnia and Somalia when the Secretary-General coordinates the political negotiations, humanitarian aid and peace-keeping operations, or approves the timing of a military action, it is not out of hunger for power but because the Security Council has placed a responsibility on the Secretary-General to do so.[42]

CONCLUSION

Differences in style and temperament affect the conduct of the office of Secretary-General but after all is said and done, the Secretary-General, no matter who it is, faces the same set of facts that define the United Nations and his office. The most basic reality is that the UN is an organization of sovereign states which, as the third Secretary-General U Thant put it, "must work by persuasion, argument, negotiations and a persistent search for consensus."[43] The record of the UN's first fifty years indicates that the Secretary-General's ability to act and direct operations is limited since his is a position of leadership without power in the conventional sense. He has no standing military forces at his disposal. He has little control over his organization's budget. He lacks his own first-hand sources of information. He is not master in his own house as head of the Secretariat since his freedom to hire and fire is limited by staff rules and the "exclusive preserve" of a government to a particular post.[44] He has no political base, such as a political party to rally in his support. His constituency, if he has any, is the world but it is so diffuse as to make it unreliable and difficult to marshall. The tasks heaped upon him are great, beyond the normal capacity of a single human being. His independence is circumscribed since he is beholden to the governments who elected him. He has no power of veto, nor is his approval required for a Security Council resolution or a General Assembly recommendation. Most significant is that the prestige, influence and significance of the office rises and falls with the prestige, influence and significance of the UN as a whole determined by the international political climate at any given moment.

Despite this litany of negative attributes with which every occupant of the office has had to cope, the Secretary-General can be a significant player on the world stage. Here is where style and temperament come in. Skilful use of the limited power at his disposal under the Charter can bring the Secretary-General the international respect he must have. Although he is primarily a servant of the main political bodies of the UN, he is not confined to the thirty-eighth floor waiting for his marching orders. The world is his bailiwick and those who have held this high office have travelled widely carrying the message of the UN – the quest for a better world through collective effort. He may or may not be the conscience of the world, but he is in a way the embodiment of the ideals of the United Nations widely looked up to by governments and people. Through his speeches and his annual report on the work of the organization, which actually is a report on the state of the United Nations, he can use his office as a "bully pulpit" to inspire, persuade, exhort and cajole. Ideally, he should be the "eyes and ears" of the world on the lookout for brewing trouble spots, short- and long-term, hence he should be engaged in preventive diplomacy. In fact, the Secretary-General does not have a diplomatic and intelligence network comparable to that of major governments and he frequently depends on them for information. And, while everyone believes in the value of preventive diplomacy, there are relatively few instances where the circumstances and the attitudes of the parties permit the Secretary-General to carry it out successfully.

At the outset of this essay, two questions were posed: as the fiftieth anniversary of the United Nations approaches, how does the Secretary-Generalship fit into the scheme of world affairs and how has it changed? To answer the latter question first, the role has basically not changed. All of the negative limitations and positive attributes of the office that governed the first Secretary-General are still in force. As to the first question, the Secretary-General's role in the overall scheme of world affairs is dependent on the role of the UN. If it is playing a vital and effective role, the Secretary-General can be expected to play a similar role. He is instrumental to the successful operation of the UN but he cannot be up front as a policy maker. The Secretary-General can not be expected to substitute his leadership for that of the Security Council or of the General Assembly in their areas of competence.

With all the limitations of his office, the Secretary-General has a critical role to play in the broad area of peace-keeping. The Security Council decisions are not self-executing; somebody has to manage and coordinate the collective effort, whether it be to monitor a cease-fire or facilitate the distribution of humanitarian assistance. On the rare occasions when Chapter VII action is authorized by the Council, such as the Gulf War, implementing the decision is the responsibility of members of the Council who have the necessary military capabilities. But in almost all other instances, which do not involve massive military intervention, the responsibility falls primarily on the Secretary-General to organize the operation, recruit the required military and civilian personnel, arrange for logistical support and financing, and keep the parties to the dispute supportive of the operation.

For a short time after the end of the Cold War, it appeared that a new collaborative ethos was taking over in the world and the United Nations and its Secretary-General were the agencies through which this was to be articulated. The Security Council summit meeting of January 1992 was the high point of this vision. It raised expectations of a more autonomous Secretary-General to go along with a more powerful and relevant United Nations. The question has not been resolved. An intense debate is taking place over the future of UN peace-keeping. [45] It is as yet an open question, at the fiftieth anniversary of the founding of the United Nations, as to how far in the direction of a strengthened and more effective United Nations and its Secretary-General will the world move.

NOTES

1. Cyril Foster Lecture delivered in Oxford on 13 May 1986, reprinted in Adam Roberts and Benedict Kingsbury (eds.), *United Nations, Divided World: The UN's Role in International Relations,* 2nd ed., (Oxford: Clarendon Press, 1993), p. 125.
2. *International Documents Review,* vol. 5, no. 5, (14 February 1994), p. 4.
3. Richard L. Armitage, "Bend the U.N. to Our Will", *The New York Times,* 24 February 1994.
4. See Alan James, "The Secretary-General as an Independent Political Actor" in Benjamin Rivlin and Leon Gordenker, *The Challenging Role of the UN Secretary-General: Making "The Most Impossible Job in the World" Possible,* (Westport, CN and London: Praeger, 1993).
5. Articles 97-99. Emphasis added.

6. Leon Gordenker, "The Secretary-General", in James Barros (ed.), *The United Nations: Past, Present and Future*, (NY: The Free Press, 1972) p. 106.

7. *Report of the Preparatory Commission of the United Nations*, Doc.PC-/20, 23 December 1945, p. 87.

8. Pérez de Cuéllar, note 1, p. 127.

9. Thomas M. Franck and George Nolte, "The Good Offices Function of the UN Secretary-General", in Adam Roberts and Benedict Kingsbury (eds), *United Nations, Divided World*, note 1, pp. 172-173. This chapter contains details on the various authorizations and uses of good offices by the Secretary-General.

10. *Ibid.* p. 37. See also Seymour Maxwell Finger and Arnold A. Saltzman, *Bending With the Winds: Kurt Waldheim and the United Nations*, (Westport, CN: Praeger, 1990) pp.42-45.

11. Pérez de Cuéllar, note 1, p. 125.

12. Brian Urquhart and Erskine Childers, *A World in Need of Leadership: Tomorrow's United Nations*, (Uppsala, Sweden: Dag Hammarskjöld Foundation, 1990) p. 21.

13. *Ibid.*, p. 20.

14. Max Jakobson, "Filling the World's Most Impossible Job", *World Monitor*, (August 1991).

15. James S. Sutterlin, "The UN Secretary-General as Chief Administrator", in Rivlin and Gordenker, *The Challenging Role*, note 4, p. 44.

16. See Paul Lewis, "The Peacekeeper in Chief Needs More Soldiers," *The New York Times*, 4 March 1994.

17. UNGA Emergency Session I, Res. 998 and Res. 999. This extraordinary exercise of authority by the General Assembly in the area of maintenance of international peace was carried out in accordance with the provisions of the Uniting for Peace Resolution of 1950, which called upon the Assembly to take over when the Security Council could not act for fear of a veto. Since two of the three forces that invaded Egypt came from Britain and France, both permanent members of the Security Council with the right to veto, the United States and the Soviet Union resorted to the General Assembly.

18. UNSC Res. 186, 1964.

19. S/PV.1102, 4 March 1964, p. 39.

20. *Ibid.* p. 32.

21. Security Council, *Official Records*, 31 October 1956.

22. Trygve Lie, *In the Cause of Peace*, (NY: Macmillan, 1954) p. 99.

23. Thomas G. Franck, *Nation Against Nation*, (New York: Oxford University Press, 1985) p. 134.

24. Speech before the Council on Foreign Relations, New York, 13 June 1993. Emphasis added.
25. UN Doc. S/PV.3046, 31 January 1992, pp. 144-145.
26. *Ibid.*
27. S/PV.3046, 31 January 1992.
28. UNGA Res. 46/59, 9 December 1991. Emphasis added.
29. In Roberts and Kingsley (eds), *United Nations, Divided World*, note 1, p. 136.
30. David Cox, "Exploring *An Agenda for Peace*: Issues arising from the Report of the Secretary-General", *Aurora Papers 20*, Ottowa: Canadian Centre for Global Security, (October 1993), p. 1.
31. Boutros Boutros-Ghali, *An Agenda for Peace*, (NY: United Nations, June 1992, publication number DPI/1247).
32. UN Doc. A/47/277; S/24111, 17 June 1992, par. 44.
33. See for example David Cox, "Exploring *An Agenda for Peace...*", note 30; Leon Gordenker, "The UN Secretary-General, Intellectual Leadership and Maintaining Peace", *International Spectator*, (The Hague), vol. 47. no. 11, (November 1993); Adam Roberts, "The United Nations and International Security", *Survival* vol. 35. no. 2, (Summer 1993); Thomas G. Weiss, *An Agenda for Peace: Some Conceptual Problems*, paper presented at the ICRA/ACUNS Symposium on "Strengthening the United Nations - Peace and Environment", Tokyo, 7-9 January 1993.
34. U.S. Congress, "Collective Security in the Post-Cold War World," *Joint Hearings before the Subcommittees on Europe and the Middle East and International Security, International Organizations and Human Rights of the Committee on Foreign Affairs*, House of Representatives, 103rd Congress, statement by former Secretary of State Lawrence Eagleburger, 11 March 1993, p. 97.
35. Louis Wiznitzer, "Boutros-Ghali's Sinking Ship," *The Japan Times*, 25 March 1993.
36. An editorial in *The New York Times* on 8 October 1993 referred to "the highly personalized vendetta that has developed between the UN Secretary-General, Boutros Boutros-Ghali, and a single Somali warlord, Mohammed Farah Aidid."
37. Former US Ambassador to the UN, Jeane Kirkpatrick in *Newsweek*, 15 February 1993.
38. *Press Release USUN 140-(93)) Rev.1*, 27 September 1993.
39. Boutros Boutros-Ghali, *Report on the Work of the Organization from the Forty-seventh to the Forty-eighth Session of the General Assembly*, par. 22, p. 6, DPI 1420, September 1993. The Secretary-General told the Security Council, in reply to a member's observation that the UN was

taking on too much, "we would be accused of discrimination and double-dealing if we tried to impose priorities." *The New York Times*, 25 January 1993.

40. *The Japan Times*, 21 December 1993.

41. U.S. Congress, "Management and Mismanagement at the United Nations, *Hearings Before the Subcommittees on Europe and the Middle East and International Security, International Organizations and Human Rights of the Committee on Foreign Affairs*, House of Representatives, 103rd Congress, 1st Session, 5 March 1993, p. 2.

42. Boutros-Ghali, "Don't Make the U.N.'s Hard Job Harder," *The New York Times*, 20 August 1993.

43. U Thant, "The Role of the Secretary-General", speech delivered on 16 September 1971, UN OPI/449-19594-October 1971, p. 11.

44. See Theodore Meron, "'Exclusive Preserves' and the New Soviet Policy Towards the Secretariat," *The American Journal of International Law*, vol. 85, no. 2, (April 1991), p. 322.

45. Important contributions to this debate include Gene M. Lyons, "A New Collective Security: The United Nations and International Peace", *The Washington Quarterly*, vol. 17, no. 2, (Spring 1994); Marrack Goulding, "Strengthening Multilateral Peacekeeping: Current Rapid Expansion Unsustainable Without Major Changes", *The Trilateral Commission, 1993 Washington Meeting*; Laura W. Reed and Carl Kaysen, *Emerging Norms of Justified Intervention*, (Cambridge, MA: American Academy of Arts and Sciences, 1993); Brian Urquhart, "For a UN Voluntary Military Force", *New York Review of Books*, 10 June 1993; Kevin M. Cahill, "A Necessary Balance", *Brown Journal of Foreign Affairs*, (Winter 1993-1994); Adam Roberts, "The United Nations and International Security", note 33; and Paul Lewis, "The Peacekeeper in Chief Needs More Soldiers," *The New York Times*, 4 March 1994.

6 UN Peace-keeping: Recent Developments and Current Problems

Alan James

In United Nations history, peace-keeping has been distinguished from enforcement. The latter refers to the UN operation in Korea in the early 1950s,[1] and the Coalition authorized by the UN in 1990-91 to eject Iraq from Kuwait.[2] The former encompasses behaviour of an impartial and non-threatening kind conducted with the consent and cooperation of the parties to the dispute in question. Peace-keepers therefore enter, and remain on, a state's territory only with its consent, however "formal" that formal requirement may in particular cases be – Lebanon's consent to the renewal of the UN Force's mandate throughout the 1980's is an instance of this. And the armed elements of any such mission are entitled to use their arms only in self-defence, including the defence of their positions and maybe also to ensure their freedom of movement. But that is all. Peace-keeping is more like counselling than combat.[3]

This does not mean that peace-keeping has been of less value than enforcement. The two activities relate to two quite different situations, and each of them, in its appropriate context, has been of considerable worth. This point deserves emphasis so far as peace-keeping is concerned, for there has been a tendency to assume that because it does not enforce the peace it has little to offer. But although it is of a secondary nature, in the sense that its success is dependent on the policies of the primary actors – the disputants – peace-keeping missions nonetheless often have made a valuable contribution to the maintenance of peace. The reason for this is that even when disputants are in principle willing to live in peace, they sometimes find that the tension between them is such that it is hard to implement their pacific intentions. They could make good use of the help of an impartial third party. Sometimes, indeed, that kind of help has seemed essential for the peace to be preserved.

105

CONCEPTS

Hitherto there has been no difficulty in distinguishing between peace-keeping and enforcement, and in this area there have been no other candidates to consider. Now, however, there is a conceptual problem which arises out of the mounting of, for the UN, relatively large, often more powerfully armed, and sometimes more assertive bodies. The missions in Cambodia, Bosnia-Herzegovina, and Somalia are the instances of this. They hardly amount to enforcement, at least not in the established understanding of that term. But are they sufficiently distinct from traditional peace-keeping to require a separate conceptual category?

A mixed answer is offered. It is doubted whether there is viable ground between enforcement and consent. One either makes war on a major party to a dispute, or one tries to encourage peace by working with the parties. Thus there is an insufficient basis for a third concept. A peace-keeping operation may shift, temporarily or partly, to enforcement, which is what happened in Somalia during the latter part of 1993. But it is likely that an operation will on the whole fall into one or other of the two established categories. The three operations mentioned in the previous paragraph seem predominantly of the peace-keeping type.

However, a distinctive sub-category does seem to be called for. Perhaps it would be useful to distinguish between pacific peace-keeping (operations of the traditional sort) and prickly peace-keeping (Cambodia, doubtfully; Bosnia-Herzegovina, possibly; Somalia occasionally). On the analogy of the prickly pear, the sub-category refers to operations with which it is painful to tangle. They do not have an offensive purpose, and are not established with partial intent, but they are equipped in a way which makes their right of self-defence a substantial consideration for those who would obstruct them. And, it may be that a prickly mission is also in a position to implement its mandate notwithstanding the contrariness of lesser local groups. (In North America such operations are often referred to as "muscular" peace-keeping. But it is thought that that term implies a more positive assertiveness than the operations in question justify.)

POLITICS

Demand

Since the end of the Cold War there has been a remarkable increase in the number of UN peace-keeping operations.[4]   No attempt is made at forecasting, but it is assumed that peace-keeping is likely to be on the international agenda for some time.   It will be interesting to see if plans for an Israeli-Palestinian accord involve the use of peace-keeping devices.

Availability

The possible problem here is that the demand for peace-keeping may outrun the supply of men and money.   Without knowing the demand, comment on this matter is not likely to be helpful.   But a few observations may be ventured.

Participation in peace-keeping does seem to be widely valued by defence ministries.   Perhaps in reflection of this there has been a remarkable increase in the number of states contributing to UN peace-keeping to about 75 (getting on for half the UN's membership of 184).[5] However, the supply of troops perhaps could become a problem, and not just because of the sheer lack of individuals or units with the required skills.   There may now be less of a difficulty arising out of the political susceptibilities of host states (although it ought not to be assumed that that problem has entirely gone away).   But potential contributor states may sometimes have political or even military reservations about certain operations, more particularly those of the prickly kind.

In February 1993 the Security Council decided to "upgrade" the Iraq-Kuwait Observation Mission from an observer operation to a force with the capability and the right to prevent small-scale violations of the demilitarized zone between the two states.[6]   There was then a long hiatus, and not until November 1993 was it announced that the requisite troops – from Bangladesh – had been found.[7]   There were also delays in finding the extra 7,600 troops authorized in June 1993 to protect certain "safe areas" in Bosnia-Herzegovina[8], and in the recruitment of an extra 10,000 troops to control that state's borders (so as better to enforce sanctions) which the Secretary-General was asked to investigate[9] at about the same time.

On finance, it may be noted that, dire though the UN's financial position always seems to be, it is perhaps unlikely that it will be unable to find the money (on a *per diem* basis) for the officers making up observation missions and for the civilian administrators of both forces and observer missions.   Nor until very recently have the long delays in the reimbursement of states who provide battalions for UN forces seemed to be a strong discouragement to participation.   It is true that this factor may have influenced the decisions of Finland (1977) and Sweden (1987) to withdraw from the UN Force in Cyprus. But for both financial and political reasons that was probably a special case. In 1993, things seem to have taken a turn for the worse in this respect, for a number of developing states have turned down invitations to join new peace-keeping operations or to expand their participation in existing ones. In all cases they have cited delays in reimbursement as a principal factor in their decisions. Furthermore, Finland is withdrawing from the Force on the Golan Heights (between Israel and Syria) and Sweden from the one in South Lebanon, reportedly for financial reasons in both cases. (Scandinavian peace-keepers are expensive for their Governments, so that the UN's slowness in making its standard $900 per month per soldier payments may be a significantly aggravating factor.)

Finance is at bottom a political problem. The member states strongly in favour of a particular peace-keeping body are unlikely to let it die for financial reasons − or at least they should not, in their own interests, let that happen. It may be noted that at the start of UNPROFOR II (the operation in Bosnia-Herzegovina [10]) certain contributor states agreed to pay their own way. With a short experience of this arrangement behind him, the Secretary-General decided that it was not, after all, a good idea. But there is no reason in principle − although one can foresee some possible political reservations − why a sufficiently interested state should not make a voluntary contribution to cover its cost to the UN.

Impartiality

A reputation for impartiality is one of the strongest assets of any peace-keeping body. It was doubt on this score which led some NATO states to view the UN operation in the Congo in the early 1960s with grave suspicion; and doubt about the impartiality of certain other aspects of the operation led a number of states, particularly in Africa, to feel uneasy about UN peace-keeping for a couple of decades.[11] Also, it was the abandonment of this principle by the American and French contingents in the non-UN peace-keeping force in Beirut in 1983 (representing a shift from peace-keeping to attempted enforcement) which set in train a series of events which ended in their humiliating withdrawal.[12]

Currently the principle of impartiality is coming under greater strain. This is because of the locale of the great majority of recently-established UN peace-keeping operations. This analyst can identify 26 new operations since the start of 1988 (adopting a somewhat more liberal set of criteria than the UN), together with three quasi-peace-keeping initiatives. Of these 26, no fewer than 24 operate within all or part of a national jurisdiction or in relation to a problem which has a domestic base, rather than at or in relation to a tense international divide, such as a frontier or cease-fire line. Contrary to what is often thought,[13] this is by no means a complete change of focus for peace-keeping. Nor is it novel for internal operations to encounter problems: the Congo has already been mentioned; another case is the anger of Lebanon's President in 1958 when UN Observers failed to endorse his allegations about interference in his country.[14]

But the present heavy predominance of internal peace-keeping operations is new. It means that such peace-keepers are more than ever before exposed to the fluid nature of domestic politics, and more particularly to the struggle for the reins of government.[15] In this context, impartial behaviour will not necessarily be seen by all the contestants, all of the time, as impartial. Instead, even when the peace-keepers' role is chiefly humanitarian, they may be judged by the impact which their activity has on the fortunes and ambitions of the local contestants.

This is why virtually all of the UN's current internal operations are in some kind of trouble. It suggests that peace-keepers should take special care to give no ground for charges of partiality. It may be noted that such charges are perhaps likely to be most vehement in respect of prickly operations, due to the greater ability of such operations to make a positive impact on the local scene.

UN or non-UN?

In principle there is no reason why peace-keeping should always be conducted by the UN. It could be done equally well by other international organizations, or even by an ad hoc group of states, as has been happening, admirably, in Sinai since 1982.[16] One also thinks of the European Union's Monitoring Mission in the former Yugoslavia.

But the UN does have some advantages. Its repository of experience in this area should perhaps not be given undue weight, but neither should it be discounted. Of greater importance is the fact that its missions are likely to be more easily seen as impartial than those of most other bodies, which adds to the UN's attractiveness to many host states. Furthermore, the range of potential contributor states is, for political and sometimes also legal reasons, wider in respect of UN than non-UN operations. There may also be merit in the fact that the UN Security Council takes its decisions on the basis of a qualified majority, whereas

NATO and the CSCE, for example, although exhibiting greater political homogeneity, give a veto to all members.

A problem could be arising, however, over the apparent preference of the United States for the use of NATO rather than the UN in connection with the implementation of any peace agreement in Bosnia-Herzegovina. That idea could give rise to greater hesitations on the part of both the local groups involved and potential contributors than if a supervisory force were under the UN's umbrella. Perhaps the point should be made that a major contributor is bound to have a big influence on an operation, so that the particular flag under which the operation flies may not be of great material significance for such a state.

The Role of the Security Council

The Security Council has been operating very smoothly in recent years, but it remains composed of states who have their own interests to consult. The end of the Cold War does not guarantee indefinite agreement on peace-keeping matters, and it is important to remember that. Already there have been some possibly ominous abstentions on certain peace-keeping resolutions, notably by China – whose observations, in another context, about the "Great Hegemon" do not bode well for Sino-American relations. The United States, too, has parted from its usual associates in the voting on a draft resolution[17] which would have lifted the arms embargo on Bosnia-Herzegovina. It would therefore not be entirely surprising if peace-keeping encountered greater politicization within the Council.

There is another, and opposite, twist to this issue. There is considerable unease among the membership at large at the dominant role now being played by the Security Council and, more specifically, at its perceived disdain for the UN's non-Council members. This was evident when the Council's report for June 1991-June 1992, dated June 1993, was debated in the General Assembly shortly after its receipt. Speakers from Africa (north and south of the Sahara), Asia, Latin America, Australasia, and Western Europe gave issue to a veritable litany of complaints about the Council's practices. Of particular interest in the present context is that the Representative of Colombia was critical of the casualness (as he saw it) with which the Council had been invoking Chapter VII – the enforcement Chapter – of the Charter.[18]

There is no immediate problem for peace-keeping here. There is little that the Assembly can do about its feeling of being left out in the cold. But it is perhaps no bad thing that the Council, and especially its permanent members, should be reminded that leaders do well to do what is possible to keep their followers happy. And it ought not to be forgotten that it is the Assembly which holds the purse strings for peace-keeping.

Legitimacy

At the moment, UN peace-keeping operations are seen almost universally as legitimate, simply by virtue of their parentage. But it is worth pointing out that this is not an automatic process. The Soviet Union used to be in varying degree suspicious of such operations, seeing them, for more than one reason, and with a measure of justification, as the instrument of the West. For many years, China stood clear of such operations (not participating in the relevant Security Council votes), regarding them (it seems) as ideologically tainted.

Things are now very different. But, pursuing the line of thought above, it should be noted that there would be much unhappiness among the majority of UN members if peace-keeping came to be seen just as the tool of the great powers. Egalitarianism is a deeply-rooted international concept,[19] however difficult it often is to match it with the practicalities of life. And peace-keeping is commonly seen, because — traditionally — of its pacific character, as something of an exemplification of this principle. If there were a marked move away from this position, controversy could easily ensue.

Should the great worry about this? Could they not say that the UN Charter itself gives them a pre-eminent role in the maintenance of peace? However, the world has changed a lot since 1945. And it is noteworthy that even the great seek approval from the UN for their international initiatives. If they seek to continue to make use of the UN as a stabilizing and peace-helping instrument, they do well not to endanger its legitimacy.

OPERATIONAL ARRANGEMENTS

Problems Arising out of the Multinational Character of Peace-keeping

Domestic Factors
Operational activity by a peace-keeping force cannot be divorced from the domestic political background of its contributor states. The Force

Commander and his political superiors do well to remember that each contingent's government has to answer, in one way or another, to its public for the well-being and fate of its men. It is easy to overlook this point when operations have a quiet life – the experience, for example, of the UN Force in the Gaza Strip and Sinai between 1957 and 1967, and of the Force which has been on the edge of the Golan Heights, between Israel and Syria, for almost two decades.

But now, with the predominance of internal operations and the emergence of prickly peace-keeping, the point has special relevance. There could be a limit to the number of casualties which contingents will accept. No state wishes to give the appearance of giving up just because the situation is getting too difficult. But on the other hand, for most states participation in a peace-keeping mission does not serve any immediate national interest. In the decision to send a contingent the possibility of injuries and deaths is likely to have been largely discounted, and if that assumption proves significantly false, the consequence could be pressing political demands at home for the contingent's withdrawal, particularly, perhaps, if it is not made up of regular soldiers. In all probability it is widely supposed – to some extent because of its very name – that peace-keeping is not a dangerous profession.

More specifically, it could be important to ensure that if there is some flexibility in the matter, specific contingents do not consistently get the worst postings. And when danger looms, a contingent should not needlessly be exposed. The embarrassing defeat of the Sudanese contingent in a local battle in the Congo in 1961 may have had a bearing on that state's subsequent withdrawal from the Force. It also has to be borne in mind that the political stance of certain states may make it unwise to use their contingents in certain aspects of the operation, and that dissatisfaction with the conduct of an operation may lead to a state's decision to withdraw its contingent. The Congo operation provides instances of both of these points, causing the Force Commanders and the UN Secretariat considerable difficulties.

The Chain of Command
In theory, national contingents are placed at the UN's disposal, and thus come under the command of the Force Commander (who, while continuing to enjoy military rank, also becomes a member of the UN Secretariat). But the practice is not as simple as that – more particularly, again, in respect of internal and prickly missions.

One problem arises out of the tendency for particular national contingents – whether out of impartial conviction, political sympathy, national disposition, the training and traditions of a particular unit, the influence of the specific problems they face, or simply (once a pattern has been set) inertia – to follow a somewhat distinctive line in its relations with local disputants. There may also be problems arising out of a misunderstanding of the character of peace-keeping. The classical instance of this is the case of the Commander of the crack French unit sent to Lebanon when the UN Force was being established there in 1978, who found it extremely difficult not to think and speak in terms of "the enemy".[20] Perhaps in part because of this attitude, and some later difficulties which the battalion encountered, it was withdrawn.[21] Subsequently, France contributed an infantry unit, but again it had to be withdrawn (in 1986) following a crisis arising out of the killing of a local leader and his bodyguard.[22]

Within limits, however, there may be acceptable gradations of assertiveness arising, quite naturally, out of the sort of factors mentioned above. In South Lebanon, for example, it is widely thought that certain battalions (the Fijian and Norwegian, for example) are tougher than others; by contrast another battalion attracted the sobriquet "PLObatt". Such developments are likely to be accentuated if, as is often the case, battalions tend to have relatively static operational areas. For this naturally encourages the making of local agreements and the emergence of accepted practices. However, such a development does not necessarily make things easier for the Force as a whole.

In face of this type of situation it is very hard, even for the most energetic Commander, to secure fairly uniform responses – especially as individual Commanders do not usually serve long terms of duty. One response is to say that the UN should have Standard Operating Procedures, which should be adjusted to suit particular conditions with the start of each operation. Early in its peace-keeping history, the UN was often criticized for this lack. It was made good in 1990. But it may be doubted if this remedy really gets to the heart of the matter. Up to a point, the problem seems to be a concomitant of multinational activity.

The same seems to be true of another, more specific problem: obtaining immediate obedience to commands. Contingent Commanders may occasionally think that certain orders are most unwise and will unnecessarily endanger their men. Or they may apprehend that their real political masters – those at home, not at the UN's headquarters in New York – would be most unhappy if the national contingent was committed to a particular course. They may worry about the impact of that course on their own careers. In these circumstances they will wish first to secure clearance from home – formally a most improper course, but an entirely understandable one. The mid-1993 rumpus regarding the alleged propensity of the Italian contingent in Somalia to behave thus is an instance of this problem.[23] It is not new. Once (November 1962) in the Congo operation the UN Air Commander (an Indian) angrily demanded the dismissal of a Swedish Commander who said that he would have to check with Stockholm before carrying out an order.[24]

This situation reflects the existence of direct communications between contingents and their national ministries. In the early days of peace-keeping there was much concern about this. Now UN officials and Force Commanders seem to be less exercised about it. After all, there is routine national business to be transacted, and if a contingent is technologically equipped for it such links are a great convenience. Of course, they can be abused. But it seems quite unrealistic to expect a multinational force engaged on peace-keeping and not therefore involved in the heat of battle to accept every order unquestioningly in the manner of a unit in a national army or even a member of an armed coalition.

This does draw attention, however, to a parallel point which could prove troublesome. It concerns the possible tendency, especially in the context of prickly peace-keeping, of contingents from bigger states to pursue what seems to be their individual agendas. Such contingents may, in general, be less disposed than others to march closely in step with what the Force Headquarters requires; they may be less accepting than states with different military traditions of obstreperousness on the part of local factions; and they will probably be better equipped to go their own way, or in a position to call up the necessary reinforcements.

This is the sort of problem which developed in Lebanon in the non-UN Force in 1983.[25] With the ending of the Cold War and the way now open for participation in peace-keeping forces (on a regular, as distinct from the hitherto exceptional basis) of contingents from the permanent members of the Security Council, this could develop into a significant problem. It seems to have been much in the UN Secretary-General's mind when he called for an end to the self-financing contributions of certain states to UNPROFOR II.[26] From the perspective of other contributors, this is perhaps the sort of course on which the United States seemed embarked in Somalia in the third quarter of 1993, when it was vigorously trying to hunt down the warlord, General Aidid (a notably unsuccessful and arguably counter-productive enterprise, which was subsequently abandoned).

In this kind of situation more is at stake than the integrity of the chain of command. Internal tensions in the host state could be aggravated if an important element in the peace-keeping operation is thought to be adding a lot of weight to one side of the political scales. Such action could lead to serious differences between contingents, possibly jeopardizing the continuation of the operation. And the general image of peace-keeping could suffer damage if it came to be seen, however unfairly in overall terms, as a vehicle for the national purposes of certain larger states. Smaller states know that they have to live with their larger brethren as best they can. But they are very sensitive about the possibility of a formally egalitarian organization being hijacked from time to time by one or more of its leading members. Moreover, states may be much more wary of inviting peace-keepers onto their soil if they think there is some possibility of the more powerful contingents adopting too assertive a role.

Attention therefore needs to be given to how this sort of problem is best averted. It is likely to be difficult once an operation is under way. But if a strong state has clear ideas, of a muscle-flexing kind, about how a particular situation should be dealt with, there may be a case for considering whether such moves could be conducted outside the UN. If the answer to that is negative, then careful attention should be paid to the implications and responsibilities of operating within the UN's peace-keeping framework.

Logistics

The inadequacies of the logistic support for UN operations have been much lamented. It is less than entirely clear, however, how the deficiencies are best addressed. In principle there would seem to be no question about the need for the UN to have the resources on standby for the more or less instant establishment of an Observer Mission. They could be at its Pisa dump or, in a lesser way, at the headquarters of the UN Truce Supervision Organization in Jerusalem, or could be otherwise on call. There is probably also a need to be able to cover in this way the essential requirements for the headquarters of a Force. But deciding how much equipment should be acquired and maintained by the UN for these purposes is perhaps not an easy process, quite apart from the vexed question of finding the necessary finance.

Furthermore, whether the UN itself should be in a position to supply the contingents making up a Force with their basic requirements, or so to act in the case of states who cannot supply what is needed from their own resources, is another question altogether. As is the question of whether the UN should be in a position not just to keep such stockpiles but itself to have airlift for them, and for some national contingents. It may be thought that such schemes, which sound fine in speeches, go

some way beyond the present political condition of the world – and
hence of the UN.

Problems with Host States

Reference was made above to major political difficulties which a mission
may encounter with internal groups, including the government. At the
operational level, the problems are fewer. But three deserve brief
mention.[27]

Sensitivities
The presence of a peace-keeping mission is itself indicative of some
inability on the part of the host state to cope on its own with a problem.
It is therefore likely to be more than usually sensitive about the presence
of foreign forces. Accordingly, those in command of the mission do
well to go out of their way to minimize actions or situations which may
cause offence.

Status
Friction arising out of host sensitivities may be reduced partly by the
early conclusion of a Status of Forces Agreement (SOFA), setting out the
legal regime which is to apply to the peace-keepers. But this may be
easier said than done. Thus, despite the best efforts of the UN, the
majority of its peace-keeping operations function in the absence of such
an agreement. Of course, if a state is in internal disarray, a SOFA may
be virtually meaningless. But otherwise operations are likely to be
assisted by the conclusion of a SOFA.

Populace
Operations will also be facilitated by good relations with the local
people. Towards this end, cultural instruction will probably be called
for. All efforts should also be made to minimize the "licentious
soldiery" problem. In Lebanon the tours of duty of contingents from one
contributor state, Fiji, are "dry". A similar degree of resolution seems to
have been missing in Cambodia where, reportedly, the libidinous
proclivities of the Bulgarians have caused a good deal of trouble. In
Somalia there has been unwise activity on the part of the Canadian
contingent, precipitating a special military enquiry.[28] A keen eye needs
also always to be kept for the proverbial "bad apples", who may upset
at least some of the locals by engaging in a bit of gun-running on the
side, or trying to sell intelligence.

Bureaucratic Complications

Backup for the Commander

Shortly after the first UN peace-keeping force was established in 1956 the Secretary-General appointed a military adviser. Until recently this office was very small, and until very recently was not at all well equipped to give the kind of instant response which a crisis in the field can demand. (At one stage this situation attracted an appreciable amount of adverse and perhaps not wholly fair publicity.) This led, during mid-1993, to the establishment of a 24-hour, seven-days-a-week Situation Room. This, however, does not go nearly as far as some wish – those who call for the UN to have its own general staff to plan and conduct peace-keeping operations. It may be thought that many member states would be at least a little uneasy at such a prospect.

A distantly associated problem which remains to be addressed is that of the build-up in New York of an institutional memory. Generals giving up their UN command often used to complain that New York had no real interest in de-briefing them. Perhaps the Secretariat members then dealing with peace-keeping – a small and long-serving group – felt that they had sufficient acquaintance with the problems which arose in the field. They may have done. Now, however, with some expansion of the Peace-keeping Office in New York and a proliferation of missions, it would be highly desirable for some mechanisms to be established for distilling and preserving for future reference the multitudinous experiences which are presently being gained. Possibly something of this kind is already in hand. But one does not feel confident about that.

Civilian Head – Force Commander Relations

Internal peace-keeping missions are sometimes multi-faceted, involving a large civilian element as well as the military. In consequence, they have a civilian head – the Representative of the Secretary-General as he may be called. This may also reflect the perception that a delicate internal situation requires a quasi-diplomatic rather than a military touch on the local tiller. In such circumstances the Force Commander is no longer in overall command. Such an arrangement was instituted in the Congo in 1960 (where certain lesser but very influential civilians seemed to inject a byzantine element to the headquarters). But with the exception of the UN's administration of West New Guinea/West Irian in 1962-63 it was not again resorted to where there was a significant military presence until the operation in Namibia in 1989.

One wonders how this arrangement is working out in practice. It could perhaps give rise to a problem or two. In Somalia where the civilian in command (in this case an Admiral!) was from the same state as the biggest national contingent – the United States – the Force Commander in the middle maybe accepted that his may not be an influential role. But other situations may be differently structured. And it may be that not all Generals will like the idea of not being top man, given that this had been their position in most peace-keeping operations. One General with considerable peace-keeping experience has been heard by the writer speaking dismissively of the prospect of just being number two or, as came to be so in the case to which he was referring, number three. Some tension between the civilian and military side was reported in respect of the Namibian mission. But as the principle of civilian control is orthodox (albeit not always practised) in virtually all national contexts, maybe the UN – if it is encountering some trouble – is just going through a necessary transition period.

The Administration of Peace-keeping
From an operational perspective, the one matter to be noted here is the dual system of control which until very recently was always in place with regard to UN peace-keeping operations. The Force Commander, or civilian Head, reports to what since 1992 has been called the Department of Peace-keeping Operations (previously it was the Office of Special Political Affairs). This is a high-level politico-diplomatic part of the Secretariat, chiefly located on the 37th and 36th floors of the Secretariat building in New York (just below the Secretary-General's floor). But alongside the mission head sits the Chief Administrative Officer who reports to the Field Operations Division. This used to be part of the administrative side of the Secretariat, being located within the Department of Administration and Management.

No doubt there were good reasons for this system. But it also had its drawbacks, and led to some uneasy relationships in the field. It is unclear whether in operational terms they have ever been more than an aggravation. But certainly there were sometimes problems. In September 1993, however, the Field Operations Division was at last integrated into the Department of Peace-keeping Operations, which on the face of it should serve to eliminate the previously-experienced difficulties. [29]

EDUCATIONAL AND TRAINING ISSUES

Given the huge increase in peace-keeping activity, the possibility that the demand for it will not markedly diminish, and the much larger number of states who provide troops for it, the issue of preparational measures has assumed a higher profile than hitherto. The training needs of civilian participants must also not be forgotten. But it is perhaps an open question whether the present rather slim and fragmented arrangements have proved so disadvantageous to peace-keeping, or threaten to be so, that a substantial expansion is required. In part the answer turns on the question (to which more than one answer has been offered) of whether a sound military training is by and large enough for efficient peace-keeping.

States

Undoubtedly, there would be an advantage in officers being exposed, at national staff colleges and the like, to some instruction and discussion about the political character of peace-keeping and the military requirements to which it gives rise. The writer does not know to what extent this takes place. In the United Kingdom some (but perhaps not much) attention has for some time been given to the matter at the Royal Navy Staff College, the Joint Service Defence College, and the Royal College of Defence Studies. Now a tri-Service module on peace-keeping has been introduced at the Army Staff College at Camberley. Joint arrangements of a more substantial kind have long operated among the Scandinavian countries (where the heavy reliance on Reserve Forces for peace-keeping duties possibly makes the need more acute). Canada, too, is thought to provide education in peace-keeping.

It is also unquestionable that units which are about to leave for a peace-keeping mission should receive detailed briefings both about the distinctive nature of what they are about to do, and the political and cultural context in which they will find themselves. It would be interesting to know the extent to which present arrangements of this sort are considered to be satisfactory. It was something of a surprise to learn, in respect of a country with such a wealth of peace-keeping experience as Canada, that the recent enquiry focusing on Somalia found it necessary to recommend that preparatory briefings should be better, that it should be emphasized that certain symbols are in bad taste, and that peace-keepers should be taught to avoid racial or derogatory ethnic epithets.[30]

At a slightly different level, and in a small way, the lack of training could be addressed by ministries of defence being sympathetic to the idea of officers taking leave to engage in studies of peace-keeping at universities and similar institutes. Indeed, there might be some positive encouragement for them to do so. It would not be every officer's cup of tea. But for academically-inclined people it could be a stimulating use of, say, a year, and the knowledge gained could then sometimes be directly fed back into the military system through appointments at staff colleges. Possibly more of this type of thing occurs outside the UK than it does there. It would be interesting to know.

The United Nations

On the face of it the UN would seem ideally placed to train officers and prepare briefing material. At one time any such activity would have been viewed with grave suspicion by those states, notably the Soviet Union and France, who had serious reservations about the UN's peace-keeping role, and particularly about anything which smacked of planning therefor. This attitude on occasion even stood in the way of Secretariat officials attending conferences which focused on peace-keeping. But now the idea that there should be a UN peace-keeping staff college and an associated research unit is often advanced with some enthusiasm. As it happens, the UN already has the framework for such a body, in the shape of its Institute for Training and Research. But that very fact should induce a measure of caution into the staff college scheme. For even its best friend would find it hard to assert that UNITAR has a distinguished intellectual history, and in financial terms its experience has been particularly chequered. In at least some measure this has to do with the belief that a UN body should not be in the business of criticizing the UN or, and perhaps more especially, any of its member states. It cannot be assumed that this approach will have evaporated with the end of the Cold War. This raises at least a question about the UN staff college concept. And, as always, there is the financial question.

However, it remains that the UN *is* very well positioned to give instruction in the practicalities of peace-keeping, and to conduct studies of such operations. And while not every state (one thinks particularly of the bigger ones) might be enthusiastic about the prospect of their officers spending time at the feet of UN-employed faculty, one imagines that many states would be glad to take advantage of such an opportunity. Perhaps, therefore, the matter should be explored further. Certainly, if the UN were willing to give it a free hand, so that it would enjoy a position somewhat analogous to that of the International Court of Justice, a UN Peace-keeping College (maybe the word "Staff" would have discouraging overtones for some) would be an exciting prospect, and would be of much value in academic as well as in practical terms; always providing, of course, that adequate money was forthcoming, which could enjoy a high degree of insulation from political currents (one has a troubling recollection of an Assembly threat to the International Court's financing some while ago).

Non-Governmental Bodies

There is no reason, in principle, why the non-governmental sector should not try to do some, if not all, of the things which might be on the agenda of a UN Peace-keeping College. Any such enterprise would need to gain the confidence of a wide variety of states, so that a viable number and a worthwhile mix of personnel would be sent on its courses. But again, in principle, there is no reason at all why that should not occur. The New York-based International Peace Academy (founded after his retirement by the UN Secretary-General's first Military Adviser) has done sterling work of this kind, attracting very gratifying attendances at its annual Vienna Seminars. As to finance, one can fantasize about a munificent grant from a well-endowed foundation to provide a sufficient measure of financial security (something the IPA, even in its relatively small way, has never had). But lesser sums would go quite a long distance.

There are many problems on the peace-keeping front. But this is another way of saying that there are many challenges, with much to be thought about and done. For peace-keeping, these are indeed exhilarating times.

NOTES

1. See Goodrich, L. M., "Korea", *International Conciliation*, No. 494 (New York: October 1953).
2. Paul Taylor & A.J.R Groom, *The United Nations and the Gulf War, 1990-91: Back to the Future?* (London: Royal Institute of International Affairs, 1992).
3. A. James, "Introduction", *Peacekeeping in International Politics*, (London: Macmillan, in association with the International Institute for Strategic Studies, 1990).

4. For an annotated list of 44 such operations, 28 of which have been established since 1988, see A. James, "A Review of UN Peacekeeping", *International Spectator*, vol. 47, no. 11 (The Hague: November 1993), pp. 623-8.
5. For a list of 75 contributor states, see *Peacekeeping and International Relations*, vol. 22, no. 6 (November/December 1993), pp. 2-3.
6. Security Council Resolution 806, 5 February 1993.
7. See *The Times*, 22 November 1993. A large part of the problem related to obtaining troops who could bring the necessary equipment with them. It may be that the eventual availability of Bangladeshis was related to the winding up of the operation in Cambodia, which had included a sizeable element from that state. (This observation, like a number of others in this chapter, is based on private comment to the author from a source having first-hand or authoritative knowledge of the matter in question).
8. Security Council Resolution 844, 18 June 1993.
9. Security Council Resolution 838, 10 June 1993.
10. The UN speaks only of one UNPROFOR. But its activity in ex-Yugoslavia has three separate and very distinct commands: in Croatia, Bosnia-Herzegovina, and Macedonia. It therefore seems helpful, as a number of commentators have done, to distinguish them with the numbers I, II, and III respectively.
11. See E.W. Lefever, *Uncertain Mandate: Politics of the U.N. Congo Operation*, (Baltimore: Johns Hopkins, 1967).
12. See A. McDermott & K. Skjelsbaek (eds), *The Multinational Force in Beirut 1982-1984*, (Miami: Florida International University, 1991).
13. For the argument to this effect, see A. James, "The History of Peacekeeping. An Analytical Perspective", *Canadian Defence Quarterly*, vol. 23, no. 1 (September 1993).
14. See G.L. Curtis, "The UN Observation Group in Lebanon", *International Organization*, vol. XVIII, no. 4, (1964).
15. A. James, "Internal Peacekeeping: A Dead End for the UN?", *Security Dialogue*, vol. 24, no. 4, (December 1993).
16. M. Tabory, *The Multinational Force and Observers in the Sinai*, (Boulder: Westview, 1986).
17. UN Document S/25997, 29 June 1993. The draft resolution was not carried.
18. General Assembly Document A/47/PV.106, 12 July 1993 (Forty-seventh session, Provisional Verbatim Record of the 106th Meeting, 22 June 1993).

19. A. James, "The Equality of States: Contemporary Manifestations of an Ancient Doctrine", *Review of International Studies*, vol. 18, no. 4, (October 1992).

20. B. Urquhart, *A Life in Peace and War*, (London: Weidenfeld and Nicolson, 1987), p. 293.

21. B. Skogmo, *UNIFIL: International Peacekeeping in Lebanon*, 1978-1988, (Boulder: Lynne Rienner, 1989), Table p. 236.

22. A. James, *Interminable Interim: The UN Force in Lebanon*, (London: Centre for Security and Conflict Studies, 1986), pp. 22-4.

23. *The Times*, 15 July 1993, and immediately subsequent issues.

24. Public Record Office (UK), FO371 161550, JB1224/21. The incident will be discussed fully in a forthcoming book by General Nils Skold.

25. McDermott & Skjelsbaek, *The Multinational Force*, note 12.

26. UN Document S/25264, 10 February 1993, para. 31-2.

27. A. James, "International Peacekeeping: the Disputants' View", *Political Studies*, vol. 38, no. 2, (June 1990).

28. For the results of this enquiry, see *Globe and Mail* (Toronto), 1 September 1993.

29. For further discussion of the matters considered in this section, see M.R. Berdal, *Whither UN Peacekeeping? An Analysis of the Changing Military Requirements of UN Peacekeeping with Proposals for its Enhancement*, (London: Brassey's, for the International Institute for Strategic Studies, Adelphi Paper no. 281, 1993).

30. *Ibid.*

7 UN Sanctions Against Yugoslavia: Two Years Later

Vojin Dimitrijevic & Jelena Pejic

Security Council resolution 757 (May 1992) imposing sanctions against the Federal Republic of Yugoslavia (Serbia and Montenegro) is the most comprehensive set of measures ever implemented by the United Nations.[1] From the outset, the package aimed at politically and symbolically evicting the country from the community of nations. An almost complete trade embargo[2] was the backbone of Res. 757, coupled with a prohibition of fund transfers to and from Yugoslavia, the rupture of air traffic, and the suspension of all officially sponsored scientific and technical cooperation and cultural exchanges. The resolution also required UN members to reduce staff levels at Yugoslav diplomatic and consular missions and banned Yugoslav sports teams from competing in international events.

The shipment of foreign goods through Yugoslav territory was not immediately prohibited, but this loophole was subsequently closed through Security Council resolution 787 which prevented the transportation of certain strategic commodities through Yugoslavia and implemented tighter transport controls along the Adriatic coast and the Danube.[3] Almost a year after the first sanctions came into effect, Security Council resolution 820 prohibited the transit of all goods through Yugoslavia, mandated both the freezing of Yugoslav funds abroad and the confiscation of Yugoslav vessels, freight vehicles, rolling stock and aircraft beyond its borders, and banned all commercial maritime traffic in the country's territorial sea. The few outlets left to Yugoslavia for communication with the outside world were "telecommunications, postal services, legal services consistent with resolution 757 and, as approved, on a case-by-case basis by the Committee established by resolution 724 (1991), services whose supply may be necessary for humanitarian or other exceptional purposes".[4]

Security Council resolution 757 was prompted by a determination that "the situation in Bosnia and Herzegovina and in other parts of the former Socialist Federal Republic of Yugoslavia constitute[d] a threat to international peace and security". After two years this situation has changed little; the prospects for a durable peace in Bosnia-Herzegovina remained remote, while the government that was targeted with international isolation was still in power. In fact, most Serbian conquests in Bosnia occurred while economic coercion was being applied. For the UN, there are some valuable lessons to be drawn concerning the manner in which sanctions should be applied and the circumstances under which they may or may not prove effective in promoting international peace and security.

THEORETICAL ASSUMPTIONS

The political and economic effects of internationally applied coercive measures are difficult to determine. Whereas sanctions are applied in the hope of creating internal political pressure on a target state's government they usually have the opposite effect of "rallying [the nation] round the flag".[5] Sanctions usually strengthen rather than weaken political support for a government. As the "collective nature of economic sanctions makes them hit the innocent along with the guilty", it is little wonder that the "attack from the outside is seen as an attack on the group as a whole, not only on a fraction of it". If there is a "very weak identification with the attacker ... and a ... belief in the value of one's own goals"[6] there is a probability that group solidarity will develop. When a government needs to arouse national sentiment, it resorts to propaganda and media manipulation; the outside world is divided into a few friends and a greater number of conspiratorial enemies.

Historically, states have proven fairly successful in wriggling out of the squeeze of economic sanctions. To mitigate the impact, countries have been known to resort to a "post-sanctions defense of the economy"[7] involving a variety of measures: sacrificing certain goods, substituting imported commodities with domestic ones (restructuring the economy), and smuggling. Relying on states not participating in the sanctions is also standard procedure; the universality of application is generally cited as the single most important condition for the success of any type of collective sanctions.[8]

What is of interest is not the degree to which an economy can be crippled, but whether sanctions bring about desired political change. The general conclusion is that sanctions are not effective. According to recent comprehensive research covering 115 cases, economic coercion was judged "successful in ... 34% of the cases overall". The study concluded that "at most there is a weak correlation between economic deprivation and political willingness to change. The economic impacts of sanctions may be pronounced, both on the sender and on the target, but other factors in the situation often overshadow the impact of sanctions in determining the political outcome".[9] Moreover, sanctions usually give target governments a perfect excuse for poor economic performance whether caused by economic coercion or not.[10]

David Baldwin puts these conclusions in a different light. He believes that in order to assess statecraft, it is important to determine as precisely as possible the goals, both primary and secondary, of an attempt to influence conduct.[11] Before judging economic sanctions as inefficient, one should ask what alternatives were at the sender's disposal. One should also bear in mind that other techniques such as diplomacy, propaganda, or military force suffer from more or less the same drawbacks as economic sanctions. War, as Baldwin points out, can work just as slowly as sanctions, is usually more costly, and the expenses incurred tend to be even less equally distributed. Also, Baldwin suggests that "the 'rally round the flag' effect is not an iron law of politics".[12]

THE TRIPLE TARGET OF SANCTIONS AGAINST YUGOSLAVIA

The formal target of UN sanctions was the Federal Republic of Yugoslavia (FRY), a state created on 27 April 1992 and comprising the territories of Serbia and Montenegro, both former republics of the former Socialist Federal Republic of Yugoslavia (SFRY).[13] As the result of a severe political crisis in 1990, several of the SFRY's republics asserted demands for independence. Armed conflict followed between forces commanded by the federal government and military units controlled by the authorities of the republics striving for independence. The highest governing bodies of the federal state were reduced to the representatives of Serbia, its two autonomous provinces Kosovo and Vojvodina, and Montenegro. This rump body eventually acquiesced to the factual "loss" of Slovenia, Croatia and Macedonia; its attitude toward the independence of Bosnia-Herzegovina remained equivocal. Despite the fact that the former Yugoslavia had been reduced by more than half in size, it continued to exist legally as the SFRY until the FRY's April 27 Constitution was adopted.

Serbia, although not openly pushing for independence, was by 1990 acquiring all the attributes of statehood. A new Constitution established the Presidential post which was very powerful by any criteria and unusually strong for a federal unit, to which Slobodan Milosevic was elected that same year. Milosevic gradually succeeded in his efforts to dominate the governing bodies of the federation and he came to exert a strong influence on political developments in the other republics; in the eyes of many observers, the SFRY and its army became identical with the Serbian regime. This regime was held responsible for the trouble in Bosnia-Herzegovina which erupted into armed conflict in early April 1992. Sanctions followed; the new FRY was punished for what had been done formally by the SFRY, but which was thought to have been engineered by Serbia, or more precisely, by Milosevic himself.

Confusion between the "formal" and the "real" target of sanctions arose immediately after they were imposed, with the election of Dobrica Cosic and Milan Panic to the posts of FRY President and Prime Minister, respectively. Cosic, not a member of the ruling Socialist Party of Serbia (SPS), enjoyed the reputation of a long-standing dissident nationalist writer; Panic, a successful businessman, had returned to Yugoslavia from the United States after more than four decades abroad. The Serbian authorities' support of Panic was interpreted as an attempt to soften the intransigent and communist reputation of the new Yugoslavia by offering the West an interlocutor who could better present the "truth" about the Serbs. As a result, it took both foreigners and domestic political factors some time to distinguish between the new federal government and the government of Serbia: the former was initially considered the puppet of the latter. The anti-Milosevic opposition in Serbia cautiously supported Panic, while pressure on him from abroad was as strong as it was on Milosevic himself.

As time passed it became obvious that Panic was shouldered with the impossible task of trying to improve international attitudes towards Serbia while lacking the power to influence events in Bosnia-Herzegovina. That leverage was commanded by Milosevic, who tolerated Panic only as long as Panic's public relations success demanded no concessions on his part. For reasons that remain unclear, the federal government entered into international commitments unacceptable to Milosevic's nationalist-communist supporters. The Serbian President became increasingly irritated by Panic's insistence on treating Bosnia-Herzegovina as a foreign country and by his effort to reduce support for the Bosnian Serbs to its moral and humanitarian dimension. Panic's open criticism of Milosevic's domestic and foreign policies was met with an orchestrated media campaign against him which peaked in December 1992, when

Panic announced that he was going to run against Milosevic for President of Serbia.

Regarding the target of sanctions, another relevant issue was the position of Montenegro, the second unit of the newly created Yugoslav federation. Admittedly, its leaders had come to power as Milosevic's protégés, but they showed signs of increasing displeasure at his rigid stand. Immediately after sanctions were introduced this displeasure was translated into support for Panic. Thanks to a parity in the number of deputies elected by Serbia and Montenegro to the upper chamber of Federal Parliament, the Montenegrins were able on two occasions to thwart Socialist Party attempts to oust Panic's government by means of a no-confidence vote.

To sum up, when sanctions were introduced, the formal target was the Federal Republic of Yugoslavia. In reality, however, coercion was directed against three distinct actors. Two were the federal government and the Montenegrin authorities, who were willing to cooperate in finding an internationally acceptable solution to the Yugoslav crisis. Official Serbia, the third and most powerful player, was opposed to any concessions and openly supported various self-styled governments of ethnic Serbs in Croatia and Bosnia, earning their fierce allegiance in return.

AIMS AND MESSAGES RELATED TO SANCTIONS

If determining the target of sanctions gives rise to some confusion, so too does the attempt to determine the goals of the internationally mandated coercive measures. Using Baldwin's methodology, the primary goal was to force the FRY to stop assisting the Bosnian Serbs in the war in that Republic in order to end the fighting. The secondary goal, not officially expressed, was to oust Milosevic. However, as a reading of the relevant Security Council resolutions shows, it was only in the Council's first resolution, 757, that a direct link between FRY support for the Bosnian Serbs and sanctions was made. The Council "condemned" the failure of the FRY/Serbian and Montenegrin authorities, including the Yugoslav People's Army (JNA), to take effective measures to cease all forms of interference in Bosnia-Herzegovina, to respect its territorial integrity and to withdraw, disband, disarm or place under Bosnian government control JNA units in Bosnia.

Sanctions were imposed several days after the Yugoslav government had announced that all JNA units from the FRY (but not the military hardware) had been withdrawn from Bosnian territory, which gave the Serbian authorities ground to claim that Serbia is not a participant in the Bosnian war. In addition, the Security Council received a UN report confirming the FRY's compliance regarding the troop withdrawal two days after the sanctions vote, further strengthening the Yugoslav authorities assertion that the sanctions were unjust. Security Council resolution 787 was imposed because, with the war still going on, it became necessary to prevent widespread violations of the embargo. It made no direct reference to the FRY's responsibility for the continued hostilities in Bosnia: it "condemns" the refusal of all parties in the Republic of Bosnia and Herzegovina, in particular of the Bosnian Serb paramilitary forces to comply with previous resolutions, and "demands" that all forms of outside interference in Bosnia, including the infiltration of irregular units and personnel, "cease immediately".[14] The only outside units involved in the conflict to be explicitly named were "elements of the Croatian army" which were to be either withdrawn, subjected to Bosnian government authority, disbanded or disarmed. Needless to say, the failure to apply sanctions to Croatia has had an important psychological effect in Serbia.

By the time Security Council resolution 820 came into force on 27 April 1993 the FRY and Serbian governments were given ample room to argue, at least for domestic purposes, that the new sanctions were a "gross injustice".[15] The application of these harsher measures came after the Bosnian Serb Assembly rejected the Vance-Owen peace plan which the other two sides in the war had accepted. The overwhelming vote against the plan, which provided for the reorganization of Bosnia-Herzegovina into 10 provinces, was taken despite an impassioned appeal made by the Presidents of the FRY, Serbia and Montenegro for its endorsement. On the surface, it seemed that the FRY/Serbia and Montenegro were being punished for not delivering Bosnian Serb acquiescence, although they had tried and were unable to do so.

Resolution 820 — and the events surrounding it — marked both the beginning of Milosevic's apparent softening towards international demands for a peaceful resolution of the Bosnian crisis and his seemingly increasing inability to meet them. It also marked the beginning of tacit Western acceptance that Bosnia-Herzegovina would have to be divided into ethnically distinct units, and the beginning of uncertainty on the precise primary goal of sanctions. These developments were confirmed when international mediators abandoned the Vance-Owen plan, substituting for it a Serb-Croat proposal to create a Union of Republics of Bosnia-Herzegovina. The tripartite division of Bosnia-

Herzegovina agreed at the Geneva Conference of July 1993 has since been paralysed by the warring factions' inability to settle how much territory each should get.

The primary aim of the sanctions has become increasingly confused. While coercion initially was meant to prevent FRY assistance to the Bosnian Serbs, it now appears that its main aim is to ensure that the Bosnian Serbs relinquish some of the territories under their control. This became open Western policy in November 1993 after the French and German foreign ministers launched their "territories versus sanctions" plan, which was endorsed later that month by European Union foreign ministers. By the end of May 1994, this materialized in the "peaceful ultimatum" that the "contact group" of the US, Russia and the EU issued to the parties to the conflict on 5 July 1994.[16]

There are no other goals for sanctions left. If Serbian defiance continues, some other vaguely stated aims, known as "globalization", may be revived. This denotes efforts to simultaneously resolve problems in various parts of the former Yugoslavia, for example the political stalemate in Croatia which has existed since the 1992 implementation of the UN/Vance peace plan. "Globalization" of aims would mean that the FRY would be expected not only to exert its influence over the Bosnian Serbs, but over the Serbs in Croatia as well. Security Council resolution 871 of 5 October 1993 explicitly exemplifies such a policy, as it calls on the FRY (Serbia and Montenegro) to "cooperate" in the full implementation of the UN peace plan and confirms that a further lack of cooperation will be taken into account when a "normalization" of relations with the parties involved comes up for consideration.[17]   Other demands on the FRY under "globalization" include a solution to the problem of the Serbian province of Kosovo and to Serbian cooperation with the international war crimes tribunal.[18]

Finally, regarding the removal of Milosevic, the West has sent mixed signals. At first it seemed that his ouster was not an aim, but rather the intention was to influence him because he was perceived as the only figure who could deliver the internationally desired political goods. Foreign envoys never failed to meet with him, thereby reinforcing his stature as leader of all Serbs in the former Yugoslavia. The Western media continually reported that the opposition in Serbia differed from Milosevic only to the extent that it rejected communism, but not the megalomaniac dream of a Greater Serbia. Moreover, there was an obvious lack of enthusiasm in the support of the most serious electoral rival of Milosevic, Milan Panic, who, even as he managed (under very adverse circumstances) to muster more than a third of the votes in the

Serbian presidential elections in December 1992, was forgotten and even ridiculed by the West. It appeared that the West upheld Milosevic for the same reasons that the populist leader was adored by his domestic followers: for being a strongman.[19]   Moreover, he seems to have persuaded the West that he was a moderate in comparison with the monsters he helped to create.[20]   There have been occasional messages that could be interpreted as signals that Milosevic must go in order for sanctions to be lifted, but they remain vague and veiled.[21]

Overall, the messages are so mixed in the average Serb mind that in a telephone poll conducted on the eve of the second anniversary of the sanctions, 42.5% of those interviewed said that they no longer knew what conditions the FRY was expected to fulfil in return for the easing of sanctions.[22]

UNIVERSAL APPLICATION?

It is difficult to establish the extent to which UN sanctions have been put into practice. Judging from the complaints of Yugoslav officials, their application is total: the public is led to believe that even those items not covered by the embargo do not reach the needy (e.g. foodstuffs and medicines). Neighbouring countries also complain of economic losses. On the other hand, even goods that cannot be smuggled in discretely, such as oil and modern household appliances, reach the Yugoslav market in sufficient quantities. The SRY is surrounded by ex-communist countries with low standards of living and poorly paid administrations which succumb easily to corruption. The tendency seems to be to slacken enforcement with time; neighbouring countries become tired of sustaining the burden of economic coercion with no compensation. Nevertheless, the sanctions against SRY have been implemented comparatively strictly, partly because of the lack of interest of multi-national companies in trading with Yugoslavia.

THE POLITICAL EFFECTS OF SANCTIONS

The reactions to sanctions, both of the Serbian authorities and of the opposition, illustrates that there was not, at least in the first stages of enforcement, a "rallying round the flag" effect. In fact, events after 30 May 1992 suggests that sanctions deepened existing political differences and spurred the opposition to vehement criticism of the government. The

December 1992 general elections, however, were the dividing line: while they marked the opposition's arrival as a substantial political force, they also demonstrated that national radicalism was, finally, on the rise. In 1993, following still more hardship, the situation remained basically unchanged. The pendulum of public opinion, admittedly, did swing back more towards the centre, yet the opposition was for all practical purposes still remote from power. While political opposition against Milosevic and his regime continued, public opinion concerning the wars in Bosnia and Croatia and the support for Serb militants there became internally divided: those supporting the latter tended to support the regime in its refusal to bend to foreign pressure. It would appear that, at the two year mark, confused messages and internal political fatigue had taken their toll. Contrary to international expectations – though not to theoretical findings – when daily life becomes a battle for survival, political issues figure less prominently in the average person's mind.

Regardless of the many warning signals, the Serbian leadership was not immediately aware of the magnitude of the misfortune that had befallen the Republic. One of the first statements of the then Serbian Prime Minister Radoman Bozovic is illustrative of the type of rhetoric that was initially in use. Calling the sanctions "unjust", Bozovic had said that: "the dignity of a nation cannot be bought by taxes or embargoes of any kind" and added that "a collapse (of the economy) under sanctions was out of the question".[23] The idea that sanctions were imposed as the result of a global conspiracy against the people and not the regime of Serbia was also a recurring theme in official public pronouncements. Serbian President Slobodan Milosevic's statements have at least for domestic purposes remained more or less defiant to this day. In a rare interview given to the Western press near the second anniversary of the imposition of sanctions, Milosevic reiterated the position that "[Serbia] can't be blocked. For a thousand years maybe [an embargo would have an effect]. But for a couple of years? It's nothing!".[24] The extreme nationalist Serbian Radical Party (SRS) had sided with the government when sanctions were introduced. Its leader Vojislav Seselj declared that the imposition of sanctions against the FRY signalled "the beginning of the end of the United Nations" and of the "American empire", explaining that "what is based on injustice cannot be of long duration".[25] Even much later, official government and state-run media presentations of the situation largely repeated these views; only assessments of the sanctions' effects have changed.

In hindsight, the imposition of sanctions was ill-timed in terms of supporting moves for policy and personnel changes in Serbia. Rather than leaving the opposition, which was gaining strength daily, to wrestle with Milosevic on its own terms, resolution 757 burdened it with the additional task of fending off constant official accusations of "unpatriotic behaviour". Despite fairly widespread Western views of a politically monolithic Serbia, the power base of the ruling SPS had been gradually eroding before sanctions came into effect. Opposition to government policy had erupted in March 1991 in massive demonstrations which claimed two lives and prompted the authorities to roll federal army tanks into the streets of Belgrade. These were followed by several days of student protests. The wars in Croatia and Bosnia-Herzegovina had not only led to a mass exodus from Serbia of young men unwilling to fight, but also to the creation of a peace movement unparalleled in any of the other former Yugoslav republics. The imposition of sanctions did not silence the opposition; international isolation was, in fact, regarded as decisive proof of what opposition groups had been saying for a very long time — that the regime had to be changed.

Belgrade students launched two "silent protests" in the beginning of June 1992 and, at a mass rally on 15 June, demanded the dissolution of the Serbian government, the resignation of Slobodan Milosevic, and multiparty elections for a Constituent Assembly. The occupation of some university buildings lasted for 26 days, during which the entire University went on strike. Other Serbian university centres followed suit. Three protest marches through the streets of Belgrade were held: one of them ended in a several-hour-long blockade of the city centre. Almost simultaneously with the student protest, a group of members of the Serbian Academy of Sciences and Arts publicly appealed for the resignation of Slobodan Milosevic. A petition signed by more than half of the Academy members stated that Milosevic's "withdrawal from political life" would be considered a "gesture of patriotism of the highest level". They also demanded the immediate creation of a provisional government with two aims: "to run state affairs until general elections for a Constituent Assembly were held" and to "most energetically, using all means to curb war activities, start negotiations with institutions that imposed sanctions on Serbia".[26] The petition divided the Academy, previously regarded as the mastermind of official Serbia's national policy.

The imposition of sanctions against Yugoslavia led, in mid-June 1992, to a flood of public calls for Milosevic's resignation. The high point of protests was the St. Vitus rally (*Vidovdanski sabor*). From 28 June to 5 July 1992, tens of thousands of people demanded in the streets of Belgrade that Milosevic resign, that a transitional government of national salvation be created, that "round table" talks between the authorities and the opposition be convened, that elections for a Constituent Assembly be organized and that the electronic media be freed. The St. Vitus rally was the biggest opposition gathering in Belgrade since the events of March the previous year;[27] its political effects, admittedly, were meagre, as none of the demands were met directly. But if sanctions added a new facet to public dissatisfaction with Milosevic's policies, they indirectly contributed to increasing pressure for change which, in turn, eventually led to the general elections of December 1992.[28]

Public protests, including street demonstrations against official Serbian policy, subsided for several reasons. First, they did not gain enough momentum to effect a peaceful change of government and the opposition had made it clear that it would not resort to force. Second, the federal government had to a large extent become representative of all of the segments of society that demanded policy changes. Third, there was an impression that foreign powers refused to support the opposition or even to deal with it. Finally, the "rallying round the flag" effect had finally started to sink in. Official propaganda continuously focused on Serbs outside Serbia, claiming that their fate would be unfairly sealed by a compromise in Bosnia. It tried to create a guilty conscience among members of the opposition and relied heavily on Serb leaders from Croatia and Bosnia who took a clear pro-Milosevic and anti-federal government stance.

The general elections of 20 December 1992 were strongly influenced by the atmosphere described above. Elections were held for one chamber of the Federal Parliament, for the parliaments of Serbia and Montenegro, for the Presidents of the two republics, and at the local level. To determine how well the targets of sanctions fared, the results of elections for the federal and Serbian parliaments and of the Serbian presidential race are of prime importance. Although the election results were widely disputed as fraudulent, we are relying on official data because opposition demands for a nullification of the elections were not met and because the results, even if rigged, still expressed basic electoral trends.

Initial forecasts that Serbian President Slobodan Milosevic would not win in the first round of the presidential race were unfounded. Milosevic received 56% of the votes cast; his main rival, then federal Prime Minister Milan Panic, received 34%. Compared to the presidential elections of December 1990, the figures show that support for Milosevic had fallen by about 7%.[29]

Table 1   **Serbian Parliamentary**
                          Election Results

Party	December 1990 Seats	December 1992 Seats
SPS	195	101
SRS	--	73
Opposition	55	76

In the contest for seats in the Federal Parliament, a comparison of the election results with those of May 1992 (an election for the Chamber of Citizens, the lower House) shows that the SPS had lost ground to the opposition, while the number of seats taken by the Serbian Radical Party had remained almost the same.

Table 2   **Federal Parliament – Chamber**
                          of Citizens Election Results

Party	May 1992* Seats	December 1992 Seats
SPS	75	47
SRS	33	34
DPS**	23	17
Opposition	7	40

* The Serbian Radical Party participated in the May 1992 elections for the (lower) Chamber of Citizens of the Federal Parliament; the opposition, with the exception of a few minor parties, boycotted them.
** Democratic Party of Socialists (DPS), the ruling party in Montenegro.

What is interesting is that the results of elections for the parliament of Serbia showed on one hand a decrease in popular support for Milosevic's ruling Socialist Party of Serbia (SPS), and on the other an increase in the influence of the Serbian Radical Party (SRS) at the expense of the SPS, attesting to an upsurge of the extreme nationalist right, xenophobia, and warmongering.[30]

From the December 1992 election results, some basic trends can be discerned: the Socialist Party of Serbia lost support; the Serbian Radical Party increased its influence;[31] the opposition held its turf although it did not become significant enough to be able to substantially influence future policy. Judging by the combined SPS-SRS showing it seemed that the national solidarity syndrome definitely had started to set in.

The Socialists and Radicals did not enter into a formal parliamentary coalition. For all practical purposes, however, their unofficial alliance functioned as such, relentlessly pursuing an authoritarian and xenophobic domestic political agenda. One of the first joint SPS-SRS moves was to amend the Serbian electoral law to prevent the proportional representation of opposition parties in the (upper) Chamber of Republics of the Federal Parliament. The opposition walked out of the Serbian parliament after this took place, but the new Serbian minority government was dutifully endorsed by the Radicals on 10 February 1993, as was the new federal Cabinet under Radoje Kontic from Montenegro a month later. The SPS-SRS condominium will probably be remembered as one of the lowest points in Serbian/Yugoslav parliamentary history due to brutish bullying by the deputies of the two parties in the conduct of parliamentary affairs. Hostility towards opposition proposals, and almost as importantly, towards opposition figures, was constant, climaxing in May/June 1993 when the FRY President Dobrica Cosic was impeached by the votes of SPS and SRS and street protests erupted once again.

What prompted Milosevic to sack Cosic remains a mystery, especially as the latter's domestic stature and international reputation had lent at least some credibility to the FRY. Western analysts generally believed that Cosic's dismissal implied a further consolidation of Milosevic's power. What is certain is that it was a message of defiance and a disavowal of Cosic's feeble attempts to compromise with the international community.

The Federal Parliament session resulted not only in Cosic's removal, but also in physical violence directed by an SRS deputy against a representative of the opposition Serbian Renewal Movement (SPO). Enraged by what they perceived as unendurable Socialist-Radical brazenness, thousands of people, joined by some opposition leaders, gathered spontaneously in front of the Federal Parliament building on 1 June to protest. Efforts to break up the rally led to clashes in which a policeman was killed, while scores of demonstrators were badly beaten and arrested. In the early morning of 2 June, special police units stormed the nearby SPO headquarters and arrested its president Vuk Draskovic, his wife, and several prominent Party members for having allegedly organized the rally. The Draskovices were severely beaten upon arrest and after being taken into custody; intimidation was clearly the order of the day.

Despite international appeals and weekly opposition rallies in support of Draskovic's release, Milosevic relented only after the SPO leader's hunger strike began to pose a serious threat to his life. The couple finally were freed on 9 July 1993 by an abolition decree of President Milosevic, in which he unrepentingly claimed that "the events accompanying the criminal proceedings against Vuk Draskovic are creating a very ugly picture" and that "the participants in these events, particularly from the opposition, are disgracing our country". The decree also included a reference to states enforcing the sanctions which, it read, were "killing even unborn children".[32] Needless to say, the clearly manifested police brutality against opposition figures and supporters did not merit even a formal inquiry.

Soon afterwards, however, events took an unexpected turn. The deteriorating economic situation and the Serbian government's inept attempts to contain it stimulated Vojislav Seselj to bid for power in the fall of 1993. The SRS first announced that it had created a "shadow Cabinet" and, in late September, that it would table a no-confidence motion in the Serbian Parliament to topple the minority SPS government. It is likely that Seselj did not throw down the political gauntlet with the prospect of new parliamentary elections in mind, but rather intended to take over the Serbian government smoothly. However, his strategy unwittingly resulted in new elections. After the raucous parliamentary no-confidence debate had run into its eleventh day, and with anti-government momentum mounting, Milosevic announced that he was dissolving the Serbian Parliament and calling early elections. His underlying calculation was to preempt political defeat by not giving his now tactically unified opponents the satisfaction of ousting the SPS government. Also, he was determined to prevent them from using their newly acquired majority to amend a crucial law − that regulating the management of Radio-TV Serbia. Milosevic's move was widely considered a gamble; winter was setting in, inflation was out of control and there was hardly any food in the stores.

The ensuing SPS election campaign was fairly low-key in comparison to that of the previous year, with the Serbian President making few pre-election appearances. The job of swaying voters was left to the official media, already well-versed in the art of journalistic manipulation, whose wrath was directed for the first time at Seselj and his party. Several SRS officials were arrested on charges ranging from murder, rape, and kidnapping, to the illegal possession of arms. Almost simultaneously, the activities of a newly founded party headed by Zeljko Raznatovic Arkan called the Party of Serbian Unity (SSJ) sprang to prominence in the state-run media.[33]

All along, the treatment and behaviour of the opposition remained more or less unchanged. Alternately ignored or attacked by the official media, it failed to create a much needed pre-election coalition. If anything, the moderate to nationalist (yet democratic) opposition parties continued to drift apart, as evidenced by the decision of one of the major DEPOS members, the Democratic Party of Serbia (DSS), to weather the elections on its own. If sanctions had produced a sense of solidarity within the opposition in the initial stages, by the end of 1993 the camaraderie was gone. The wars in Croatia and Bosnia-Herzegovina and one and a half years of isolation had completely shrunk the political agenda. All opposition parties, except the SPO and the small Civic Alliance, began to move towards militant nationalism, to support and seek contacts with the leaders of the rebel Serbs outside Serbia, to distrust foreigners and to posit the "Serb national interest" as the supreme political value. The concern for national survival gradually overshadowed the image of Milosevic as the common foe. War and sanctions finally deformed political life.

When reading the results of the 1993 parliamentary elections, bear in mind the expectation of the senders of international sanctions that dire economic circumstances would turn an electorate against those in power. The outcome is illustrated in Table 3.[34]

The Socialist Party of Serbia did not achieve a hoped for majority in the new Parliament — falling only three seats short — but it did recover 22 seats in comparison with the election results of 1992. If ever the electorate meant to punish the ruling party for Serbia's isolation and its slide into penury, December 1993 was the time to do it, but it did not.

The DEPOS coalition, comprised of the Serbian Renewal Movement (SPO), the Civic Alliance of Serbia (GSS), the New Democracy Party (ND) and the Peoples' Peasant Party (NSS), showed that its followers were faithful but it could not win over SPS or SRS voters. Coming in as the second group in strength, DEPOS proved that a significant segment of the population still desired political change, but was not as yet weighty enough to effect it. Put bluntly, only a fifth of the deputies in the Serbian Parliament were truly committed to make concessions to end the war and lift sanctions.

Table 3   Serbian Parliamentary Election Results

Party	*December 1992* Seats	*December 1993* Seats
Socialist Party of Serbia	101	123
DEPOS	50	45
Serbian Radical Party	73	39
Democratic Party	7	29
Democratic Party of Serbia	--	7
Democratic Alliance of Hungarians in Vojvodina	9	5
Party for Democratic Action/ Democratic Party of Albanians	--	2
Group of Citizens (Arkan)	5	--
Others	5	0
TOTAL	250	250

By now, all other political parties (except those representing minorities, whose concerns ended where the interests of their community were not immediately at stake), were rallying around the "national interest". They supported the Serb war effort and wooed the fanatics waging the war in Bosnia-Herzegovina (sometimes in the vain hope of winning them over against Milosevic). The condemnation of the international community was not an argument against the regime any more: some of them even felt embarrassed by foreign support and all forgot their earlier claims that international sanctions had been deserved by the actions of the regime. Since there were no parallel presidential elections, some parties sought accommodation with Milosevic in the hope of sharing power with his party.

The rift with the Socialists cost the Serbian Radical Party a total of 34 seats compared to December 1992. Nevertheless, Seselj's loss was not as big as the Socialists would probably have liked. By securing third place in Parliament Seselj proved that his extreme nationalism had genuine appeal for a sizable part of the population.

By adopting a somewhat more nationalist stand and yet successfully projecting itself as pragmatic and middle of the road, the Democratic Party (DS) did much better in 1993 than in 1992. Due to the party leader's (Zoran Djindjic) opposition background, but just as much to his alleged willingness to compromise with the SPS, the DS seemed to have succeeded in attracting at least some disillusioned SPS or even Radical votes. The poor showing of the Democratic Party of Serbia (DSS) indicated that conversion to nationalism by a group perceived as intellectual was not convincing to nationalist voters, who could get much stronger medicine from the SPS and the SRS. Widespread belief that the Serbian Unity Party (SSJ) would at least cross the five percent threshold for entry into Parliament proved to be unfounded.

If any message can be extracted from the 1993 Serbian parliamentary election results, it would seem to be that international coercion failed to increase internal pressure. One and a half years after isolation was enforced, Milosevic's party was still the single most popular political force in the Republic. The decreased number of SPS and SRS seats in the new Serbian parliament was compensated for by the switch of some opposition parties to nationalism, xenophobia and support of war as the only means to secure Serb national interests. If any (relatively) positive change should be noted, it is the swing of the pendulum of public opinion back towards the centre in comparison to the election of 1992. Radical and SSJ losses seemed to indicate that national solidarity was not going to be carried to its fascist extreme.

In the six months following the Serbian parliamentary election there was no substantial political change. What it lacked in parliamentary majority the SPS made up for in skilful political manoeuvring and absolute control of the media, police and the army. It took the Socialists all of two months to get parliamentary life back on track both in Serbia and at the federal level. Milosevic made overtures to the opposition on the creation of a government of national unity but did nothing specific to support this offer. When Mirko Marjanovic finally was appointed Serbian Prime Minister in late February 1994, the New Democracy party (hitherto part of DEPOS) announced that it was willing to serve in such a government. With the hurdle of a lack of majority temporarily cleared, the SPS had, once again, little to fear, especially since economic measures introduced in the beginning of the year had started to produce good results.

THE PSYCHOLOGICAL EFFECTS OF SANCTIONS: THE MEDIA AND PUBLIC OPINION

The political effects of sanctions can hardly be separated from their psychological effects, defined for our purposes as the perceptions individuals have about why sanctions were introduced and what should be done to remove them. The media's role in moulding perceptions is crucial at any given time; it becomes vital when a target government needs to convince the population that its internationally condemned policies were right and that it is being ostracized groundlessly. That media manipulation is the key instrument used by the authorities to drum up support through calls for national solidarity has been confirmed in the Yugoslav case.

Radio-TV Serbia is the major source of information for a huge majority of the population of Serbia, a fact which the regime exploits to maximum advantage.[35] Being state-owned and state-run, i.e. effectively under SPS control, its programmes have been carefully designed to carry every story, fact and opinion supportive of government stands. The principal messages broadcast almost entirely mirror official views. Hence the widely held belief in Serbia proper that the Bosnian Serbs are fighting only a defensive war to preserve their lives and land. The use of (outside) force against them is popularly interpreted as an unwarranted act of aggression. The only victims ever seen or heard on official radio-television are the Bosnian Serbs, just as they are the only group presented as being forcibly evicted from their homes.

Coverage of domestic political events by the official media is similarly biased. Opposition viewpoints are rarely transmitted but often criticized; facts about human rights abuses are rarely explored but regularly denied. While TV Serbia does inform of politically controversial topics, commentary follows instructing the viewer how to interpret what has just been presented.

The officially-run electronic media would not be of such importance were it not for its monopoly. Radio-TV Serbia is the only broadcasting organization that reaches the entire Republic. With complete government control of frequency allocations it is also clear that only media organizations sympathetic to the SPS can hope for any visibility beyond the perimeter of the city of Belgrade. Fully aware of the strength of electronic media in a semi-literate population, the regime has crushed all attempts to broaden the area where independent radio and TV stations could reach. The independent media also have been hampered by a lack of resources. Their occasional acceptance of Western technical assistance has raised considerable controversy and faced them with the task of fending off accusations of being foreign hirelings.

The role of the printed press in Serbia has diminished greatly since the imposition of sanctions, for almost exclusively financial reasons. Due to reduced budgets, buying a daily newspaper has become too expensive for most, while magazines have become prized commodities. There is a significant number of independent dailies and weeklies, but their influence is negligible (none print more than 30,000 copies). In spite of virulent attacks against them and their staff, they have not been persecuted. The government, quite reasonably, prefers to boast of a modicum of (harmless) freedom of expression.

Given the discrepancy between official media messages and logical reasoning, Yugoslav public opinion has been confused. Opinion polls show that people feel badly hit by sanctions, but fail to establish the link between the internationally imposed measures and domestic government policy.[36] In a May 1993 survey conducted shortly after resolution 820 was passed, only 10% of those interviewed believed that the SPS and Slobodan Milosevic were to blame for the Bosnian war; 44% thought the FRY should do "everything possible" to lift the sanctions, while 40% thought it should resist international pressure. However, only 23% replied affirmatively when asked in the same poll if Yugoslavia should meet UN conditions to enable a cessation of hostilities in Bosnia; 18% were convinced that it should not, 22% claimed that Yugoslavia already had fulfilled UN demands, while 25% thought the FRY was not responsible for the conflict anyway.

In the final analysis, at the second anniversary of sanctions there was no willingness to work towards overcoming international isolation: people had become resigned to their fate. In a late May 1994 survey, 60% said that they "were used" to life under sanctions.[37]

THE ECONOMIC EFFECTS OF SANCTIONS

The goal of sanctions is not the deterioration of the economy or ensuing hardship to a population, but compliance with the demands of the sender, in this case the United Nations, as a direct or indirect consequence of economic deprivation. Estimating the effects of sanctions is difficult because the Yugoslav economy was very poor even before they were introduced. According to independent economists, the rupture of economic relations between the republics of the former Yugoslavia affected the FRY harder than sanctions, as the volume of trade within the SFRY had far surpassed foreign economic activity. In addition, the new Yugoslavia's economy was undergoing a transition regarding property status. The economic effects of sanctions are difficult enough to determine in a market economy; they are even less calculable in a system primarily based on "social ownership" such as Yugoslavia's. Finally, it is no secret that Yugoslavia has supported the Serb war effort in Bosnia-Herzegovina and Croatia, at considerable but officially undisclosed cost.

If people are meant to starve as proof that sanctions "bite", then this has not happened in Yugoslavia, yet. The worst-case scenario excluded starvation due to the country's relative self-sufficiency in basic foodstuffs and electricity. Nevertheless, the economy has suffered severely. Initially, Government officials either played down the effect of sanctions or presented them as a "challenge". They took very little anticipatory action. In surveys published right after SC res. 757 was passed, the managers of most industrial plants said that their stocks of raw materials and supplies could last between one and three months. Government confidence rested on a belief that sanctions would not work because they would somehow be circumvented by "the interests of capital".[38] However, the official attitude that "sanctions effects will not be particularly severe" has changed completely: they now have "tragic" consequences, which better suits the propaganda effort to present them as part of a genocidal scheme against the Serb nation.[39]

Independent economists and company managers differed with the government right from the start, warning not only that sanctions would last, but also that they could not be lifted soon enough given the dependence of the Yugoslav economy on foreign trade. Given such opposing forecasts, the public reacted instinctively. Right after sanctions were imposed, people spent whatever surplus money they had creating stocks of basic foodstuffs. Huge queues formed at petrol stations almost immediately, as Yugoslavia's dependence on imports of crude oil and petroleum products was well-known. As predicted by foreign experts, the oil embargo proved to be one of the most efficient tools in the sanctions package. Out of an estimated 6 to 6.5 million tons of crude oil and petroleum products, Serbia's planned annual consumption for 1992, only 1.1 million could be expected to come from domestic sources.[40]

The oil embargo was violated frequently in 1992, so much so that passenger cars were back in the streets of Belgrade by October. Violations of the embargo were mentioned as one of the reasons for the adoption of resolution 787 imposing stricter controls on sanctions implementation. The impact of these violations (as well as of later ones) was insignificant from the point of view of average living standards. Car traffic bouncing back to a third of its pre-sanctions level is one thing; the revival of industrial production, currently at 40% of its pre-sanctions level, is quite another.[41] Individual "importers" of petroleum products were able to meet limited private demand but proved incapable of supplying cities to run central heating plants or the public transportation systems.

Each winter spent under sanctions was in that respect progressively worse. In 1992/93 the heating period was shortened, with temperatures in homes and offices reduced to levels the population had not experienced before. With the aim of saving energy (and lives), schools and universities were closed for a considerable period in the winter of 1993/94. Medical services of all types were crippled. The public transportation system in Belgrade and other major cities could not accommodate a 50% increase in the number of passengers alongside an equal decline in the number of operative vehicles. Traffic in the countryside nearly came to a halt.

The population has faced a constant struggle with inflation. By the end of 1992, the annual inflation rate in the FRY stood at 20,000 percent, just an indication, as it transpired, of what was to come. In November 1993 it had reached 286,000 million percent at the annual level, reaching an all time high in January 1994, when the monthly rate alone came to a staggering 313 million percent.[42] Apart from decreased output, the single most important cause of the price spiral was money printing, which the central bank did little to control. It was used to stop up a huge budget deficit constantly being widened by additional public spending.[43] Furthermore, the quarter of Serbia's 2.3 million work force which had been sent on "forced leave" (effectively laid off) had to be handed out its government-promised salaries.[44]

As inflation rose, the exchange rate of the national currency fell, reducing average monthly earnings by October 1993 to just 10 German marks (DM) at the black market rate. Not only did purchasing power fall, but there was a shortage of goods as well. Producers and retailers in the socially-owned sector were unwilling to sell at government-fixed prices. Food coupons did little except add to the queues in the already gloomy Belgrade streets.

Estimates of the losses suffered by the FRY economy after two years of sanctions were officially released just prior to the second anniversary of international isolation. Even allowing for the discrepancies in figures presented by various government sources, the damage appears to be staggering. According to a statement by current Serbian Prime Minister Mirko Marjanovic, sanctions have so far cost the FRY US$30 billion.[45] A Federal Government assessment published previously — and which included losses attributable to the rupture in former Yugoslav economic relations — put the total damages at US$45 billion. Whatever the exact data may be, sanctions have largely contributed to widespread poverty. The annual per capita income in 1994 was no more than US$600 dollars, five times less than in 1989.[46]

What kept the social peace and why was Milosevic's party voted back despite such a desperate situation? The simple answer, it seems, is that economic deprivation does not produce political dissatisfaction. Nationalist feelings fanned by the war in Bosnia and supported by defiant media messages were undoubtedly an important impediment. So also was the constant struggle to survive, which leaves little room for reflection on the cause of events. But there were other factors that eased the average existence.

Foreign currency reserves are widely believed to have been a significant buffer against total impoverishment, at least for a segment of the population. According to pre-sanctions estimates, FRY citizens had between DM 1.7 and 2 billion saved.[47] These funds were used to supplement meagre guaranteed pensions and wages. Also, while socially-owned banks had frozen individual foreign currency savings deposits long before sanctions were introduced, several new private banks guaranteed monthly interest rates of 14% from 1992 until the system collapsed in early 1993.

Because the majority of the population of Yugoslavia lives in villages and small towns, food hunting never became an overriding concern, except for city dwellers. Most of the land is privately owned, and it is supposed that rural families helped out relatives and friends living in the cities, thus contributing to social stability.

Smuggled goods were a buffer against economic hardship, provided individuals had foreign currency reserves. Smuggling permitted the continued operation of small privately-owned shops and street vendors. Prices were very high and daily purchases of smuggled goods were limited to a fairly small segment of the population.[48]

If none of these factors that eased survival was the direct result of government effort, the regularity of monthly wages and pension payments, however scant, were paramount to maintaining social peace. Rather than allowing speedier economic privatization, the government chose to guarantee entitlements regardless of their burden on the crippled economy. Some 1.2 million pensioners, a staunch SPS constituency, were also catered to, reinforcing the impression that the government was concerned about the plight of the people.

The bulk of industry remained state-owned, but small businesses had started to flourish already in the time of the pre-war federal government of Ante Markovic. His legislation has been generally kept in place and everyday life was alleviated by typically "capitalist" resourcefulness, initiative, flexibility and skill of small industries, merchants and artisans. Another important factor has been the virtual absence of trade unions. The regime inherited an old trade union, which remains a transmission of ruling party policies. New, independent trade unions have been created, but they are mostly limited to the white-collar work force. It goes without saying that their leaders have been vilified as traitors. In an attempt to thwart their activity, the official trade unions have staged a number of small strikes with demands that the government has been only too willing to accommodate.

The accelerated down-slide of the Yugoslav economy was unexpectedly halted in late January 1994 when a Programme of Monetary Reconstruction was launched. Its author, Dragoslav Avramovic, devised a strategy to battle hyperinflation: to create a new dinar at par with the German mark, backed by gold and foreign exchange reserves worth DM 500 million.[49] The plan included strict control of money printing, cuts in public spending, more efficient tax collection, and wider distribution of consumer goods to restart the trade and production cycles. This programme has produced remarkable results. In February 1994, inflation had dropped to just 1% from the 313 million percent recorded just a month before. The new dinar held firm against the DM, retailers were encouraged to return food and other commodities to the stores, and the black market exchange rate was effectively undermined. There was even a slight recovery in living standards. From 10 DM in December 1993, average wages had risen to 116 dinars/DM by the following April.[50] Prices were still far above monthly wages, but a significant psychological respite had been achieved. The accompanying propaganda succeeded in blaming the sanctions for the economic nadir at the end of 1993 and crediting the regime for the subsequent recovery.

The main question currently in the focus of domestic and international interest is how long the economic hiatus can be expected to last. Avramovic, appointed Governor of the National Bank of Yugoslavia in March 1994, exuded confidence in mid-May claiming that the "program was sustainable whatever happened".[51] His prediction is based on an alleged rise in industrial production and the country's self-sufficiency in basic foodstuffs.[52] Sceptics argue that with no access to new funds, increased production can be upheld only if the government eventually foots the bill, which would obviously entail a new spiral of inflation.

At the two year sanctions mark, a mood of cautious optimism could be felt among the population. The resulting political boost to the incumbent, internationally isolated government, hardly needs to be mentioned.

CONCLUSIONS

At the second anniversary of their implementation, it would appear that sanctions against the FRY have not fulfilled international expectations. The war in Bosnia does not seem to be drawing to an end unless the stalemate on the ground, accompanied by a lesser level of fighting and limited reward for Serb conquests, could be termed an aim. Although the sanctions bite has been hard, isolation has not unseated the internationally repugnant government. Theoretical wisdom proved to be true in its assessment that resignation, not revolt, would be at least the short-term consequence. Ostracism, as evidenced by the Yugoslav case, is not conducive to democracy or a free press, obviously essential prerequisites for countering the "rallying round the flag" effect.

The aim of the sanctions was never clear and it has become fuzzier with time. The original demand that the FRY stop supporting the Serb army in its attempt to destroy Bosnia-Herzegovina as a multinational entity was replaced by appeals to the FRY to exert influence to stop the war in return for a Serb state that would comprise about half of the territory of the old republic. The wish to convey the message that the regime in Serbia should be changed was abandoned, if it was ever there, and replaced either by attempts to cajole Slobodan Milosevic as a wise and strong statesman or by veiled hints that something should generally change in Serbia, easily interpreted as pressure on the otherwise immovable Serbian president to grant some peace and autonomy to non-

Serb minorities in Serbia. Coupled with the absence of sanctions against Croatia (despite its involvement in the war in Bosnia), this has only strengthened the impression that outside powers are siding with other nations against the Serbs.

In a society that has remained basically socialist, even clearer messages could have been easily distorted by the omnipresent propaganda machinery. The population was encouraged to believe that sanctions were not caused by any action on the part of the government, but were the result of an international conspiracy against the Serbs. This explanation, while contradictory and incoherent, proved politically effective. The Serbs are "guilty", it is argued, only of a desire to exercise their right to self-determination: "If others are bent on the extinction of Serbs, what is left to them but to endure and resist in the hope that some eternal justice would be done?".[53]

Economic suffering resulting from both sanctions and the war effort did not change this attitude. The power holders have not even found it necessary, as they did in the beginning, to deny the proportions of the economic catastrophe: paradoxically, economic disaster tends now to strengthen the belief that sanctions are "genocidal".

In accordance with theoretical predictions, it can be concluded that, after two years, sanctions have failed.[54] It is not too early to make this statement; whatever the continuation of sanctions may produce, it will certainly not be the original aim of their senders, especially the military and political disengagement of the Serbian regime, via Yugoslavia, in Bosnia and Herzegovina. At present, sanctions are being transformed from a threat to a promise: they will be lifted if "Serbs accept and carry out" the plan put before them by the foreign ministers of the US, Russia and the EU to get 49% of the territory of Bosnia and Herzegovina.[55] Everyone seems resigned to the final outcome: the regime in Serbia will eventually control that territory, either through a local government it sponsors or through outright incorporation (Great Serbia). If the Serbs do not agree, there is a clear threat of military force looming on the horizon: the rearmament of the Bosnian Muslims (and Croats, now their allies) after the lifting of the UN arms embargo on former Yugoslavia. This would be another admission that sanctions have failed.

Because of the constantly shifting agenda in the former Yugoslavia and the irrationality of many actors, we offer no prediction as to what direction future events might take. But we do suggest that as a tool of international policy sanctions should be reconsidered seriously. At the very least, there are questions the UN needs to answer before once again utilizing this "feelgood" solution: What exactly is the aim of the international community in a given situation? Can this aim be achieved by economic coercion? If an aim cannot be stated with great clarity, if the message cannot reach the target population, if the society has become closed and militarized, if the situation at hand involves ethnic strife, and if, because of that, the dilemmas can be presented as matters of life and death of the whole nation, sanctions do not appear to be an appropriate means for conflict resolution.

NOTES

1. Security Council Resolution 757, 30 May 1992, UN Doc. S/Res/757 (1992).
2. Excluding medicines, foodstuffs, and technical equipment for the independent media. See also Michael P. Scharf and Joshua L. Dorosin, "Interpreting UN Sanctions: The Rulings and Role of the Yugoslavia Sanctions Committee", *Brooklyn Journal of International Law*, vol. 19, no. 3, (1993), pp. 771-827.
3. Security Council Resolution 787, 16 November 1992, UN Doc. S/Res/787 (1992).
4. Security Council Resolution 820, 17 April 1993, UN Doc. S/Res/820 (1993).
5. Johan Galtung, "On the Effects of International Economic Sanctions", *World Politics*, vol. 3, (1967), p. 409; Peter Wallensteen, "Characteristics of Economic Sanctions", *Journal of Peace Research*, vol. 3, (1968), p. 258; Margaret Doxey, *Economic Sanctions and International Enforcement* (Oxford: Oxford University Press, 1971), p. 131; Vojin Dimitrijevic, "The Efficacy of International Sanctions", *Review of International Affairs*, 726-7, (1980), pp. 31-33.
6. Galtung, *ibid.*, pp. 389-390.
7. Doxey, *Economic Sanctions*, note 5, pp. 120, 125.
8. Galtung, "On the Effects of International Economic Sanctions", note 5, p. 411.
9. Gary Hufbauer, Jeffrey Schott, and Kimberly Elliott, *Economic Sanctions Reconsidered*, (Washington: Institute for International Economics, 1991), pp. 93 & 94.
10. Doxey, *Economic Sanctions*, note 5, p. 133.
11. David A. Baldwin, *Economic Statecraft*, (Princeton: Princeton University Press, 1985), p. 149.
12. Baldwin, *ibid.*, p. 204.

13. On the dissolution of the SFRY see Misha Glenny, *The Fall of Yugoslavia: The Third Balkan War*, (Harmondsworth: Penguin, 1992).
14. Security Council Resolution 787 (1992), paras. 4 and 5.
15. *Keesing's Record of World Events*, vol. 39, no. 4, (1993), p. 39427.
16. *Keesing's Record of World Events*, vol. 39, no. 11, (1993), p. 39743. *International Herald Tribune*, 6 July 1994, p. 1.
17. Security Council Resolution 871, October 5, 1993, U.N. Doc. S/Res/871 (1993).
18. The former was expressed by a British diplomatic source to a Yugoslav journalist; the latter has been raised primarily by the US. *Politika*, 30 May 1994, pp. 4-5.
19. Asked about Milosevic after the 1992 elections and the demise of Milan Panic, David Owen, co-chairman of the Conference on Former Yugoslavia, said: "When we visited Belgrade, Vance and I always sought him out, even when he was electorally unpopular, because we could see he was potentially a very powerful figure. We naturally treat him warily, but also as if he is somebody who is ready to play a constructive role. I think that Milosevic is the most important figure in the whole region... It seemed to me unrealistic to expect him to have helped the peace process in December, which would only have benefitted the then Milan Panic government in Yugoslavia. We sensed we had to wait until the elections had been held before we could get a constructive response on Bosnia from Milosevic... We must persuade him to play a role in forcing the Bosnian Serbs to accept the peace plan." "The Future of the Balkans: An Interview with David Owen", *Foreign Affairs*, vol. 72, no. 3, (Spring 1993), p. 9.
20. "The question is, will he stand up to the likes of Seselj and Arkan or go with them further down the path of repression? I sense a realistic politician who will distance himself from them." Owen, *ibid.*
21. In an interview with the BBC, US President Bill Clinton was reported as saying that the lifting of sanctions was (also) conditional on "...certain changes in Serbia itself". *Politika*, 30 May 1994, p. 5.
22. The poll of 21 May 1994 comprised a random selection of some 200 individuals in Serbia. *NIN*, 27 May 1994, p. 14.
23. *Borba*, 3 June 1992, p. 3.
24. *Vanity Fair*, June 1994, p. 131.
25. *Borba*, 1 June 1992, p. 8.
26. *Borba*, 5 June 1992, p. 16.
27. Foreign news agencies estimated the number of people assembled on the first day at 100,000; the organizers said it was between 250,000 and 300,000; and the official Belgrade police count was 23,000. *Politika*,

28 June 1992, p. 6.

28. This election was called two years ahead of time at the level of Serbia (the previous ones had taken place in December 1990) and only seven months after the opposition had boycotted the federal elections of May 1992, which were called after the FRY's 27 April Constitution was adopted.

29. In the December 1990 elections, Milosevic obtained 63.34% of votes cast. In December 1992, this was 56%. Voter turnout was 69.04%. Consequently, Milosevic was favoured by 39.67% of the electorate in Serbia.

30. Five seats won by a citizens' association, led by Zeljko Raznatovic Arkan are included in the 76 opposition seats for the purpose of comparison with 1990 and also because Arkan was formally in opposition to the SPS. Proportional representation favoured SPS and SRS, while the opposition included a number of small parties; some of the votes cast for the latter eventually went to the pro-Milosevic parties.

31. In December 1992 the extent to which the popularity of the Radicals was attributable to the effect of sanctions is debateable because they had already done fairly well in the May 1992 federal elections. The 1993 election results showed, however, that the Radicals were "here to stay" in spite of the fact that their influence had slightly diminished in the meantime.

32. Economist Intelligence Unit, *Serbia-Montenegro Country Report*, (3rd quarter 1993), p. 29.

33. The Serbian Unity Party was launched officially on 3 November 1993. Arkan is best known as the leader of a paramilitary formation reputed to have committed war crimes in Croatia and Bosnia-Herzegovina. He is internationally sought as an alleged criminal and also believed to be one of Serbia's wealthiest and most dangerous men, according to the *New York Times*, 23 November 1993, p. 1.

34. Voter turnout was 62.3%

35. In an October 1992 public opinion survey conducted by the Belgrade Institute for Social Sciences, 76% of a total of 2,000 people said that radio and TV were their "most frequent" sources of information. Jugoslovensko javno mnenje, Centar za politikoloska istrazivanja i javno mnenje Instituta drustvenih nauka Univerziteta u Beogradu, p. 4.

36. According to a poll of 2,000 people conducted by the Belgrade Institute for Social Sciences at the one year sanctions mark (May 1993), 49% said that their financial situation was "much worse" than the previous year, while 37% believed it would continue to deteriorate the following year. *Vreme*, 21 June 1993, pp. 26-29 and *passim*.

37. *NIN*, 27 May 1994, p. 11.

38. Opinion of then Serbian Prime Minister Radoman Bozovic, a professor of economics. *Borba*, 3 June 1992, p. 3.

39. The federal Prime Minister Radoje Kontic said in April 1993, just before resolution 820 was passed: "The sanctions have completely isolated our economy, and so far they have had tragic consequences...We have no illusion that any spectacular results can be achieved under the present oppressive circumstances". *Review of International Affairs*, vol. XLIV, no. 1015, (April 1993), pp. 1, 3.

40. Depending on the source, domestic production was estimated to be between 20-28% of annual consumption.

41. *Politika*, 29 May 1994, p. 1.

42. *Keesing's Record of World Events*, vol. 39, no. 4, (1993), p. 39427; vol. 39, no. 12, 1993, p.39785. Economist Intelligence Unit, note 32, (1st quarter, 1994), p. 32.

43. Three quarters of the federal budget was earmarked for the Yugoslav army. However, federal spending was estimated to be only 20% of all public expenditures, the rest being generated in Serbia and Montenegro. Economist Intelligence Unit, note 32, (2nd quarter, 1993), p. 38.

44. It was estimated that 900,000 people were on forced leave in Serbia by March, 1994. Economist Intelligence Unit, note 32, (1st quarter, 1994), p. 32.

45. *Politika*, 30 May 1994, p. 5.

46. Assessment of the Centre for Development and Economic Policy of the Federal Ministry for Science and Technology. *Politika*, 30 May 1994, p. 5.

47. Economist Intelligence Unit, note 32, (1st quarter, 1994), p. 33.

48. An advertisement published in *NIN* on 29 April 1994, is irresistible: "Maxima International Department Store. New Dimension of Purchase... In accordance with high European standards offers rich, high quality, carefully selected imported and domestic assortment and top service... Furniture from Denmark, glass and ceramics from Italy, French wines and cheese, products of Sony, Philips, Moulinex."

49. Most foreign economic experts doubted that the FRY had that amount at its disposal when the Program started. "Yugoslavia-Economy: Reforms Reap Rewards Despite Sanctions" *Inter Press Service*, 17 March 1994.

50. *Vreme Novca* no. 29, 30 May 1994, p. 5.

51. *New York Times*, 30 May 1994, p. A3.

52. Avramovic told the New York Times that "industrial production was up 40% since the end of last year". *New York Times*, 30 May 1994, p. 3.

53. In this respect, the papers and the discussion at the "Second Congress of Serb Intellectuals", held in Belgrade on 23 April 1994 were the most indicative. See *Republika* (Belgrade) no. 91, 1-15 May 1994, p. 15.
54. David Gompert, "How to Defeat Serbia", *Foreign Affairs*, vol. 73, no. 4, (1994), pp. 30-47.
55. *International Herald Tribune*, 6 July 1994, p. 1.

8 New Directions in Disarmament

Dimitris Bourantonis & Marios Evriviades

Fifty years ago representatives from fifty states signed the Charter of the United Nations, the primary aim of which was to maintain international peace and security. The means to achieve this aim was through collective security; disarmament and arms limitation were considered to be secondary. Even in its more limited sense as a limitation of armaments, disarmament was not discussed in detail either at the Dumbarton Oaks or at the San Francisco conferences.

On the issue of disarmament, it was agreed by the founders of the UN at San Francisco to authorize the General Assembly to "consider principles governing disarmament and the regulation of armaments" (Article 11 (I)). Authority was also given to the Security Council to formulate with the assistance of the Military Staff Committee referred to in Article 47, plans to be submitted to the members of the UN for the establishment of a system for the regulation of armaments (Article 26) and "possible disarmament" (Article 47). The underlying reason for this peace and security planning action of the Security Council was to minimize withdrawals for armaments from "the world's human and economic resources" (Article 26).

With the advent of nuclear weapons, priorities changed abruptly. The use of nuclear weapons against targets in Japan shortly after the signing of the Charter made members of the UN recognize that immediate steps had to be taken to avert their further use. Disarmament thus attracted an urgency that was not envisaged in the Charter. A flurry of activity ensued, beginning with the first session of the General Assembly, to arrest the nuclear arms race before it began. But the post-war political climate was not conducive to this. The Cold War, and the acquisition of atomic bombs by the USSR and later by the United Kingdom, China and France led to an unprecedented race in conventional and nuclear arms. In the inter-bloc competition, the world witnessed a race for refurbishing arsenals for the purpose of increasing power, acquiring allies and friends and extending influence in the emerging Third World.

154

In this setting, disarmament negotiations were adversary proceedings from the start. Even so, for half a century the UN never ceased to exhort states to act and sponsored negotiations for this end. For fifty years, the disarmament fora of the UN were utilized to focus attention on and to coordinate pressures concerning the arms race which facilitated agreement on a number of measures to limit it. The Outer Space Treaty of 1967, the Non-Proliferation Treaty of 1968, the Sea-Bed Treaty of 1971, the Convention on the Prohibition of Bacteriological (Biological) and Toxin Weapons and on their Destruction of 1972, the ENMOD Convention of 1977 and the Convention on a Comprehensive Prohibition of Chemical Weapons of 1992, were all the result of negotiations carried out within UN organs. There are also a number of agreements, such as the Partial Test Ban Treaty of 1963 and the Treaty of Tlatelolco of 1967 which although concluded outside the UN framework, had benefitted to a considerable degree from the cooperation of the world organization.

As a result of the changes that have taken place on the international scene over the past few years, the prospects for a greater involvement of the UN in disarmament and arms limitation have improved considerably. The end of the Cold War has created a climate conducive to the conclusion of effective disarmament agreements. A direct consequence of this is that more progress in disarmament has taken place since 1987 than in all previous years combined. Such evidence may be found in five agreements: the Treaty on Intermediate Range and Shorter Range Missiles (INF); the Treaty on Conventional Forces in Europe (CFE); the START I and START II agreements between the United States and Russia for far reaching reductions in strategic arms; and the Chemical Weapons Convention.

These developments have generated a momentum of interest in disarmament and have provided a focus for policy oriented action. This momentum has acquired considerable urgency because of the interest displayed by the states which enjoy a preponderance of power. In an unprecedented UN Security Council summit meeting on 31 January 1992, the Security Council members pledged their full support to the UN and expressed their commitment "to take concrete steps to enhance the effectiveness of the UN in these [disarmament and arms limitation] areas."[1]

The focus of this chapter is on the role that the UN may be able to play in the years ahead in disarmament and arms limitation. It is designed to contribute to the ideas about how to maximize the UN's potential to deal effectively with the new global security requirements, especially where disarmament is concerned. Disarmament is understood as the process of actually reducing or renouncing weapons systems. Arms limitation, on the other hand, denotes any measure or restraint − not involving the actual reduction of weapons − on the testing, manufacture, possession, deployment, or use of weapons.   Arms limitation also includes all the measures which promote confidence among states.

THE DECISION STRUCTURE OF THE UN

The essential starting point for any discussion concerning the performance of the UN *vis-à-vis* disarmament should be an understanding of certain key political assumptions upon which the UN was founded. Foremost among these is that the UN was designed to be a body of sovereign states, not a prototype of world government.   As a non-supranational authority the UN's potential for the attainment of its major goal − to afford a more or less comprehensive regime for all international affairs by way of conduct and oversight − depends exclusively on the authority that individual governments and particularly the major powers are willing to grant it. As far as disarmament is concerned, the fundamental constraint inherent in the UN is that it cannot dictate; at most, it can be used to encourage and facilitate disarmament amongst member-states.

As an arena of sovereign states, the UN's structure of decision-making authority reflects this reality.   The history of disarmament negotiations reveals that the UN can act effectively only if members reach unanimous agreement over certain issues. These include, first, the position that the UN should occupy in the global negotiating process (either central or peripheral), second, the agenda and, finally, the form which the institution-building of the UN disarmament machinery should take.   All of these issues are closely related.   As long as states disagree on the role that the UN should play in the global negotiating process, there does not exist even the most remote possibility for agreement on an institutional format and agenda for negotiations.   Institutional arrangements[2] do have a special importance in organizing disarmament issues in one way or another.   Similarly, the perspectives of independent states, as expressed through their preference for any of the roles that the UN could play in disarmament negotiations, are influential in the decisions reached by states about the way disarmament institutions should be shaped and implemented.

THE NEED TO CLARIFY THE ROLE OF THE UN

It is clear that, with the end of the Cold War, the machinery used by the international community to address problems of disarmament has to be reassessed.   It is in this context that the Secretary-General of the UN submitted a report on *New Dimensions of Arms Regulation and Disarmament in the Post-Cold War Era*.[3] This calls for a comprehensive review of the functions of and the relationships between the various disarmament fora with a view to making the international machinery for disarmament negotiations more forward looking, efficient and results oriented.

Today the most important issues of disarmament and arms limitation are negotiated in UN fora, the Russian-American bilateral institution of SALT/START and in certain other regional institutions such as the Conference on Security and Cooperation in Europe (CSCE), within which talks on European conventional armed forces are taking place. The central issue is how to organize and harmonize the work of these institutions to ensure that each of them contributes as effectively as possible to disarmament. This presupposes agreement on a comprehensive world structure for negotiating disarmament wherein these institutions may play distinct roles as approved by the world community.

In this context, it would be appropriate for the UN to take on a clearly defined role that complements, not competes with, the roles assigned to other disarmament institutions, bilateral or regional. This would entail some rethinking of issues of the international agenda to which the UN is best suited to respond.   The universalization of principles, practices and approaches that govern disarmament negotiations in the UN lead to the conclusion that it might be better for the UN to focus on purely multilateral aspects of certain issues, such as the strengthening of the non-proliferation regime. The great virtue of global multilateralism is that, since it requires the cooperation of a large number of states representing all regions, it offers all a chance to participate in the negotiations of issues that confront humanity as a whole. Experience has shown that when the UN has addressed issues that are worldwide in scope, it has been relatively successful. When it attempted to deal with East-West nuclear issues which had direct repercussions on the strategic balance of power, its efforts ended in failure.[4]

The application of a global approach to East-West issues of nuclear disarmament, which are currently under discussion within the bilateral institution of SALT/START is questionable. The UN should avoid the duplication of work which is being done there successfully since it has achieved a record of accomplishments, the most recent being the break-through in START II in which the United States and Russia have agreed to scale down their strategic arsenals. The functioning of this forum should continue uninterrupted to yield even further results. Global and bilateral negotiations should be pursued simultaneously, since progress in each is partly dependent on movement in the other. For instance, the extension of the non-proliferation regime is clearly dependent on the parallel conclusion of agreements by the US and Russia on nuclear disarmament. Disarmament can be effective only if both of these aspects interact cooperatively; for many years, the UN and SALT/START have failed to cooperate with each other. The tendency that existed in the UN after the General Assembly convened in 1978 its first special session devoted exclusively to disarmament was to focus mostly on the nuclear weapons of the two superpowers, a bilateral issue, and to brush aside aspects such as conventional weapons and questions of arms transfers in which the multilateral-global approach is more suitable. As a result, the SALT/START institution acted for a long time as an institutional alternative to the UN.

While realizing the need for a division of labour between the UN and SALT/START, stress should be laid equally on determining a role for the UN in a regional context. Given the persistent stockpiling of sophisticated arms in various parts of the world and the growing interest among states in developing regional approaches to disarmament, this is a particularly timely, important, and urgent task.

Indeed, in recent years the regional approach to disarmament and arms limitation has been gaining ground steadily both at the conceptual and practical levels. In light of the European achievements in disarmament through the CSCE, the importance of regional disarmament and arms limitation is confirmed not only as a confidence building measure, but also as an endeavour to establish a mutually acceptable equilibrium between regional states. This equilibrium could be achieved, *inter alia*, through the renunciation of certain types of weapons, agreed ceilings on conventional weapons, the creation of fully or partially demilitarized zones, nuclear-free zones and arrangements for inspection.

There are a number of regional organizations which are active in the field of disarmament and arms limitation including the Organization of American States (OAS), the Organisation of African Unity (OAU), and the Association of South-East Asian Nations (ASEAN). In these regions, the European experience is being assessed and its possible application to their own security needs is being weighed.[5] There appears to be a widespread concern for confidence-building measures, first developed in

Europe, as a means of reducing tensions and improving the prospects for disarmament. In the Middle East, for example, discussions are taking place in arms limitation as part of the peace process. Consequently, what is called for is an exploration of possible mechanisms and procedures that would strengthen interaction between the UN and various regional organizations in promoting disarmament and arms limitation at the regional level.[6]

Regional disarmament is entwined with political and security choices which are region specific and therefore are addressed best within the framework of regional institutions. These should be guided by the need to maintain a delicate balance between the rights and the responsibilities of all the participating states. Disarmament proposals should take into account the particular characteristics of the region concerned and the differing threat and security perceptions of individual states.

The UN may not be the institutional focal point for disarmament work at the regional level, but it could help the regional process in various ways. It could encourage the trend towards regional approaches to disarmament and arms limitation; formulate basic principles and general guidelines for regional disarmament negotiations; promote institutional mechanisms for regional security dialogues, particularly in regions where institutions for such discussions have not yet developed fully or are lacking altogether; and assume a role in the verification and implementation of regional agreements.

THE AGENDA OF THE UN

There appears to be a realization that changes in the UN agenda are required if the world organization is to remain relevant in the rapidly changing arms limitation and disarmament environment. The existing agenda is a little diffused and includes items such as the Comprehensive Programme of Disarmament, the Cessation of the Nuclear Arms Race and Nuclear Disarmament, and the Prevention of Nuclear War including all Related Matters, that are too obsolete or too broad to lend themselves to negotiation.

A restructured agenda should be without these broad-ranging and unsuitable issues. Restructuring should aim at devising a sharper focus on more pragmatic objectives to address issues of immediate concern to all states. A majority of member states are in favour of reshaping the agenda of the UN by reducing the number of items and concentrating on well-defined, practical and result-oriented issues. Notwithstanding differences of opinion between member-states on the order of priorities, there is substantial consensus on four important issues which should rank high on the international agenda of security and disarmament: non-proliferation of nuclear weapons, security assurances to the non-nuclear-weapon states, a comprehensive nuclear test ban treaty and transparency in armaments. [7]

On nuclear non-proliferation, the cornerstone of all international efforts should continue to be the Non-Proliferation Treaty (NPT). Over the past twenty-five years the NPT has made a significant contribution to slowing down the spread of nuclear capability. However, nuclear weapons have proliferated enormously despite the fact that the NPT requires non-nuclear weapon states to forgo nuclear-weapons capability, not to transfer or receive nuclear related technology and to submit facilities to International Atomic Energy Agency (IAEA) safeguards.

Although the NPT now has more than 155 signatories, it has not yet gained universal adherence. However, the benefits to global and regional security are dependent largely on universal adherence. Therefore, the UN should seek to ensure that the NPT is universally implemented in letter and spirit. It is gratifying to note that China and France recently have acceded to the NPT thereby bringing all permanent members of the Security Council into it. Another positive development is the accession of new independent states to the NPT, namely Estonia, Latvia, Slovenia, Uzbekistan and Azerbaijan, and the undertaking of Belarus, Kazakhstan and Ukraine to become parties to the NPT in the near future. All this augurs well for the 1995 fifth review conference of the NPT with a view to strengthening the non-proliferation regime.[8]

Important steps should also be taken to improve further and to strengthen the safeguards system of the IAEA. There has been much needed action to tighten nuclear export controls and to establish such full-scope safeguards as the international standard for the supply of nuclear and other sensitive materials. In addition, the IAEA should continue to carry out inspections of nuclear facilities. However, the agency should be provided with adequate financial resources to maintain a credible level of inspection. This important function of the IAEA could be enhanced further if the Security Council could function as a key forum for non-proliferation enforcement. The Security Council is entitled to and should adopt measures that curb proliferation and even apply sanctions against states that violate international norms and pose a threat to international peace and security. In this regard, reference should be made to the decision taken by the members of the Security Council, at the summit meeting of January 1992, "to take appropriate measures in the case of any violations notified to them by the IAEA."[9]

Nuclear-weapon states (NWS) should act decisively to enhance the viability of the non-proliferation regime by offering credible security assurances to the non-nuclear-weapon states (NNWS) in addition to those provided by Security Council Resolution 255 of 1969. The issue of guaranteeing the security of NNWS is a high priority issue of global and regional security. NNWS have asked for security assurances in a positive as well as a negative form.[10] Positive assurances would be promises on the part of the NWS that they would come to the defence of NNWS in the event of a nuclear attack against any of them. Negative assurances would be promises whereby the NWS undertake that they would never use or threaten to use nuclear weapons against the NNWS. The granting of comprehensive security assurances to the NNWS is a part of the commitments that the NWS undertook under the terms of the NPT with a view of correcting, even partially, the imbalance of rights and obligations of parties to the Treaty. Effective and legally binding international arrangements should, first, guarantee the deterrence of any use or threat of the use of nuclear weapons by NWS.[11] Second, they should provide for action, including the imposition of sanctions against parties or non-parties to the NPT, in any case concerning the use or threat of the use of nuclear weapons against a NNWS.

A comprehensive test ban treaty (CTBT) has a very important place among all the measures envisaged in the context of nuclear disarmament. A complete ban on nuclear testing would halt the development of new types of nuclear weapons and the emergence of more NWS. The Partial Test Ban Treaty of 1963 prohibited nuclear tests in the atmosphere, underwater and in outer space at a time when the nuclear powers had been mastering the techniques of underground testing. Since then, the UN has given the issue of a CTBT continuous consideration, but no satisfactory results have been achieved so far. The objective of a CTBT, as spelt out in the preamble of the Partial Test Ban Treaty, is to seek the permanent discontinuance of all nuclear tests. To be truly comprehensive, such a treaty should extend the ban on nuclear underground testing and attain broad adherence which would include all the NWS.

For the first time in many years, the international political climate is favourable for the prohibition of all nuclear tests. The NWS have adopted an attitude of self-restraint towards nuclear tests. A remarkable decline in the number of nuclear tests carried out during the period 1987-1992 is indicative of this. The US, the UK, France and Russia are currently observing a temporary cessation of nuclear testing. The US Congress has enacted legislation that places severe restrictions on US nuclear testing programmes. Henceforth, the US cannot conduct more than five nuclear tests per year. Existing legislation provides that "no underground tests of nuclear weapons may be conducted by the United States after September 30, 1996, unless a foreign state conducts a nuclear test after this date", thus compelling efforts to negotiate a CTBT.[12] All five declared nuclear weapon states have been inclined to make the fight against proliferation of nuclear weapons a serious objective of their foreign policy. They appear to share the view that a universal and effectively verifiable CTBT should be kept in the forefront of the UN negotiations because it would serve to deter NNWS from becoming members of the nuclear club[13] and also because the NNWS see a CTBT as a litmus test of the NWS's commitment to the non-proliferation regime. As a result of this change in the policy of states possessing nuclear weapons, the UN has decided to tackle the issue of a CTBT. A mandate already has been given to the UN Conference on Disarmament to negotiate a CTBT at the earliest time.[14]

Another equally important question is that of transparency in armaments. The conflicts in various parts of the world clearly show the consequences that can ensue from the uncontrolled flow of armaments into volatile regions. Openness and transparency in armaments cannot replace reductions in the number of weapons. They could, however, be conducive to confidence-building measures among states, reducing suspicion and removing misunderstandings, thus paving the way for disarmament measures both at regional and global levels.

As part of the universal measures to promote transparency, the UN Register of Conventional Armaments was set up by the General Assembly in 1991. According to General Assembly Resolution 46/36 of December 1991, the Secretary-General was requested to establish a register of conventional arms by January 1992, and to provide data annually on the import and export of certain categories of equipment, such as battle tanks, armoured combat vehicles, artillery, combat aircraft, attack helicopters, warships, missiles and missile launchers.[15]

If vigorous control of conventional arms trade were to be introduced it should be comprehensive to be effective. International action is required to expand the scope of the UN Register by the addition of further categories of equipment and data such as military holding, procurement through national production and stockpiling of conventional weapons. A follow-up step in establishing a more comprehensive and non-discriminatory register could be the further extension of the Register to cover the production and stockpiling of other types of arms, in particular nuclear weapons, as well as the transfer of technology.

Furthermore, the Register will be effective only if all UN members provide the required information and make sufficient resources available for the UN Secretariat to operate it.[16] As the UN Secretary-General noted in his report on *New Dimensions of Arms Regulation and Disarmament in the Post-Cold War Era*, "nothing would undermine the Register's operations more quickly than inadequate attention to the funding which is necessary to make it an effective instrument."[17]

The strengthening of the chemical and biological weapons regimes is also a matter of immense significance for the UN. The UN should appeal to all members to ratify the Chemical Weapons Treaty.[18] The strengthening of this treaty will result from the effective implementation of its provisions and, especially, those provisions which provide for inspections of national chemical industry installations by the world organization. The Biological Weapons Treaty has been criticized for many years for its lack of enforcement provisions. The identification and implementation of effective verification measures under this convention is therefore a matter for immediate international action.

A considerable part of the current debate in the UN has turned to proposals which call for the establishment of an autonomous and integrated multilateral verification system within the UN.[19] There are reasons to have reservations about these proposals. Verification under the authority of the UN would be a cooperative exercise and would require, as a precondition, cooperative input by all states to place their trust in the world organization in advance. Furthermore, the cost of installing such a verification system may not be affordable in this time of financial restraint. What is considered to be feasible, in the short run, is for the UN to assist verification on an *ad hoc* basis in the context of multilateral agreements on disarmament or arms control, provided the parties to these agreements so request. This would enable the UN gradually to gain experience and to develop some expertise. Following such a course and provided that the UN's credibility can be increased, its involvement in the verification business could be augmented. Thus, one day the stage could be reached where the UN will be entrusted with an autonomous mechanism for monitoring agreements. Additionally, the UN should continue to take enforcement action in specific cases where peace is threatened by individual states with weapon capabilities. The step taken by the Security Council and the IAEA[20] following the war in the Persian Gulf to carry out immediate on-site inspection of Iraq's biological, chemical and missile capabilities is in the right direction. In so doing, the UN demonstrated a capacity to organize intrusive inspections and to ensure the destruction of proscribed weapons systems.

THE UN DISARMAMENT MACHINERY

Over the last three years, questions concerning the adequacy of the existing UN disarmament machinery were raised by many member-states[21] which appear to agree with the UN Secretary-General's view that the machinery, established during the Cold War, "should be reassessed in order to meet the new realities and priorities of our time."[22]

There is clearly scope for improved efficiency, better functioning and coordination among the three main bodies that make up the UN disarmament machinery, namely the First Committee of the General Assembly, the Conference on Disarmament, and the Disarmament Commission. One approach to improve the efficiency of the UN disarmament machinery would be to establish a definite demarcation of roles among its component parts.

As agreed at the first special session of the General Assembly devoted to disarmament in 1978, the First Committee should continue to be the main forum for discussions in which priorities on the multilateral agenda of disarmament and arms limitation are identified for negotiation. An urgent task for the First Committee would be to streamline its own agenda to reflect the generally acknowledged reality that arms limitation and disarmament issues must be examined while bearing in mind their interrelationship with international and regional security. As the UN Secretary-General pointed out, "the time has come for the practical integration of disarmament and arms regulation issues into the broader structure of the international peace and security agenda."[23] The joint consideration of disarmament and international security questions during the 47th and 48th session of the First Committee marked a positive step as well as a good beginning for reform. Further measures should be taken towards making the First Committee more action oriented. This could be achieved by a more focused debate on a limited number of issues, the merging of related questions, a continued reduction in the number of resolutions, and the adoption of a growing number of resolutions by consensus.

The Conference on Disarmament is the only body which negotiates agreements that are global in scope. To fulfil its task to the satisfaction of the greatest number of states, the 39-member Conference has begun a reassessment of its agenda and a review of its working methods and composition. Many members have stressed the need to reduce its agenda and to concentrate on substantive issues that are ripe for intensive consideration, thus limiting the number of specialized groups functioning under its aegis. There is widespread agreement among the members of the Conference that it should continue to take decisions on the basis of consensus, which "implies the right of veto for all the participants in the negotiations."[24] As to its membership, the prevalent feeling is that if the Conference is to continue credibly to negotiate agreements for which universal adherence is required, its current composition must be altered. However, there is no agreement yet on the degree of expansion and the criteria on which such an expansion would be based. Some members have expressed their preference for a limited expansion, while others maintain that this body should be open to all states that wish to join it, otherwise its output may lack universal adherence and negate the very purpose of global negotiations; all states would accept an expansion by approximately twenty members and the Conference on Disarmament is currently in the process of defining criteria for changing its membership.[25]

The Disarmament Commission provides a forum for inter-sessional discussion of disarmament matters while the First Committee of the General Assembly is not in session. It is a subsidiary organ of the General Assembly, open to all members of the UN, and reports annually to the General Assembly and to the Conference on Disarmament. This forum has been the subject of increased criticism in recent years. Due to the apparent lack of specific goals, the Disarmament Commission has failed to provide a specialized forum for in-depth deliberations on specific disarmament issues and, therefore, to submit useful recommendations to the General Assembly. There is only a wide-ranging debate which many states have tended to view as untidy and, to a large extent, a duplication of the debate taking place in the First Committee. Over the last three years the Disarmament Commission, under pressure from the General Assembly, began to move its agenda towards a three-item approach providing for a stage-by-stage consideration of the following questions: the process of nuclear disarmament in the framework of international peace and security; a regional approach to disarmament within the context of global security; and the role of science and technology in the context of international security, disarmament and other related fields. The adoption of the three-item rolling agenda represents a modest but nevertheless important first step in reforming the Disarmament Commission with a view to making it a productive component of the UN disarmament machinery.

The essential fourth part of the UN disarmament machinery is the Office of Disarmament Affairs, which is a Secretariat coordination centre whose primary function is to service the First Committee, the Disarmament Commission and the Conferences on Disarmament. Its technical and administrative support is at the heart of the work of these organs. The Office of Disarmament Affairs has been facing an expanding number of activities including the operation of the Register of Conventional Armaments and the coordination of the regional centres for disarmament, while it is expected to play a crucial role in the inter-departmental task force to give advice on the political, economic and technical aspects of arms conversion. Given its growing workload, the Office of Disarmament Affairs should be provided with adequate personnel and funding and should continue to be located at the UN headquarters.

Recently, the Security Council has strengthened its role in disarmament and arms limitation. It is actively participating in a number of ways in the implementation of various measures, especially in the area of non-proliferation. The reference to the Security Council in the Biological and Toxic Weapons Convention (Article VI), and the Chemical Weapons Convention (Article XII-4) are examples of how this organ can be integrated into multilateral instruments to ensure compliance to them. The Security Council could also encourage the conclusion of regional disarmament agreements. Finally, the UN Institute for Disarmament Research should continue to carry out analyses, studies and research activities. The Institute could serve the UN in the field of disarmament better if it were to be linked institutionally with the activities of the Conference on Disarmament.

CONCLUSIONS

The time has arrived for the UN to assume a clearly defined role in the global negotiating process on disarmament. While the UN should not attempt to form an alternative to bilateral and regional disarmament negotiations, except in a complementary and supporting fashion, it must focus on agreements that are global in scope. It must also restructure its disarmament agenda to reflect the new global realities and priorities. Such priorities could be the strengthening of the non-proliferation regime, the granting of assurances to the NNWS, the conclusion of a comprehensive ban on testing, and transparencies in armaments. Finally, the UN disarmament machinery needs to be reformed to ensure the better coordination and functioning of its component parts.

NOTES

1. See "Joint Statement Adopted by the Security Council on Maintenance of International Peace and Security" *United Nations News*, Press Release 22/92, 1 February 1992, pp. 3-4. See also "Security Council Meets at Heads of State and Government Level", *United Nations News*, Press Release 20/92, 1 February 1992, pp. 1-9.

2. As Epstein rightly observes; see William Epstein, "UN Special Session on Disarmament: How Much Progress?", *Survival*, vol. xx, no. 6, (1978), p. 252.

3. UN Document A/C.1.47/7, 23 October 1992. This report supplements the Secretary-General's earlier report entitled *An Agenda For Peace*.

4. Dimitris Bourantonis, *The United Nations and the Quest for Nuclear Disarmament* (Aldershot: Dartmouth, 1993) pp. 152-160.

5. "Confidence and Security-Building Measures: From Europe to other Regions", *Disarmament Topical Papers*, no. 7 (New York: UN Department for Disarmament Affairs, 1991), pp. 3040 and 77-148.

6. Warwick Mckibbin, "A New Military Equilibrium?', *The Brookings Review*, vol. 11, no 4 (1993), p. 44. See also the following UN documents: A/C.1/47/PV.7, 16 October 1992, p. 26; A/C.1/47/PV.8, 16 October 1992, p. 16; A/C.1/47/PV.10, 20 October 1992, p. 53; A/C.1/47/PV.17, 23 October 1992, p. 52; A/C.1/47/PV.19, 27 October 1992, p. 21; A/C.1/47/PV.21, 28 October 1992, pp. 37-41.

7. See Secretary General of the United Nations, *Report on the Work of the Organization* (New York: United Nations, 1993), pp. 161-163.

8. The recent United States led attention on the potential nuclear capability of North Korea raises a host of issues that are beyond the scope of this paper. But these issues cannot and should not be confined to North Korea alone. There are a number of other states that are on the threshold of joining the nuclear club. They include India, Pakistan, Israel, Iran, Iraq, Argentina, Brazil and others. The politics of the issue are explosive but it cannot be ignored indefinitely. Neither should the nuclear club countries consider their possession of nuclear weapon sacrosanct. See note 13 below.

9. See "Joint Statement Adopted by the Security Council on Maintenance of International Peace and Security", *United Nations News*, Press Release 22/92, 1 February 1992, p. 3.

10. For positive and negative assurances to the non-nuclear-weapon states see *Arms Control and Disarmament Agreements* (Washington D.C: United States Arms Control and Disarmament Agency, 1990), pp. 93-96.

11. See UNGA Resolution 47/50, 9 December 1992.
12. See John Tessitore and Susan Woolfson (eds.), A Global Agenda (Washington: United Nations Association of the United States of America, 1993), p. 134. Leonard Spector, "Non-Proliferation's Balance Sheet", *The Christian Science Monitor*, 26 July 1993, p. 19.
13. The nuclear club itself is coming under increasing attack by non-nuclear states especially now that the Cold War has ended. A recent effort by the 110 members of the Non-Aligned Movement to force the issue by endorsing a UN resolution calling on the World Court to declare nuclear weapons illegal, was derailed the last minute after some high handed diplomacy by the United States, the United Kingdom and France. But this issue will not go away. See especially Mark Scharpino, "Mutiny of the Nuclear Bounty", *The Nation*, vol. 257, no. 22 (1993), pp. 789-800.
14. See *Disarmament Newsletter*, vol. 11, no. 2 (1993), pp. 6-7 and *Disarmament Newsletter*, vol. 12, no. 1 (1994), pp. 1-2; see also "Conference on Disarmament Opens 1994 Session", *United Nations News* Press Release DCF/191, 27 January 1994.
15. See UN Document A/48/344, 11 October 1993. This document contains the data that members of the UN provided to the Secretary-General during the first year of the operation of the Register.
16. See UN Document CD/TIA/INF.2/Rev.1, 27 July 1993. The document contains extracts from statements of the members of the Conference on Disarmament on transparency in armaments.
17. UN Document A/C.1/47/7, 23 October 1992, p. 10.
18. See Peter Baehr and Leon Gordenker, *The United Nations in the 1990's*, 2nd ed. (London: Macmillan, 1994), pp. 95-96.
19. See UN Document A/C.1/47/PV.6, 28 October 1992, pp. 13-14; see also UN document CD/PV.646, 18 March 1993, pp. 23-24 and UN document A/S-15/27, 3 June 1988, Annex I, p. 8.
20. *The United Nations Disarmament Yearbook 1992*, vol. 17 (New York: United Nations, 1992), pp. 248-255.
21. See UN Document A/C.1/47/PV.41, 8 March 1993 and UN Document A/C.1/47/PV.42, 8 March 1993. See also the following UN documents: A/47/887, 17 February 1993, A/47/887/Add.1, 26 February 1993 and A/47/887/Add.4, 18 March 1993.
22. UN Document A/C.1/47/7, 23 October 1992, p. 12.
23. *Ibid.*, p. 3.
24. Josef Goldblat, "The Role of the United Nations in Arms Control: An Assessment", *Arms Control*, vol. vii, no. 2 (1986), p. 128.

25. For the issue of membership see UN Document, CD/1184, 18 February 1993, pp. 6-8.

9 Human Rights Organizations and the UN: a Tale of Two Worlds

Peter R. Baehr

> Indeed, the notion that individual human rights can be protected by the international community is one of the great practical and intellectual achievements of international law.
>
> — Boutros Boutros-Ghali[1]

INTRODUCTION

Human rights are very much on the international political agenda. Fundamental human rights, such as the right to life, the physical integrity of the human person and the right to freedom of thought, conscience and religion, are violated on a massive scale in many parts of the world. At the same time, international bodies meet in formal and informal meetings to discuss ways of assuring the promotion and protection of human rights. The year 1993 witnessed the second World Conference on Human Rights in Vienna, which brought together representatives of more than 170 states and as many as 2,300 non-governmental organizations (NGOs). That conference produced the "Vienna Declaration and Programme of Action", which some hailed as showing that at least the conference had not split apart; others expressed their disappointment about the meagre results of the meeting.

From its very beginning the United Nations has been involved in the struggle for human rights. One of the purposes of the organization, listed in the Charter, is to achieve international cooperation in promoting and encouraging respect for human rights and fundamental freedoms for all without distinction as to race, sex, language or religion.[2] The Universal Declaration of Human Rights, adopted by the General Assembly in 1948, contains a list of the major standards of human rights.

170

Together with the two legally binding international conventions adopted in 1966[3] and the two Optional Protocols to the International Covenant on Civil and Political Rights (1966 and 1989), it is commonly referred to as the "International Bill of Human Rights". Now, more than forty-five years later, it seems appropriate to take stock.

In an persuasive article[4], Herman Burgers made it clear that the strong language on human rights contained in the UN Charter was not so much due to the discovery of the Nazi atrocities after the Second World War, as has often been assumed, but had started already after the First World War. He does not dispute that later efforts that brought about, among other things, the Universal Declaration of Human Rights, were to a great part motivated and strengthened by what had happened in Nazi Germany.[5] By then, the idea that "such matters should never happen again" had taken root. Writing in 1994, one is forced to admit that this idea, as strongly as it may have motivated the fathers and mothers of the Universal Declaration, has now become outdated. A world confronted with genocide in Cambodia, mass killings in Somalia, torture in Iraq and ethnic cleansing in the former Yugoslavia, knows that "such matters" have happened again and again – albeit in a different fashion.

Such awareness has not discouraged NGOs from continually pressing the cause of human rights. There are now more non-governmental human rights organizations than ever before. Many of their activities are directed at, or take place in, organs of the UN, as explicitly mentioned in the Charter.[6]

These two phenomena, UN organs on the one hand and NGOs on the other, account for a major part of the efforts on behalf of the protection and promotion of human rights in the world. Their activities and their mutual interaction are the subject of this chapter.

NON-GOVERNMENTAL HUMAN RIGHTS ORGANIZATIONS

NGOs are a curious phenomenon, as they are defined by what they are *not*. They emphasize their distance and independence from governments, yet at the same time the actions and activities of governments are the very cause and purpose of their existence. If there were no governments, there would hardly be a need for non-governmental organizations. A useful definition of a human rights NGO has been proposed by Canadian human rights expert Laurie Wiseberg as a "a private association which devotes significant resources to the promotion and protection of human rights, which is independent of both governmental and political groups that seek direct political power, and which does not itself seek such power."[7] The independence is often, though not always, interpreted as a refusal to accept financial assistance from governmental sources, referring to the old saying that who pays the piper calls the tune. Refusal of government money is also a way of showing to the outside world that a particular NGO is indeed independent, which may increase its credibility. It is clearly not enough to *be* independent; the organization should also *be seen* as independent.

The size and importance of human rights NGOs varies greatly. There are large-scale organizations such as Amnesty International (which has three times as many staff members as the entire UN Centre for Human Rights), the International Commission of Jurists and the Anti-Slavery Society. On the other hand there are many much smaller organizations, some of which encompass only very few persons, or even only one. Asbjorn Eide, a human rights expert from Norway, has pointed to the variety among NGOs: "A few of them are highly competent, well informed, constructive and effective. Others are not."[8] Other authors tend somewhat too easily to identify the notion of NGOs with such illustrious examples as Amnesty International,[9] the International Commission of Jurists and the International League for Human Rights. It would be a useful exercise to look closer at the definition of the term "non-governmental organization" and the variety of groups that are covered by that concept.

Though the number of delegates does not, of course, perfectly reflect an organization's impact, it does provide an indication of the efforts made by particular organizations. There were many less publicly known groups represented at the World Conference in Vienna who sent written contributions to the Conference. Some of such "organizations" may represent not much more than one person and a letterhead. Others, such as representatives of Kurdish, Palestinian, Basque and other opposition groups, as well as sympathizers of *Sendero Luminoso*, all of which were represented in Vienna, did not quite meet Wiseberg's definition in that these groups clearly aim for political power. That was probably also true for some groups listed in Table 1, such as the Christian Democrat International and the Liberal International, both of whom have close ties with the political parties of the same name. They differ from some of the other organizations listed in that they do not deal *exclusively* with human rights.

Table 1 NGOs with fifteen or more delegates at the World Conference on Human Rights

NGO	# of Delegates
International Federation of Human Rights	56
Women's International League for Peace and Freedom	40
World Jewish Congress	38
International Conference of Free Trade Unions	36
World Federation of United Nations Associations	35
Asian Cultural Forum on Development	33
Coalition against Trafficking in Women	31
Four Directions Council	29
Arab Organization for Human Rights	28
Latin American Federation of Associations of Relatives of Disappeared Detainees	27
International Commission of Jurists	26
Arab Lawyers Union	26
World Federation of Democratic Youth	25
Third World Movement against the Exploitation of Women	23
Disabled Peoples' International	22
Baha'i International Community	20
Christian Democrat International	20
Amnesty International	18
France Libertés – Fondation Danielle Mitterrand	17
World Young Women's Christian Association	17
Liberal International	17
International Fellowship of Reconciliation	16
Pathways to Peace	15
Habitat International Coalition	15
World Council of Indigenous Peoples	15

Source: World Conference on Human Rights, Provisional List of Attendance.

Furthermore, there is now a tendency by authoritarian regimes to set up or to support "non-governmental human rights organizations" which are linked to them. These "GONGOs" (government organized non-governmental organizations) clearly do not meet Wiseberg's criteria either. It is, however, not always easy to prove such links beyond doubt. Real human rights NGOs often have their doubts about certain human rights "study groups", especially if these are formed in countries with authoritarian regimes. Some of these clearly fall in the category of GONGOs.

What all of the 2,300 organizations represented in Vienna had in common was that they wanted to have their views heard by an international audience. For some of them that was simply enough, while many others wanted explicitly to have an impact on the results of the conference. There does not exist a commonly accepted definition to account for all human rights groups that were represented in Vienna. Henry Steiner, reporting on a meeting of human rights activists held in 1989, has written "that self-perception and self-definition by NGOs constitute the only sensible method of identifying human rights organizations." [10] He added: "An attempt at authoritative definition could block a natural and important growth of the human rights movement, such as its earlier evolution toward economic and social rights, or its present initiatives towards linking human rights concerns with developmental and environmental issues."[11] This conclusion, which seems realistic and which would leave everything open, has the important disadvantage that it leaves unclear what it means when intergovernmental organizations (IGOs) or conferences recognize the role of NGOs. The World Conference on Human Rights included in its Final Document the following passage:

The World Conference on Human Rights recognizes the important role of non-governmental organizations in the promotion of all human rights and in humanitarian activities at national, regional and international levels. The World Conference on Human Rights appreciates their contribution to increasing public awareness of human rights issues, to the conduct of education, training and research in this field, and to the promotion and protection of all human rights and fundamental freedoms. While recognizing that the primary responsibility for standard-setting lies with States, the Conference also appreciates the contribution of non-governmental organizations to this process. In this respect, the World Conference on Human Rights emphasizes the importance of continued dialogue and cooperation between Governments and non-governmental organizations. Non-governmental organizations and their members *genuinely involved in the field of human rights* should enjoy the rights and freedoms recognized in the Universal Declaration of Human Rights, and the protection of the national law. These rights and freedoms may not be exercised contrary to the purposes and principles of the United Nations. Non-governmental organizations should be free to carry out their human rights activities, without interference, *within the framework of national law* and the Universal Declaration of Human Rights.[12]

Although the quoted passage gives credit to the work of NGOs, it remains unclear what type of organizations it refers to. Moreover, the italicized words imply some kind of qualification or restriction, but it is not clear which organ should be charged with the interpretation of this clause. The precise meaning of the entire passage remains very vague, which most probably is what was intended. The statement was after all drawn up by government representatives, and governments and NGOs – at least those of the type within Wiseberg's definition – which are normally at odds with each other. As Herman Burgers – who as a former government official and later board member of the Dutch section of Amnesty International has been intimately familiar with both sides – has written, the relationship between ministries of foreign affairs and NGOs "is often coloured by mutual distrust".[13] He continued:

Usually the NGOs are asking for more action than the government is prepared to take. ... Government officials may regard NGOs as one-sided in insisting on human rights objectives without recognizing the government's wider responsibility. They may perceive some NGO appeals as an inconvenient interference with what they consider reasonable conduct of foreign policy. ... As to the other side of the relationship, NGOs may suspect the government of not being sincere in its proclaimed human rights policy.[14]

For their part, governments that have been criticized by NGOs will try to discredit the veracity of such statements. The Soviet Union used to accuse Amnesty International of being financed by imperialist secret services; it alleged that members of the staff and the board of Amnesty maintained contacts with British and American intelligence services and that it was partisan in its anti-Soviet reports. The Chinese government has made similar allegations against Amnesty International and Asia

Watch, calling their reports on rights abuses biased and politically motivated.[15]   Such accusations are not limited to the (former) communist world.   During the regional meeting for Asia in preparation of the World Conference on Human Rights in April 1993, former Thai Foreign Minister Thanat Khoman criticized self-appointed private sources and accusations of violations made for "selfish political or economic gain" and said that private organizations which arrogate to themselves the right to denounce violations should themselves be investigated.   Later, outside the conference he said that he had been referring only to Amnesty International and Asia Watch and he criticized these organizations for bias by not reporting on human rights violations in western countries. He accused Amnesty of being funded by western governments and having links with the CIA.[16]

The in-built tension between governments and NGOs in the field of human rights does not preclude close cooperation.   The Dutch Government, for instance, when working on the preparation of the International Convention against Torture in 1984, sent one of its top civil servants to the headquarters of Amnesty International in London when that organization expressed too many reservations with the proposed draft convention.   The Dutch government also sends the annual reports of Amnesty International for comment to its diplomatic missions abroad.[17]

In the end, NGOs derive their greatest impact from the degree to which they can provide reliable information about human rights situations which is not (yet) available to governments or IGOs such as UN bodies.   Philip Alston, a well-known human rights expert from Australia, has made the point that the Working Group on Enforced or Involuntary Disappearances is empowered to make use of information from any "reliable sources".   In its 1990 report it listed ninety-eight different groups with which it has been in contact since its inception. The other thematic rapporteurs have been restricted to seeking or obtaining information from NGOs or even from NGOs in consultative status with ECOSOC.[18]   It is the nature and the reliability of the information which human rights NGOs command next to the views they expound that determines their influence.   Governments that criticize human rights situations elsewhere tend to refer to information supplied by major human rights organizations such as Amnesty International, the International Commission of Jurists and Human Rights Watch, because of their reputation of reliability and nonpartisanship, even if those governments have information of their own.

THE UNITED NATIONS

Through the years, human rights have acquired a place of increasing importance at the United Nations. The annual debates in the Commission on Human Rights and other UN bodies have the character of strongly fought contests; states try to score points in this field. In recent years the European Union in close cooperation with the United States and other Western governments have tried to have the Commission pass a resolution condemning human rights practices in China, which the Chinese Government has opposed successfully so far. Although resolutions carried at the Commission do not involve sanctions they *are* seen as moral condemnations, which governments dislike. Thus the Indonesian government managed in the 1994 session of the Commission on Human Rights to avoid a resolution denouncing human rights violations in East Timor. Under heavy pressure from the European Union and especially Portugal (the former colonial master of East Timor), Indonesia – as in 1992 – had to accept a statement by the Chairman of the Commission, recalling the pledge by Indonesia to promote human rights in East Timor, stressing the need to take further steps towards its implementation and calling upon Indonesia to continue its investigation of those still missing "and the circumstances surrounding the matter". The Chairman's statement said that the Commission was encouraged by the greater access recently granted by the Indonesian authorities to human rights and humanitarian organizations and the international media, and called upon them to continue this policy of expanding access. The undertaking by Indonesia to invite the Special Rapporteur on Extrajudicial, Summary or Arbitrary Executions to visit East Timor was welcomed. [19]

Such Chairman's statements may be a useful device for recording a consensus opinion about a particular situation but they lack the authority of a resolution, as Amnesty International has pointed out. [20] During the 1993 session the Chairman made a statement concerning Sri Lanka which reflected the Sri Lankan government's intention to review and revise the emergency legislation relating to arrest and to detention, and to undertake the prosecution of those found responsible for disappearances and other human rights violations. Another Chairman's statement in 1993 expressed concern at reports of human rights violations in Tadzhikistan and called on all parties to respect the human rights of the Tadzhik people. The precise content of such Chairman's statements may involve long and difficult negotiations behind the screens. As Koen Davidse, a Dutch diplomat, has pointed out, such statements can be seen as a way of helping to foster commitment and cooperation instead of a polarization between the UN and the countries concerned. Countries can be persuaded to commit themselves to changes of policy and to international scrutiny to avoid outright condemnation. However, the proliferation of such statements could lead to a watering down of monitoring.[21]

At the same time, there has been an unwillingness on the part of the member states to provide the UN with sufficient means to deal seriously with human rights. The UN Centre for Human Rights in Geneva is notoriously understaffed and underfinanced. No more than 0.7% of the UN budget has been devoted to human rights activities. In spite of the World Conference's recommendation to that effect,[22] the subsequent General Assembly has not been willing to vote for additional funding for the UNHCR.

The location of the UN Centre in Geneva, away from the central decision-making of the UN, is another case in point. In 1974 what was then called the "Division of Human Rights" was transferred from New York to Geneva, because, as Theo van Boven has written, East European and Arab nations in particular wanted it away from the American Jewish lobby.[23]   Another reason was that the Secretary-General wanted this division, "which for all political purposes was considered more of a liability than an asset" removed from the political centre.[24] Van Boven, who is a former director of the Human Rights Division, has argued in favour of either moving the Centre back to New York or of strengthening the status of the Centre's Liaison Office in New York.[25] He is right, if the Secretary-General and the member-states would be willing to give human rights the central point of political attention it deserves. However, it is extremely unlikely that this will happen in the near future. The site given to the newly appointed High Commissioner on Human Rights is a case in point. His office is going to be located in Geneva with a liaison office in New York;[26] he has been provided with rather limited staff facilities, away from the political centre of the UN. I shall return to the position of the High Commissioner later in this chapter.

NGOs and IGOs such as the UN base their human rights activities on international human rights standards such as the Universal Declaration of Human Rights, the two international Covenants of 1966 and numerous other declarations and treaties. International functionaries in the field of human rights should ideally reflect those standards in their actions and behaviour. Among these functionaries are the Secretary-General of the United Nations, the Director of the Human Rights Centre, the Chairman of the Human Rights Commission, the Special Rapporteurs and Working

Groups and, of course, the newly appointed High Commissioner for Human Rights. Should they also publicly express criticism over human rights violations and mention the names of the countries concerned?[27] Or should they rather, in the tradition of "quiet diplomacy", limit themselves to expressing their views in private? Secretary-General Pérez de Cuéllar opted for the latter course, when he refused in 1982 to renew the contract of the director of the UN human rights division, Dr. Theo van Boven, who had criticized the human rights situation in a number of countries.[28] The issue has received a great deal of attention in a book by the British journalist Iain Guest, which contains a running indictment of efforts on the part of Argentina to cover up serious human rights violations, including involuntary disappearances.[29] He shows how, for many years, a campaign was conducted to undermine Van Boven's position and he leaves no doubt that in his opinion the UN succumbed too easily to political pressure.

In such cases, effectiveness should be the major consideration. There is no reason to assume that silence on the part of UN functionaries always helps to promote human rights. UN personnel can preeminently represent the world's conscience, as codified in international instruments. It should be a source of inspiration for human rights advocates and of hope to the victims.

HIGH COMMISSIONER FOR HUMAN RIGHTS: IDEAL AND REALITY

The idea for the creation of a High Commissioner for Human Rights was launched in the United Nations more than forty years ago, in 1947.[30] In the early years it met with little positive response. In the early sixties it received a new impetus, possibly due to the efforts of John Humphrey, the first director of the Division of Human Rights.[31] Despite the efforts of Costa Rica, Uruguay and other states, it was not adopted. That, it was widely assumed, was the end of the affair. As late as 1987 the Dutch human rights expert, Willem van Genugten, had good reason to name an article about the subject "the slow death of a good idea".[32]

Since then things have turned out to be different. In 1992, in the course of the preparations for the World Conference on Human Rights, the human rights organization Amnesty International re-introduced the idea of what it then called a Special Commissioner for Human Rights.[33] The mandate of that Special Commissioner should cover the full range of rights in the economic, social, cultural, civil and political spheres. His or her task would be to maintain an overview of all the UN's human rights activities and their relationship to other programme areas, to take initiatives and coordinate UN action in response to human rights emergencies, to ensure that appropriate attention be given to human rights concerns in any country of the world; to develop programmes in areas which have been neglected or insufficiently developed, to formulate and oversee the human rights components of other UN operations, and to ensure the integration of human rights issues and concerns in the full range of other UN activities and programmes.   The new functionary should be given sufficient authority and responsibility to respond to human rights problems on his or her own initiative to ensure that the UN acts impartially and objectively in all human rights situations deserving of attention in any region of the world, based on his own independent appraisal rather than only on the specific authorization of a governmental body.   He or she should be given the authority to spur governments to greater cooperation in tackling human rights concerns addressed to them by the UN.   Finally, the Special Commissioner should be publicly accountable in all his or her activities.   Amnesty International envisaged that the new functionary should be most appropriately based in New York "to ensure that human rights are taken seriously at the political level to secure his or her close involvement in high-level consultations and discussions on all issues with implications for human rights promotion and protection and to facilitate the liaison and coordination between the New York headquarters and the Geneva-based human rights bodies and mechanisms." If based in Geneva he or she should have a high-level representation in New York.

Amnesty's proposal received a mixed reaction initially.   The first regional preparatory meeting for the World Conference in Tunis in November 1992 did not refer to the proposal in its Final Declaration. [34] But at the inter-regional meeting organized by the Council of Europe in January 1993, it met with a generally positive attitude.   The conclusions of the General Rapporteur, President Mary Robinson of Ireland, included the statement that a Special Commissioner or other office with similar functions could more efficiently address the needs for urgent action and greater coordination of resources.   As such it should be given serious consideration. [35]   At the Latin American regional meeting in San José (from 18-22 January 1993), Costa Rica proposed the establishment of a High Commissioner.   After much debate a reference to a so-called "Permanent Commissioner" was included in the Final Declaration, but only proposing that the World Conference should consider requesting the General Assembly to study the feasibility of establishing a Permanent

Commissioner for Human Rights. The proposal was not mentioned, however, in the "Bangkok Declaration" which was the result of the Asia Intergovernmental Meeting from 29 March-2 April 1993.

At the fourth preparatory meeting in Geneva, the United States expressed its support for the creation of a High Commissioner for Human Rights. The Commissioner should monitor actions of UN organs in the field of human rights and address violations of human rights in areas where the UN has stationed peace-keeping units. He or she should also have the authority to send Special Rapporteurs to investigate allegations of human rights violations and bring such violations to the attention of the Security Council.

Nevertheless, when the World Conference in Vienna began, many delegations were still sceptical about the proposal, either because they were afraid that the new official would become too powerful, or because his or her function would be at the detriment of existing UN human rights organs such as the Centre for Human Rights and the Special Rapporteurs and Working Groups in the field of human rights. Thus – at least to outside observers – it came as somewhat of a surprise that the Final Declaration of the Vienna Conference did contain a reference to a High Commissioner:

> The World Conference on Human Rights recommends to the General Assembly that when examining the report of the Conference at its forty-eighth session, it begins, as a matter of priority, consideration of the question of the establishment of a High Commissioner for Human Rights for the promotion and protection of all human rights.[36]

Although the World Conference had accepted the principle, it was by no means sure that the General Assembly would adopt the notion of a High Commissioner along the lines of what Amnesty International had in mind. Indeed, if one compares the detailed proposal, as resubmitted in a somewhat amended form by Amnesty International in October 1993[37] with the resolution adopted by the General Assembly in December[38], major discrepancies appear (see Table 2).

What Amnesty International clearly had in mind was the appointment of an official with the authority to initiate action in the field of human rights. The General Assembly opted for an official under the directorate of the Secretary-General with much more limited possibilities. It remains to be seen whether he can avoid becoming the "super-bureaucrat" Amnesty has warned against, the more so as his relationship to the UN

Centre for Human Rights remains unclear.

Table 2 The High Commissioner for Human Rights as proposed by Amnesty International and as adopted by the General Assembly

	Amnesty International	*UN General Assembly*
Initiative	Initiate action and respond immediately to human rights crises and emergency situations.	Promote and protect the effective enjoyment of all human rights; carry out tasks assigned to him by competent UN-bodies; engage in a dialogue with all Governments; play an active role in removing current obstacles and in meeting challenges to the full realization and preventing the continuation of violations of human rights
Mandate	Integrate human rights protection and promotion into other UN programmes	Coordinate human rights promotion and protection throughout the UN system
Relationship with UN Centre	Titular and political head; no administrative and managerial responsibility	Carry out overall supervision of the UN Centre
Station	New York	Geneva

In view of the discrepancies between Amnesty's proposal and the resolution of the General Assembly the choice of the first individual to occupy this post would seem to be crucial. There exists considerable doubt whether the person selected by the Secretary-General will be able to meet the demanding criteria of this post. Amnesty International and other NGOs have expressed uncharacteristically strong reservations about the individual who was named as first High Commissioner for Human Rights, Ambassador Ayala Lasso of Ecuador. Amnesty, among others, said that it was "concerned that Ambassador Lasso's former association with a government responsible for serious human rights violations may affect his credibility and undermine his vitally important work."[39]   In the late 1970s he was a high-ranking government minister in his own country at a time when grave human rights violations were taking place under the then military government. Amnesty continued: "The organization fears that this may lead to a widely-held perception that he may not meet all the criteria for the post set out in the General Assembly resolution." However, he should be judged by what he does: "It is the actions and achievements of his office which will be crucial in dispelling any doubts or concerns which have been expressed by NGOs about his past."[40]

This new proposal for a High Commissioner for Human Rights originated from a non-governmental organization. Although – against all odds – the proposal was eventually adopted by the General Assembly, the way it was dealt with and the contents of the final decision provide a vivid illustration of the gap between the two worlds in which human rights are debated: the governmental and the non-governmental one.

CONCLUSION

Human rights are very much the subject of activities of both intergovernmental and non-governmental organizations. The NGOs see it as their task to spur IGOs, such as the UN, into action. UN Secretary-General Boutros-Ghali may have been a little over-optimistic when he mentioned the protection of individual human rights as one of the "great practical and intellectual achievements of the international community", as cited at the outset of this chapter. To the extent that there exists such a thing as an international community represented by the UN, it is very much due to the urging of NGOs that it has come into action. Many governments still see these NGOs as troublesome interferers in their domestic affairs. Yet, they cannot afford to ignore them completely, because, among other reasons, of the force of domestic and world public opinion. Some governments even try to enter the fold of the non-governmental world themselves through the device of government-supported GONGOs.

Governments have on the whole different aims than NGOs. While the latter may concentrate all their efforts on the improvement of the respect of human rights, the former have different interests to pursue as well. Such interests include the preservation of law and order, the continuation of its own regime, the protection of national and international security and the development of the national economy. Even the government of the Netherlands, which traditionally has paid a great deal of attention to the protection and promotion of human rights in its foreign policy, has mentioned it as only *one* of its policy goals among others. Thus there exists an in-built tension between governments and NGOs. This tension surfaces in the debates and decisions of the UN, which – it should always be remembered – remains an organization of states.

The history of the establishment of the High Commissioner for Human Rights has shown that governments and NGOs have different interests to pursue. The High Commissioner, as originally conceived, is a potential threat to many governments. He may push human rights concerns more than is to their liking. Therefore it is in their interest to keep his powers at a minimum. The UN Secretary-General cannot and will not do more than whatever a majority of the member states will allow him to do. That is one of the reasons why human rights manifestly are not at the top of his political agenda. That is also the reason why the human rights activities of the UN are kept away from the political centre of the organization, in Geneva rather than in New York.

The discrepancy does not rule out cooperation. Governments are often in need of the reliable information gathered by NGOs. Through their expertise, NGOs may provide material which governments can use in their negotiations. The UN Commission on Human Rights and the Sub-Commission, where NGOs have access to the floor, provide a useful meeting place for the two. For their part, NGOs make use of their contacts with friendly governments and with functionaries of international organizations to push their areas of concern. They may submit draft texts for new international human rights treaties. They submit information to UN Special Rapporteurs or working groups, which may end up in the reports of these units. NGOs also make use of intergovernmental gatherings to meet each other. The regional meetings in advance of the World Conference on Human Rights and the World Conference itself provided useful meeting grounds for NGOs as well. The phenomenon of "parallel conferences" such as have taken place at the International Women's Conferences in Copenhagen and Nairobi, are a useful spin-off of international governmental gatherings. Some of the more than 2,300 NGOs represented in Vienna agreed to meet again in the future. It remains to be seen, however, whether they will be able to mount the organizational and financial means to set up such a meeting on their own.

As was said before, the precise definition of what constitutes a non-governmental organization remains unclear. That may not be such a bad thing, if looked at purely from the point of view of their activities. It becomes a problem as soon as issues such as providing facilities in conference centres and the right to take the floor at intergovernmental gatherings, let alone the provision of financial aid, are at stake. Then NGOs working for similar aims may become fierce competitors. One thing is clear: it should not be left to governments to make the selection as to which NGO should be recognized and which not. In the end it should be left to the NGOs to organize themselves.

ACKNOWLEDGEMENTS

The author would like to thank Ineke Boerefijn, Herman Burgers, Cees Flinterman and Tiemo Oostenbrink who commented on an earlier version of this chapter.

NOTES

1. Public Address by UN Secretary-General Boutros Boutros-Ghali, The Hague, 19 January 1994.
2. UN Charter art.1 par. 3. The Charter contains many other references to human rights; see also articles 13(1b), 55(c), 56, 62(2), 68 and 76(c).
3. The International Covenant on Civil and Political Rights and the International Covenant on Economic, Social and Cultural Rights.
4. Jan Herman Burgers, "The Road to San Francisco: The Revival of the Human Rights Idea in the Twentieth Century," *Human Rights Quarterly*, vol. 14, no. 4 (November 1992), pp. 447-478.
5. Written communication by Mr. Burgers. I am obliged to him for a reference to a book by Paul Gordon Lauren, *Power and Prejudice: The Politics and Diplomacy of Racial Discrimination*, (Boulder and London: Westview Press, 1988) who emphasizes another source for the human rights idea: the irritation on the part of non-western countries over western colonialism and racial discrimination.
6. "The Economic and Social Council may make suitable arrangements for consultation with non-governmental organizations which are concerned with matters within its competence. Such arrangements may be made with international organizations and, where appropriate, with national organizations after consultation with the Member of the United Nations

concerned."(United Nations Charter, article 71).

7. Laurie S. Wiseberg, "Protecting Human Rights Activists and NGOs: What Can Be Done?", *Human Rights Quarterly*, vol. 13 (1991), p. 529. She refers to Henry J. Steiner, *Diverse Partners: Non-Governmental Organizations in the Human Rights Movement, the Report of a Retreat of Human Rights Activists* (Cambridge MA: Harvard Law School Human Rights Program and Human Rights Internet, 1990), pp. 5-15.

8. Asbjorn Eide, "The Sub-Commission on Prevention of Discrimination and Protection of Minorities," in Philip Alston (ed.), *The United Nations and Human Rights: A Critical Appraisal*, (Oxford: Clarendon Press, 1992), p. 260.

9. For a discussion of the mandate of Amnesty International see: Peter R. Baehr, "Amnesty International and its Self-Imposed Limited Mandate," *Netherlands Quarterly of Human Rights*, vol. 12, no. 1 (1994), pp. 5-21.

10. Steiner, *Diverse Partners*, note 7, p. 7.

11. *Ibid.*

12. Vienna Declaration and Programme of Action, par. 38; (italics added).

13. J. Herman Burgers, "Dutch Nongovernmental Organizations and Foreign Policy in the Field of Human Rights," in P.J. van Krieken and Ch. O. Pannenborg (eds), *Liber Akkerman: In- and Outlaws in War*, (Apeldoorn/Antwerp: MAKLU, 1992), p. 157.

14. *Ibid.*, pp. 157-158.

15. "Chinese Heap Scorn on Rights Groups" *International Herald Tribune*, 24 February 1994. A spokesman for the Chinese Foreign Ministry was quoted as follows: "It is with ulterior motives, and it is irresponsible for Asia Watch to choose this moment to publish its human rights report, which makes accusations against China." A month earlier, a Foreign Ministry spokesman said: "It is also the Chinese people themselves who have the most right to evaluate how human rights are in China." ("Beijing Resists Pressure on Human Rights," *International Herald Tribune*, 14 January 1994).

16. See: *Reuter Textline: Bangkok Post*, April 1, 1993.

17. Peter R. Baehr, "The General Assembly: Negotiating the Convention on Torture," in David P. Forsythe (ed.), *The United Nations in the World Political Economy: Essays in Honour of Leon Gordenker*, (London: Macmillan, 1989), p. 47.

18. Philip Alston, "The Commission on Human Rights," in Alston (ed.), *The United Nations and Human Rights: A Critical Appraisal*, (Oxford: Clarendon Press, 1992), p. 177.

19. *Chairman's Statement on the Situation of Human Rights in East Timor*, adopted on 9 March 1994. In a joint statement, the Greek ambassador on behalf of the European Union and the Indonesian ambassador stated their understanding that the UN Secretary-General would submit a written report to the UN Commission on Human Rights.

20. *Amnesty International's Concerns at the 50th session of the United Nations Commission on Human Rights*, (AI Index: IOR 41/38/93), (November 1993), p. 17.

21. Koen M. Davidse, "The 48th Session of the UN Commission on Human Rights and UN Monitoring of Violations of Civil and Political Rights," *Netherlands Quarterly of Human Rights*, vol. 10, no. 3 (1992), p. 294.

22. "The World Conference on Human Rights stresses the importance of strengthening the United Nations Centre for Human Rights." *Vienna Declaration and Programme of Action*, adopted by the World Conference on Human Rights on 25 June 1993, II A, par. 13. In this context it was significant that it failed to use words such as "high priority" or "from the regular budget".

23. Theo C. van Boven, "The Role of the United Nations Secretariat," in Philip Alston (ed.), *The United Nations and Human Rights: A Critical Appraisal*, (Oxford: Clarendon Press, 1992), p. 561.

24. Van Boven, *ibid.*

25. With regard to this subject the Vienna Declaration uses similar words: "The Centre for Human Rights should play an important role in coordinating system-wide attention for human rights. The focal role of the Centre can best be realized if it is enabled to cooperate fully with other United Nations bodies and organs. The coordinating role of the Centre for Human Rights also implies that the office of the Centre for Human Rights in New York is strengthened." (*Vienna Declaration and Programme of Action*, IIA, par. 14).

26. UNGA resolution A 48/141, 20 December 1993.

27. The remainder of this paragraph as well as the following paragraph are taken from Peter R. Baehr, "Human Rights: A Common Standard of Achievement?" *Netherlands Quarterly of Human Rights*, vol. 9, no. 1 (1991), pp. 13-14.

28. Cambodia, Uganda, Chile, Iran, El Salvador and Guatemala. Cf. Howard Tolley Jr., *The UN Commission on Human Rights*, (Boulder and London: Westview Press, 1987), p. 107.

29. Iain Guest, *Behind the Disappearances: Argentina's Dirty War Against Human Rights and the United Nations*, (Philadelphia: University of Pennsylvania Press, 1990).

30. See: R.S. Clark, *A United Nations High Commissioner for Human Rights*, (The Hague: Martinus Nijhoff, 1972).

31. John P. Humphrey, *Human Rights and the United Nations: A Great Adventure*, (Dobbs Ferry N.Y.: Transnational Publishers, 1983), pp. 296 ff.

32. W.J.M. van Genugten, "Hoge Commissaris voor de Rechten van de Mens: de Langzame Dood van een Goede Gedachte," ["The High Commissioner for Human Rights: Slow Death of a Good Idea"], *Internationale Spectator*, vol. XLI, no. 9 (September 1987), pp. 463-467.

33. Amnesty International, *World Conference on Human Rights, Facing Up to the Failures: Proposals for Improving the Protection of Human Rights by the United Nations*, AI Index: IOR 41/16/92, (December 1992).

34. Although formally launched only in December 1992, it had been discussed before on an informal basis.

35. Mary Robinson, "Human Rights at the Dawn of the 21st Century: Interregional Meeting organized by the Council of Europe in advance of the World Conference on Human Rights, Strasbourg, 28-30 January 1993, Conclusions by the General Rapporteur," *Human Rights Quarterly*, vol. 15, no. 4 (November 1993), p. 634.

36. *Vienna Declaration and Programme of Action* II A. "Increased coordination on human rights within the United Nations system," par. 18.

37. Amnesty International, *United Nations: A High Commissioner for Human Rights, Time for Action*, AI Index: IOR 41/35/93, (October 1993).

38. UNGA resolution 48/141, 20 December 1993. For paragraph 4, which contains the mandate of the High Commissioner, see appendix.

39. AI INDEX: IOR 41/WU 02/1994, (1 February 1994).

40. *Ibid.* When interviewed, the newly appointed High Commissioner acknowledged that his mandate was "vague but also very wide". He said that he would not be neutral. In regard to governments that refused to cooperate, he said: "If nothing else works, we will go public. We will shame them into compliance." ("Q&A: UN Human Rights Chief 'Won't Be Neutral'", *International Herald Tribune*, 14 March 1994).

APPENDIX

United Nations General Assembly resolution 48/141: High Commissioner for the Promotion and Protection of Human Rights, (adopted 20, December 1993)

Paragraph 4. **Decides** that the High Commissioner for Human Rights shall be the United Nations official with principal responsibility for United Nations human rights activities under the direction and authority of the Secretary-General; within the framework of the overall competence, authority and decisions of the General Assembly, the Economic and Social Council and the Commission on Human Rights, the High Commissioner's responsibilities shall be:

(a) To promote and protect the effective enjoyment by all of all civil, cultural, economic, political and social rights;

(b) To carry out the tasks assigned to him/her by the competent bodies of the United Nations system in the field of human rights and to make recommendations to them with a view to improving the promotion and protection of all human rights;

(c) To promote and protect the realization of the right to development and to enhance support from relevant bodies of the United Nations system for this purpose;

(d) To provide, through the Centre for Human Rights of the Secretariat and other appropriate institutions, advisory services and technical and financial assistance, at the request of the State concerned and, where appropriate, the regional human rights organizations, with a view to supporting actions and programmes in the field of human rights;

(e) To coordinate relevant United Nations education and public information programmes in the field of human rights;

(f) To play an active role in removing the current obstacles and in meeting the challenges to the full realization of all human rights and in preventing the continuation of human rights violations throughout the world, as reflected in the Vienna Declaration and Programme of Action;

(g) To engage in a dialogue with all Governments in the implementation of his/her mandate with a view to securing respect for all human rights;

(h) To enhance international cooperation for the promotion and protection of all human rights;

(i) To coordinate the human rights promotion and protection activities through the United Nations system;

(j) To rationalize, adapt, strengthen and streamline the United Nations machinery in the field of human rights with a view to improving its efficiency and effectiveness;

(k) To carry out overall supervision of the Centre for Human Rights.

10 Realpolitik and the CNN Factor of Humanitarian Intervention

Edward Newman

The relationship between the needs and rights of humans and the norms and practicalities of international relations has been prominent in the mainstream post-Cold War political agenda. An apparently greater willingness on the part of many governments to address the issue, the improved capacity of the United Nations to orchestrate collective humanitarian operations, and a number of well-publicized tragedies have helped to achieve this. However, while the possibilities of humanitarian intervention seem increasingly to exist, there remain doubts regarding its worthiness and practicality. Even with the potential for strides in humanitarian collective internationalism, there are perennial tensions in the interaction between multilateral possibilities and international realities, and these are systemic, aside from the much touted Cold War/post-Cold War dichotomy. These tensions – largely political, legal, practical and financial – are inevitably reflected in the UN, and are central to the wider debate regarding the future of multilateralism, especially in the field of international peace and security. Indeed, the international community is in an era of transition; collective approaches to humanitarian assistance and intervention constantly challenge the mechanisms of international organization and precariously pave the way to the future. In interpreting the developments of recent years, however, one must remain open-minded when identifying trends. Academics and journalists have in particular succumbed to the temptation of prematurely formulating "post-Cold War trends" which have been overtaken by events; the post-Cold War "honeymoon", Iraq and Resolution 688, and a number of isolationist scares are examples of this.

The Iraqi case has encouraged the attitude that state sovereignty does not represent an insurmountable obstacle to action on behalf of the international community in situations of grave human suffering. This article aims to address this whilst illustrating that policy making at the national and international level in this area is usually an amalgamation of divergent standpoints, competing interests and ad hoc decision making. In addition, it aims to demonstrate that discussion has centred too much on legality and the question of whether there is a right or a duty — *droit* or *devoir d'ingérence*[1] — to alleviate human suffering, whereas the question of the will, capability, and political coherence on the part of governments and the UN is equally as important, especially now that intervention is increasingly associated with situations where the traditional conception of consent and sovereignty is not clear. This, in turn, is underpinned by the exigencies of public pressure and geopolitics.

WHAT IS HUMANITARIAN INTERVENTION?

Humanitarian intervention is action across recognizable territorial boundaries ostensibly aimed at alleviating grave human need, be it the result of starvation, disease, atrocity or gross persecution, widespread dispossession, or the imminent danger of these or other threats. It has been used to describe short term action in response to immediate need, either with or without the consent of the recipient territory, longer term reconstruction involving the distribution of food, medical equipment, shelter, and also military protection and rescue. This type of action has been conducted on a unilateral or multilateral basis. Humanitarian intervention has been associated with situations of government persecution of the citizens of its state, government persecution of the citizens of another state within its territory, civil war, conditions of failed statehood and anarchy, and in cases of natural disaster.

It is essential to emphasize that failing statehood has prompted much of the debate concerning humanitarian intervention. Although this is not a new phenomenon, if one were seeking a point of departure from the Cold War to the post-Cold War humanitarian agenda, this would undoubtedly form part of the equation. As Falk has stated, "the challenge of the weak state is moving to the centre of concern,"[2] and the attitude of the international community in response forms a major part of the subject of humanitarian intervention. Vulnerable states are those chiefly of the Third World, typically struggling under the legacy of spurious colonial boundaries in the case of Africa, the collapse of dictatorial rule and the semblance of authority and order, premature decolonization, and abject poverty. Although many tribal and ethnic animosities are indigenous in origin, there is a strong argument to suggest that the colonial overlords, where they existed, and in turn the interference of Cold War politics, severely weakened or destroyed traditional structures of authority. During the Cold War the sovereignty of many such states was partly propped-up by aid and the support of vying superpowers. Now that the support is gone, the corrupt leaders are being toppled, leaving anarchy and a glut of weapons. Fragmentation and ethnic hostility are the only identities which exist, and the lawlessness which often accompanies this can result in the most harrowing of human suffering. It is, therefore, correct to suggest that the "[i]nstabilities and insecurities that abound in the Third World are largely a function of the historical juncture at which most Third World states find themselves."[3]

In addition to the moral responsibility to intervene where possible to alleviate the suffering which usually follows state collapse, there is a real need to consider the international repercussions of state failure. The spill-over from such circumstances can create innumerable problems; as Boutros-Ghali has suggested "[y]ou will pay the price sooner or later if you don't intervene. And later it could cost you 10 times more."[4] However, humanitarian intervention in such circumstances almost inevitably leads to further tasks of reconstruction. There is no hope of the "surgical operation" so beloved in the West, and a host of problems arise requiring great commitments by the international community. Yet if the failing of states becomes "a familiar facet of international life",[5] the international community must respond with more understanding and farsightedness than has been demonstrated so far.

An important distinction must be made between intervention which is under the auspices of the United Nations — either directly coordinated, or authorized, by the Security Council — and that which is not. The most important distinction, however, is between action which has the consent of the recipient state — either expressly or tacitly — and that which does not, through the opposition of the government or in circumstances where a government can no longer be said to exercise legal jurisdiction. From these factors — the *what, when,* and *who* of humanitarian intervention — one can draw a loose legal and political framework which has a bearing upon the usual questions raised with this subject: is intervention necessary and legal in a particular case? Is humanitarian intervention the prerogative of the strong against the weak, or the North against the South? Can it involve structural change in the recipient state? Is humanitarian intervention a mask for ethnocentrism or neo-colonialism? Or can humanitarian intervention in the post-Cold War world, free from the geopolitics of bipolarity and spheres of influence, finally live up to its altruistic rhetoric? What is the relationship between the United Nations and non-governmental organizations (NGOs) in the provision of humanitarian assistance? Can the international community devise an acceptable blueprint and multilateral mechanisms for intervention which could overcome the present disagreements on when to assist, and how to coordinate and pay for these operations?

Before addressing such questions it is essential to distinguish between the different agendas underpinning humanitarian intervention. In particular, one can identify the separate, but by no means mutually exclusive, political,[6] strategic,[7] legal,[8] moral,[9] practical,[10] and financial dimensions which sometimes converge but often compete behind the stances of governments and by extension the activities of the UN. This is an important exercise: it is the alignment of these factors which largely determines whether a humanitarian operation will be initiated under the UN and if it will have the support necessary for success. These factors should be the focus of attention, for they form the basis of unilateral and collective action under the UN; theoretically the activities of NGOs, discussed below, should be more objective and single-minded. As a starting point, one FCO participant at the conference was candid in stating that amongst the numerous issues at play in humanitarian intervention, "realpolitik forces our hand at all times."[11]

INTERNATIONAL LAW

The legal basis for humanitarian intervention should not be regarded simply as a convenient complementary factor; legal mistakes can and do cause problems. Nevertheless, the British Foreign Office does not deny that humanitarian intervention is surrounded in a vague legality.[12] The fundamental factor is the question of consent and sovereign territorial integrity, whereby a state occupies a definite part of territory and exercises jurisdiction over persons and things to the exclusion of other states or entities.[13] Further to this, the existence and nature of Security Council support for humanitarian intervention is of great importance.

Historically, humanitarian intervention in breach of the sovereignty of a state has been condemned by treaty and customary international law. The statist Westphalian conception of international society, reflected in countless legal instruments, has culminated in the legal, if not actual, sanctity of state sovereignty. The UN Charter, most notably Article 2(4) and 2(7), and a number of landmark resolutions, support this.[14] Generally, state practice also reflects this, including the questionable legality of forceful humanitarian intervention. For example, in 1979 after Vietnamese forces overthrew Pol Pot in Cambodia, Vietnam made no claim of humanitarianism and the action was widely condemned: "[n]ot a single state spoke in favour of the existence of a right of humanitarian intervention."[15] In the same year in Africa three oppressive regimes were overthrown — Bokassa in the Central African Republic, Macias Nguema in Equatorial Guinea, and Idi Amin of Uganda — with the presence of external involvement, yet none of the foreign parties attempted to "invoke" the principle of humanitarian intervention. State practice is likewise unsupportive of such intervention even in cases of the emergency rescue of nationals without the consent of the target state. Cases such as the successive Belgian interventions in the Congo, the US intervention in the Dominican Republic in 1965, the 1976 Israeli raid at Entebbe in Uganda, and the 1980 attempt by the US to release members of its embassy from Iran, were widely questioned from a legal standpoint and often defended more in terms of an extended form of self defence. This norm of nonintervention is not significantly challenged by the argument that force can sometimes be used and not necessarily be directed against the territorial integrity or political independence of a state if it is limited to legitimate and temporary humanitarian objectives and not directed against the structure or domestic institutions of the country. It is an issue of territorial inviolability.

Clearly Article 2(7) of the Charter does not preclude action authorized by the Security Council without the consent of the target state if a threat to the maintenance of international peace and security in the context of Chapter VII exists. For much of the post-1945 period, however, this has been defined very much in a traditional international security sense, whether or not a grave humanitarian issue constitutes such a threat to order. In fact the British Foreign Office has suggested that there is a problem of legal precedence which acts as a significant influence, and therefore limitation, on action. Indeed, the Security Council may often wish to act on humanitarian grounds, but can be reluctant, even when China is not an obstacle, due to the fear of future repercussions.[16] There is no doubt that the UN, reflecting the pervading state-centric attitude which is inseparable from the present structure of international relations, places more emphasis on the need for order and stability expressed in Article 2(4) and 2(7) than on the rights of humans expressed in Article 1 and indeed the rights of civilians embodied in the Geneva Conventions and their two Protocols.[17]

However, since the end of the Cold War there arguably has been progress in state practice through the United Nations, and in attitudes, towards an adjustment of the balance between human needs and state sovereignty. Central to this is the question of humanitarian need within the UN conception of peace and security. In this respect a most important legal trend would be a wider acceptance of the idea that humanitarian suffering on a large scale represents a threat to international peace and security and that there is an obligation to respond to this new dimension of collective security. This is clearly a popular theme, rejecting as it does the distinction between international and domestic sources of conflict. A second fundamental trend would be a wider acceptance of the principle that, irrespective of international peace and security, grave humanitarian suffering must be addressed by the international community within the framework of the UN, either by right or obligation, even without the consent of the recipient territory.[18] Finally, one might expect a greater recognition from the legal perspective that the concepts of sovereignty and consent, in the context of failed statehood, are no longer inviolable in absolute terms.

THE POST-COLD WAR: NEW DAWN OR FALSE DAWN?

Some years after their publication, Pérez de Cuéllar's famous words appear to have greater relevance:

> It is now increasingly felt that the principle of non-interference with the essential domestic jurisdiction of States cannot be regarded as a protective barrier behind which human rights could be massively or systematically violated with impunity. ... [T]he case for not imping-ing on the sovereignty, territorial integrity and political independence of States is by itself indubitably strong. But it would only be weakened if it were to carry the implication that sovereignty ...includes the right of mass slaughter or of launching systematic campaigns of decimation or forced exodus of civilian populations in the name of controlling civil strife or insurrection.[19]

It is not difficult to find such sentiment; in fact, many commentators would take the argument further.[20] This should be seen in the context of the immediate post-Cold War "honeymoon"[21] of the United Nations, characterized by a renewed sense of vigour and collective international-ism. Indeed, duties to non-nationals and respect for human rights within the framework of the United Nations was one tenet of the New World Order. The case which apparently embodied this historic development was that of Resolution 688 of 1991, which insisted that Iraq allow access by humanitarian organizations to alleviate the suffering and danger to the civilian population of that country. Although there is some disagreement concerning the exact status of Resolution 688 the British Foreign Office insists that, although it cites "international peace and security", the resolution was not adopted under the mandatory language of Chapter VII and therefore did not include enforcement provisions.[22] Nevertheless, this was greatly significant through the threat or use of force on behalf of the international community in the interests of humanitarianism, at least on the face of it. According to one commentator, "[o]ne precedent does not constitute a pattern but Security Council Resolution 688 and the efforts to assist Kurdish refugees have blurred considerably the distinction between domestic jurisdiction and international responsibilities."[23]

THE UN FRAMEWORK

In the context of a number of other cases and institutional developments, the Iraq provisions could be looked upon as something of a watershed. In Somalia, despite the eventual problems, it has been suggested that the Council gave a clearer mandate in Resolution 794 where there are copious uses of the word "humanitarian".[24] According to Boutros-Ghali, this "established a precedent in the history of the United Nations: it decided for the first time to intervene militarily for strictly humanitarian purposes. By that resolution the Council authorized the use of all necessary means to establish as soon as possible a secure environment for humanitarian relief operations in Somalia."[25] Also, international efforts in the former Yugoslavia have at times attained the status of coercive protection and relief assistance.

The significance of Resolution 688 as opening the way to an environment of interventionism should not, however, be exaggerated. It should be seen in the context of the overall effort on the part of the allies through the UN to subdue and reverse the aggression of Iraq, and perhaps the customary rights which victors have over their vanquished; 688 was not the "Holy Grail" of authorization.[26] The assistance was in the context of wider events. In addition, it is important to note how much the actual implementation of 688 involved, or even relied upon, the cooperation and consent of Iraq through the Memorandum of Understanding.[27] Finally, it is essential to recognize how the alignment of political and geopolitical factors — both within the allied countries and internationally — was conducive to the commitments made by the allies.

In different circumstances since and before that case, especially when media interest — the "CNN factor"[28] — has not played such a significant role in whipping up domestic support in the West for action, the UN and its prominent members have been much more reluctant to act with force on humanitarian grounds. It might be overstating to assert that the intervention in Iraq was "blatantly politically motivated",[29] although the domestic political and geopolitical motives are no secret. The allies had encouraged a Kurdish insurgence, which created an element of responsibility for humanitarian assistance in response to the subsequent well-publicized Iraqi crackdown; Western domestic pressure was central. Simultaneously the UN action, whilst it was part of a program to keep Iraq down and to remind the world of the morality of the New World Order, never contemplated the creation of a more autonomous Kurdish territory, or the territorial or internal dismemberment of Iraq. Such action would have set a precedent most unsavoury to the permanent members of the Security Council and upset the local power-balance *vis-à-vis* Iran. Thus, while the Iraqi case broke new ground, it was contingent upon an alignment of circumstances in New York and in the capitals of the most powerful states. Most importantly, because the situation in Iraq already had been "internationalized" and there was a visible threat to the regional stability — not least through the movement of refugees — it was not a case of intervening into the purely internal affairs of a state possessed of the full rights of sovereignty.

How have UN and NGO efforts risen to the challenge of increasing burdens and wider mandates? It is necessary to make a distinction here between the drama of the above cases which involved the forceful delivery of relief, an element of peace enforcement, and even state-building in situations of state breakdown or widespread human suffering, from the actual organization and coordination of relief in these and less high-profile cases. This relates to the command and control of military personnel when involved, the coordination of UN agencies, and the relationship between them and NGOs. Within the UN there has been a movement towards a model of "post-conflict peace-building" aimed at integrating the protection of human needs and the repatriation of refugees in "comprehensive efforts to identify and support structures which will tend to consolidate peace and advance a sense of confidence and well-being among people."[30] The current catch-phrase, "towards a coordinated United Nations response,"[31] suggests coordinated planning and implementation involving the departments of Political Affairs, Peace-keeping Operations and Humanitarian Affairs in New York, and the UN Children's Fund, the Joint UN/FAO World Food Programme, and the

UN High Commissioner for Refugees on the ground. New thinking thus stresses the importance of linking humanitarian action and refugee assistance with peacemaking and peace maintenance, in particular with regard to the infrastructural requirements of the societies in need: "[r]ehabilitation and reconstruction must accompany emergency relief."[32] The Administrative Committee on Coordination — chaired by the Secretary-General — strives to improve the efficiency and coordination of departments and agencies. Progress is under way, although there are bureaucratic obstacles — even inter-office "turf wars" — to be overcome.[33]

Concrete developments arose out of the "pioneering debate"[34] on the capacity of the UN to coordinate humanitarian assistance, leading to Resolution 46/182 of 1991 and the Department of Humanitarian Affairs (DHA) in March 1992. This established an Emergency Relief Coordinator and resident relief coordinators; the Inter-Agency Standing Committee due to meet every 2 years with the inclusion of leading NGOs such as the International Committee of the Red Cross and the International Federation of the Red Cross and Red Crescent Societies; and a Consolidated Appeal Fund.[35] The Revolving Fund has been a success, reaching its target of $50 million and financing urgent humanitarian action in Afghanistan, Georgia, Iraq, Kenya, Lebanon, Mozambique, Somalia, Tadzhikistan and the former Yugoslavia. By September 1993 new coordinated arrangements under the DHA have helped launch 17 inter-agency consolidated appeals for over $16 billion for relief and rehabilitation programmes in some 20 countries.[36] In particular, the wider approaches to natural and man-made tragedies, straddling the humanitarian and political realms, are reported to be proving appropriate in such countries as the Sudan, Kenya, Ethiopia, and Southern Africa, and the work of the UNHCR is recognized as being central to the containment of further suffering and preventing the spread of instability.[37] However, concerning the coordination and control of the military dimension of humanitarian intervention and the principle of preparedness there has been little progress. The military components of UN authorized operations have either remained under national control or exhibited a rather ambiguous coordination. Whilst the ideal may be, for some, that "[t]he UN needs to be able to plan, staff and launch military operations,"[38] the reality is that the UN "cannot conduct military operations on its own. That is the business of sovereign states."[39] The resulting reliance on Member States' forces, and the reflection of the political processes within those states upon an operation, can produce a less than whole-hearted performance.

NON-GOVERNMENTAL ORGANIZATIONS

There has been progress in the relationship between NGOs and the UN system in the field of humanitarian assistance in the post-Cold War world, but not to the complete satisfaction of the NGO community and a number of other observers.[40] There is an unavoidably different ethos, motive, and basis for operation underlying NGOs and intergovernmental organizations (IGOs), and it is only in recent years that the paths of both have converged productively. It is now increasingly accepted that NGOs play a vital − and officially sanctioned and funded − role in dealing with crises in cooperation with governmental aid agencies and the UN. General Assembly Resolution 43/131 of 1988 recognized the important role that NGOs have performed in the provision of essential supplies in civil strife and has been described as a "milestone".[41] Their profile has risen in line with a number of high-profile cases; they have been shown to have improved their level of professionalism; and NGOs have demonstrated greater flexibility in a number of circumstances than UN-related agencies. It has been suggested that NGOs' ability to respond quickly and single-mindedly, the freedom they have to apply action-centred and functional arrangements, can be contrasted with the procedural and "proper" restraints of their IGO counterparts.[42] This may be reflected in the high proportion of national aid which is now channelled through NGOs.[43] In addition, coordination between NGOs has existed for some time in the form of umbrella organizations such as the Steering Committee for Humanitarian Response, representing seven leading NGOs.

Despite the progress towards a closer working relationship between NGOs and the UN − in particular through the UNHCR, DHA, and the Inter-Agency Standing Committee − there has been evidence of antagonism and competition between them. One NGO representative has complained about the lack of participation in decision-making within the UN and national foreign offices, stating that "we are usually ignored."[44] Moreover in the field some NGOs fear that their impartiality and principles − and even safety − may be in jeopardy through a close association with the UN.[45] However, this should not detract too much from a basically positive trend in this area.

What is perhaps more worrying are allegations, in the midst of the burgeoning NGO community, concerning malpractice, spurious motives, and poor levels of professionalism amongst the smaller organizations. For example, at one point there were some 90 NGOs involved in

Somalia, with often little coordination and overlapping mandates. There has been criticism of the "vultures"[46] among them, attracted to disasters for the wrong reasons, and the "unseemly jealousies" that some agencies have exhibited.[47] One Southern commentator has lamented that "[m]any disaster experts turn out to be beachcombers and adventurers out to make a quick buck with doubtful credentials as relief aid administrators."[48] The FCO/BISA Conference reflected some such concerns, but the consensus was that, while there is certainly room for improving the accountability of some NGOs, the majority perform admirably a crucial service in often difficult conditions, sometimes where UN agencies cannot. Future progress depends upon a utilization of the qualities of all types of agencies in cooperation; there is no room for competition in the face of suffering.

Pitfalls

The problems associated with the theory and practice of humanitarian intervention and assistance are of a normative, political, legal, practical, and financial nature. Firstly, for a number of years there has been the suggestion that humanitarian intervention alludes to a neo-imperialist ethos or intention, in terms of ethnocentrism, geopolitics, or economic self-aggrandizement.[49] According to such a view, the only change that has accompanied post-Cold War developments is perhaps the motive behind humanitarian intervention, away from the geopolitical demands of bipolarity. However inappropriate the reference to Kipling might be, the paternalism of the "White Man's Burden" is a tradition which has not been forgotten.[50] Some commentators – most vociferously those of the South – have berated a perceived superiority behind humanitarian assistance, and "the humiliation and the degrading paternalism that have accompanied aid work for many years."[51] The neo-colonialist connotations have become clearer for two reasons: first, the trend towards failed statehood in the South and subsequent ideas of state-building and guardianship in the North; and second, the increasing significance of the military factor to humanitarian intervention and assistance. The first of these is the corollary of the idea that in the early post-war period "self determination ... was given more attention than long-term survivability."[52] Such territories are said to be unable to sustain the order and institutions necessary to support a society and qualify as a sovereign state, endangering their own citizens and regional security, and giving rise to corrupt leaders or anarchy. In the worst circumstances – such as Somalia and Liberia – there is a strong argument for such guardianship within the framework of the UN, if the elements of the Charter which preclude this and the opposition of China could be overcome.[53] The international community should not be afraid to recognize when the legal concept of sovereignty does not correlate to reality, even when the implications of this invoke the trusteeship spirit.

Support for coercive intervention is a source of great concern amongst potential target states and the South in general. This can be seen in the context of the wider North-South debate in response to the intrusive implications within post-Cold War UN developments in international peace and security, spurred on by *An Agenda for Peace*.[54] However, the North-South dimension should not be exaggerated: humanitarian intervention is not confined to this in terms of the recipients of such assistance and the composition of humanitarian operations. Likewise the development of UN mechanisms in international peace and security and the question of military force is not only a North-South dialogue; a wide variety of states and individuals dedicated to the traditional model of peace-keeping fear its contamination by "new" techniques.

The motives of intervening forces or aid agencies is relevant to the rather abstract neo-colonialist debate, yet are also important in a case-by-case sense. Even when intervention is within the framework of the UN, one must often look beyond the words of the Security Council at the interests of the states supporting the operation. According to one academic participant at the FCO/BISA conference, "we are never going to get a pure motive"; a mixture of motives must be identified.[55] Within this mixture there may not necessarily be anything wrong with a perceived interest — such as that which some observers have associated with the French presence in Rwanda in June and July 1994[56] — when it does not interfere with the humanitarian objectives, especially when there is no alternative. In fact, in an environment where the agenda of Western policy is influenced by the media, and *inter alia* the public, overlapping national interests may help to maintain a commitment; as Somalia demonstrated, public support for humanitarianism in another land can reverse when a dearer interest, that of American lives, is at stake.

However, a hazard which is involved in the idea of interests occurs when the intervening force or organization is not impartial towards local politics, or is not perceived as being so. There are painful memories of Beirut in the early 1980s in this respect, when the multilateral force became embroiled in local politics. Likewise, in an environment where regional organizations are increasingly being urged to share the burden of low level intervention and employ the advantages of their composition and geographical disposition, there are further issues of partiality. There are obvious practical advantages to a regional solution, and cultural and ethnic similarities can be less disturbing than alien assistance, especially in the environment of North-South intervention and neo-colonialist sensitivity. Indeed, there is a palpable aversion amongst much of the South to the idea of Northern, and especially European or American, troops on their soil. Moreover, a number of regional operations have been successful. However, there is much truth in the idea that "[t]he chief advantage of a regional approach — proximity to the conflict — is often also its most conspicuous disadvantage."[57] Clearly local solutions are often tied to local antagonisms and power balances; if neighbours are involved in fuelling a conflict, for example, how can they help put out the fire? The main challenge to this is the opinion that one should not necessarily condemn a local solution if a local great power has an interest — such as Nigeria towards Liberia — because it may be the only option.[58]

United Nations humanitarian operations are not above local politics and the appearance of partialities; a popular argument holds that "[i]ntervention for humanitarian purposes leads, inevitably, to political tasks."[59] This opens up a number of issues regarding the often uneasy mixture of humanitarian and military dimensions to many such operations. In the context of domestic and factional fighting — typically the environment when humanitarian assistance has a military accompaniment — the situation can be fraught with danger. Ideally, a humanitarian operation — even one with a military component — should be distinct not only from local politics, but also UN political and peace-keeping efforts, and obviously military enforcement. However, the reality is often different, especially where a humanitarian operation escalates to a *de facto* military operation as a result of developments on the ground. Somalia and the former Yugoslavia reflect this trend: the "quagmire" scenario of shifting local conditions, demanding further commitment. Military force, even when authorized by the Security Council, is incompatible with purely humanitarian assistance. When the two are combined the impartiality of the intervention can be put into question; the withdrawal of the operation may become more difficult politically; the safety of the aid workers and their protectors becomes an important issue; the command and control of the operation become more sensitive, complicated and expensive; and the interaction between the policy decisions of the governments which are providing personnel and materials and their domestic constituencies will tend to become more volatile.

This latter point relates to the triangle of the media, public opinion, and governmental support for UN humanitarian operations. Many commentators have noted the influence upon Western governments of domestic opinion, and by corollary, that foreign policy is partly for domestic consumption. When the media is so efficient in communicating the events of faraway countries the "CNN factor" is often the variable which foments pressure upon governments and the United Nations to intervene in desperate situations, yet likewise can be the key to turning public opinion against such operations when difficulties or complications arise.[60] For example, at the end of July 1994, President Clinton all but admitted that the decision to send US military personnel under UN auspices to help distribute aid to refugees in the border regions of Rwanda and Zaire was in response to media coverage of the tragedy there.[61] This is a recipe for inconsistency and vacillation; it also partly accounts for the difficulty in attempting to identify post-Cold War trends in multilateralism. The US participation in the Somalia operation and its varying support for multilateral efforts in the aftermath is the classic example of this, and the various stands of the international community in the former Yugoslavia likewise illustrate the point. Inconsistency and half-heartedness can be detrimental to humanitarian efforts in specific cases and in general; the "safe havens" programme in Bosnia, for example, has been described as "half-baked" and "damaging" to the credibility of the Security Council.[62] The late response in Somalia formed a part of one commentator's claim that "[r]elief efforts in Somalia in 1992 constitute a searing case study of failure."[63] Early efforts under the UN − urged by the Secretary-General [64] − could surely have helped reduce the scale of the humanitarian disaster in Rwanda and Zaire following the explosion of violence in the former country, and perhaps lessened the effort which became necessary when the enormity of the refugee problem became clear. However, whilst most would support an ounce of prevention in principle, the practice is well known to be hazardous. Similarly, the problem is not one of early warning, for there is plenty of this: the challenge is to act on the basis of it with prudence.[65]

Popular concerns about the "slippery slope" of intervention and images of national forces being imperilled for an ambiguous "foreign" cause, or being entrenched in a "quagmire" of local fighting, figure strongly in the foreign departments of the prominent members of the UN. There seems little doubt, for example, that the United States is still under the yoke of the "Vietnam Syndrome" and the fear of overextension; an image still invoked by Kissinger.[66]   Accordingly, the debate between neo-isolationist and internationalist feelings underlies the US support for the UN. This is something which transcends the Cold War/post-Cold War watershed, and there is evidence to suggest that, after the optimism of the post-Cold War "honeymoon", the neo-isolationist movement in the US is gaining ground. This is something which inevitably pervades the atmosphere and performance of the UN. Indeed, a recent Presidential document reflects the determination for caution and the importance of having clear goals, a specified "sunset provision", and the continuing support of Congress and the public.[67]

In line with this, the British Government has sought to clarify its position towards UN humanitarian operations. With the recognition that the international community has had its "fingers burnt" on one or two occasions recently, there is a need to tread carefully in potential minefields. This is especially so in the face of civil conflict, fragmentation and failed statehood. Indeed, the public impulse is often that "more must be done", yet the international community must be wary of slipping inexorably into war or overextension: the UN cannot do everything, "it cannot wipe the tear from every eye", and certainly not in the post-Cold War world where the freedom for Security Council activity and numerous trouble spots represent an endless agenda of possible causes.[68]

Therefore, an assessment of the theory, practice and realpolitik of humanitarian intervention would appear to raise a number of issues which must be addressed — especially within governments and the UN — and satisfied before a serious commitment is made to such operations with a military component. These are clearly centred around legal, practical and political prudence:[69]

1. There should be clear and achievable goals attached to a potential case.
2. There must be the political will — chiefly in the context of the P5 members — to maintain sight of the goals.
3. There should be the commitment and resources necessary to transform will into action.
4. The situation should warrant intervention on practical grounds; there should be no alternative short of intervention.
5. Intervention must be in response to an immediate and widespread human crisis which cannot be met locally or within the territory in question.
6. Command and control arrangements must be appropriate, and

the practical and financial burdens acceptable.

7. The scale, duration and scope of intervention must be limited; it should be adequate only to ensure the success of the humanitarian objective, and not directed towards the structural alteration of the state, if one is in existence.

8. There must be regular reports to ensure accountability and provide ongoing monitoring. In this respect, any escalation of the operation must be subject to renewed conditions and scrutiny.

CONCLUSION: COMPETING AGENDAS

The wide subject of humanitarian intervention has a number of perspectives, chiefly legal, strategic, political, normative, practical and financial. The competition between such agendas is a natural reflection of the position of parties who are relevant to this subject – politicians, civil servants, academics, the UN Secretariat, the public – and policy within the UN is a balance of the whole conglomeration, weighted in favour of those parties with greater influence. Clearly policy is not static: it is in flux during a single operation and from one operation to another, depending on a number of circumstances. For this reason the British Foreign Office, in common no doubt with its counterparts across the world, has admitted to a policy "ad hoc-ery"; something which is imperfect and reactive, yet with a reasonable track record.[70] Likewise, it is this environment which makes arguments for early warning mechanisms and effective preventive diplomacy fall upon deaf ears. Those who support such an approach are often not as vocal as those who require a disaster to be visible *before* acting, especially when the support of the public and the media is a factor. This draws us to the crux of the issue. There are many perspectives to humanitarian intervention: whether it is a right or a duty, the impact of intervention upon the territory in question, the significance of impartiality or neutrality, the issue of sovereignty and consent, and the innumerable issues of organization within the UN framework. However, the legal, practical, and normative angles should not obscure the importance of governmental will, geopolitical considerations, and public attitudes to the concept of the *responsibility* of the international community to act and intervene in all manner of circumstances. Given the trend and possibility of further civil strife and failed statehood, this is a debate which would benefit from more consensus. Unfortunately, given the primacy of realpolitik and prudence, the ad hoc approach seems likely to continue to underlie multilateral efforts as long as the UN remains a reflection of every political twist and turn within its main member states with respect to this emotive issue. It remains to be seen if the present period of transition gives way to greater consistency.

ACKNOWLEDGEMENTS

This chapter draws upon a seminar held at the British Foreign and Commonwealth Office on 21 June 1993, supported by the British International Studies Association, which sought to reflect the overlapping and divergent views of academics, diplomats, and government and non-governmental organizations represented there. Nothing in this article is necessarily the opinion of the British government. The author would like to acknowledge the help of Sally Morphet, John Groom and Richard Bone and Basil Eastwood. Other participants at the conference included Tony Aust, J. Douglas, Martin Griffiths, David Howell, Rudolph Kent, Adam Roberts, and Paul Taylor.

NOTES

1. Y. Sandoz, "*'Droit'* or *'devoir d'ingérence'* and the Right to Assistance: the issues involved", *International Review of the Red Cross*, no.288, (May-June 1992).
2. R.Falk, "Human Rights, Humanitarian Assistance, and the Sovereignty of States" in K.M.Cahill, (ed.), *Framework for Survival. Health, Human Rights, and Humanitarian Assistance in Conflicts and Disasters*, (New York: Basic Books/Council on Foreign Relations), 1993, p. 27.
3. M. Ayoob, "The New-Old Disorder in the Third World", paper at the *Roundtable Series on International Peace and Security*, UN Training Service, UN, New York, 1 June 1994, p. 1, and in T.G. Weiss and K.M Campbell (eds), *The UN and Civil Wars*, (Boulder CO: Lynne Rienner, forthcoming).
4. B.Boutros-Ghali, *Time*, 1 August 1994, p. 21.
5. G.B. Helman and S.R. Ratner, "Saving Failed States", *Foreign Policy*, no.89, (Winter 1992-93), p. 20.

6. See for example R.Falk, in K.M Cahill, (ed.), *Framework for Survival*, Note 2: "[t]he inability to disengage the normative and psycho-political from the geopolitical and the logistical generates much of the controversy about where to draw the line between sovereign rights and human rights." p. 29; also K.N. Awoonor, "The Concerns of Recipient Nations", in the same collection.

7. R.Falk, *ibid*, pp. 31-36.

8. See for example M. Akehurst, "Humanitarian Intervention", in H.Bull (ed.), *Intervention in World Politics*, (New York: Oxford University Press, 1984); C.Greenwood, "Is There a Right of Humanitarian Intervention?", *The World Today*, (February 1993); M. Stopford "Humanitarian Assistance in the Wake of the Persian Gulf War", *Virginia Journal of International Law*, vol.33, no.49, 1993: "the debate over the limits of sovereignty and the demands of solidarity have yet to define a new consensus, that elusive line in the sand between cooperation and coercion, compassion and a new colonialism." p.491; A.C. Helton, "The Legality of Providing Humanitarian Assistance Without the Consent of the Sovereign", *International Journal of Refugee Studies*, vol.4, no.3, 1992.

9. For example C.R. Beitz, *Political Theory and International Relations*, (Princeton: Princeton University Press, 1979), part two; D.R. Mapel, "Military Intervention and Rights", *Millennium*, 20, 1, 1992; J. Slater and T. Nardin, "Nonintervention and Human Rights", *Journal of Politics*, vol.48, February.

10. T.G.Weiss and K.M.Campbell, *The UN and Civil Wars*, Note 3, esp. p. 457; M. Mandelbaum, "The Reluctance to Intervene", *Foreign Policy*, Summer 1994: "The U.N. itself can no more conduct military operations on a large scale on its own than a trade association of hospitals can perform heart surgery." p. 11.

11. FCO/BISA Conference, 21 June 1993.

12. *Ibid.*

13. J.L. Brierly, *The Law of Nations*, 6th edition (first ed. 1928), (New York: Oxford University Press, 1963), p. 162.

14. For example General Assembly Resolution 2131(20) 1965; *The Declaration on Principles of International Law Concerning Friendly Relations and Cooperation Among States in Accordance with the Charter of the United Nations*, Annex to Resolution 2625(25) 1970; and Resolution 103(36) 1981 on the "inadmissibility of intervention and interference in the internal affairs of States", stressing "the duty of a State to refrain from the exploitation and deformation of human rights issues as a means of interference in the internal affairs of States..."

15. M.Akehurst, in Bull (ed.), *Intervention in World Politics*, Note 8, p. 97.
16. FCO/BISA Conference.
17. D. Plattner, "Assistance to the Civilian Population: the Development and Present State of International Humanitarian Law", in K.M.Cahill (ed.), *Framework for Survival*, Note 2.
18. G. Lewy observes that "[i]n the case of Somalia, the threat to international peace and security was essentially fiction and was used as a fig leaf to cover the absence of a satisfactory legal rationale for humanitarian intervention." "The Case for Humanitarian Intervention", *Orbis. A Journal of World Affairs*, vol.37, no.4, Fall 1993, p.628.
19. J.Pérez de Cuéllar, *Annual Report on the Work of the Organization*, (New York: UN, September 1991).
20. See for example S.E. Goldman, "A Right of Humanitarian Intervention Based upon Impaired Sovereignty", *World Affairs*, vol.156, no.3, (Winter 1994), p. 125; A.C.Helton, "The Legality of Providing Humanitarian Assistance Without the Consent of the Sovereign", Note 8, p.375; G.W.Lewy, "The Case for Humanitarian Intervention", Note 18, p.632; G.B.Helman and S.R.Ratner, "Saving Failed States", Note 5, p.11; M. Torrelli, "From 'humanitarian assistance' to 'intervention on humanitarian grounds'?", *International Review of the Red Cross*, (May-June 1992), p. 236.
21. Sir Brian Urquhart, "The UN and International Security after the Cold War", in A.Roberts and B.Kingsbury (eds), *United Nations, Divided World*, 2nd edition, (Oxford: Clarendon Press, 1993), p. 82.
22. FCO/BISA Conference. This is supported by the Chef de Cabinet to the Executive Delegate of the Secretary-General for the UN Inter-Agency Humanitarian Programme in Iraq; M.Stopford, in "Humanitarian Assistance in the Wake of the Persian Gulf War", Note 8, p. 492; and Greenwood "Is There a Right of Humanitarian Intervention?", Note 8. However other commentators at the Conference insisted that the language of 688 "surely alluded" to Chapter VII, even if there was no explicit reference.
23. T.G.Weiss and K.M.Campbell, *The UN and Civil Wars*, Note 3, p. 462.
24. FCO/BISA Conference. G.Lewy has stated that "[n]ot since the 1840s, when Britain, France, and the United States dispatched cruisers to the west coast of Africa in order to hunt down slave ships, had the world seen a major military operation devoid of any strategic or economic benefit", "The Case for Humanitarian Intervention", Note 18, p. 621.
25. B.Boutros-Ghali, *Report on the Work of the Organization from the Forty-seventh to the Forty-eighth Session of the General Assembly*, September 1993, UN, paragraph 431.

26. FCO/BISA Conference.
27. See M.Stopford, "Humanitarian Assistance in the Wake of the Gulf War", Note 8. The Memorandum was a "framework for cooperation, rather than an instrument for imposition....Quite apart from the lack of Chapter VII authority to enforce Resolution 688, it would have constituted a rather academic exercise to attempt to mount a full-scale humanitarian programme against the express will of the Iraqi government." p. 495.
28. FCO/BISA Conference.
29. M.Ayoob, "The New-Old Disorder in the Third World", Note 3, p. 15.
30. B.Boutros-Ghali, *An Agenda for Peace. Preventive Diplomacy, Peacemaking and Peace-keeping*, (New York: UN, 1992), paragraph 55.
31. B.Boutros-Ghali, *Report on the Work of the Organization*, September 1993, paragraph 480.
32. *Ibid.*, paragraph 481. UNICEF, WFP and UNHCR increased their relief outlays from $278 million in 1989 to $1,287 million during 1992. Paragraph 483.
33. Interview with a former member of the Executive Office of the Secretary-General of the UN, New York, 17 June 1994.
34. J. Eliasson, "The World Response to Humanitarian Emergencies" in K.M.Cahill (ed.), *Framework for Survival*, Note 2, p. 309.
35. *Ibid.*, p.311-314.
36. B.Boutros-Ghali, *Report on the Work of the Organization*, September 1993, paragraph 487.
37. *Ibid.*, paragraphs 492-509. A practitioner in relief assistance suggested that political efforts are an essential component of humanitarian assistance, lest assistance prove to be "ultimately futile". FCO/BISA Conference.
38. T.G.Weiss and K.M.Campbell, *The UN and Civil Wars*, Note 3, p. 457. They continue that "[t]he only large-scale delivery system for relief assistance belongs to the military establishments of the West." p. 463.
39. M.Mandelbaum, "The Reluctance to Intervene", Note 10, p. 10.
40. FCO/BISA Conference; see also P.R.Baehr's chapter in this collection.
41. T.G.Weiss and K.M.Campbell, *Framework for Survival*, Note 3, p. 454.
42. It has been suggested that the "bureaucratic" UN agencies did an "appalling job" on the ground in Somalia until the NGOs "took over". FCO/BISA Conference.
43. According to one source about 10% of public development aid world wide is now channelled through NGOs, and the United States disperses nearly a quarter of its foreign aid that way, twice the level of 10 years ago. See *Newsweek*, 1 August 1994, p. 14.

44. FCO/BISA Conference.
45. For example when the DHA accepted, in late 1992, the Iraqi conditions attached to the Memorandum of Understanding, the UN and NGO agencies had to register with the Iraqi authorities and volunteer information regarding their personnel.
46. FCO/BISA Conference.
47. K.N. Awooner, "The Concerns of Recipient Nations", in K.M.Cahill (ed), *Framework for Survival*, Note 2, p. 79.
48. *Ibid.*, p. 75.
49. FCO/BISA Conference.
50. ..Take up the White Man's burden -
       The savage wars of peace -
    Fill full the mouth of famine
       And bid the sickness cease;

    R.Kipling, "The White Man's Burden", 1899, in *A Choice of Kipling's Verse*, (London: Faber and Faber Ltd, 1963), p. 136.
51. K.N.Awooner, "The Concern of Recipient Nations", in K.M. Cahill, *Framework for Survival*, Note 2, p. 79. On intervention, K. Malik, "The West Knows Best - and Don't Forget it", *The Independent*, June 1993.
52. G.B.Helman and S.R.Ratner, "Saving Failed States", Note 5, p.4. They propose voluntary guardianship, or 'conservatorship', until failed states can be self-supportive.
53. Articles 77 and 78 preclude the UN conception of trusteeships for states which are already self-governing, but - even without an amendment - history has amply demonstrated the flexibility of the Charter.
54. See D.Cox, *Exploring An Agenda for Peace: Issues Arising from the Report of the Secretary-General*, Aurora Papers, 20, Canadian Centre for Security, Ottawa, 1993.
55. FCO/BISA Conference.
56. France was a supporter of the ousted Hutu government and has been accused of seeking to promote francophile interests in Africa. See, for example, "France's Risky Rwandan Plan", *New York Times*, editorial, 24 June 1994, p. 26; "Before We Applaud France's Mission to Rwanda", *New York Times*, 1 July 1994, letters page; "Nice Idea, Wrong Army", *Newsweek*, 4 July 1994, p. 18.
57. E.C.Luck, *op.cit.*, p.143.
58. FCO/BISA Conference.
59. M.Mandelbaum, "The Reluctance to Intervene", Note 1, p. 8.
60. FCO/BISA Conference.

61. See *Time*, 1 August 1994, p.17; also G.Szamuely, "Clinton's Clumsy Encounter with the World", *Orbis. A Journal of World Affairs*, vol.38, no.3, (Summer 1994).
62. FCO/BISA Conference.
63. J. Leaning, "When the System Doesn't Work: Somalia", in K.M. Cahill (ed.), *Framework for Survival*, note 2, p. 103.
64. "Boutros-Ghali Angrily Condemns All Sides for Not Saving Rwanda", *New York Times*, 26 May 1994, p. 1.
65. FCO/BISA Conference.
66. H.Kissinger, "Humanitarian Intervention Has Its Hazards", *International Herald Tribune*, 14 December 1992; "If the United States wants to avoid the extremes of overextension or abdication, it must develop new criteria separating challenges affecting American well-being and security from those which, however unpalatable, cannot have that impact."
67. US Presidential Document - Unofficial: *US Policy Guidance on Reforming Multilateral Peace Operations*, March 1994. The decision for UN personnel to participate in any peace operations will be based, amongst other considerations, on "[t]he extent to which the operation advances U.S. interests; the risks to U.S. personnel are acceptable; personnel, funds and resources are available; U.S. participation is necessary for the operation's success; an endpoint for U.S. participation can be identified; domestic and Congressional support exists or can be marshalled; and command and control arrangements are acceptable."
68. FCO/BISA Conference.
69. The following are partly the reflection of discussion at the FCO/BISA Conference.
70. FCO/BISA Conference.

Index